Transnational Jean Rhys

Transnational Jean Rhys

Lines of Transmission, Lines of Flight

Edited by Juliana Lopoukhine, Frédéric Regard
and Kerry-Jane Wallart

BLOOMSBURY ACADEMIC
NEW YORK • LONDON • OXFORD • NEW DELHI • SYDNEY

BLOOMSBURY ACADEMIC
Bloomsbury Publishing Inc
1385 Broadway, New York, NY 10018, USA
50 Bedford Square, London, WC1B 3DP, UK
29 Earlsfort Terrace, Dublin 2, Ireland

BLOOMSBURY, BLOOMSBURY ACADEMIC and the Diana logo
are trademarks of Bloomsbury Publishing Plc

First published in the United States of America 2021
This paperback edition published 2022

Volume Editors' Part of the Work © Juliana Lopoukhine, Frédéric Regard
and Kerry-Jane Wallart, 2021
Each chapter © of Contributors, 2021

Cover image © Antoine Boureau/Millenium Images

All rights reserved. No part of this publication may be reproduced or transmitted in any form or by any means, electronic or mechanical, including photocopying, recording, or any information storage or retrieval system, without prior permission in writing from the publishers.

Bloomsbury Publishing Inc does not have any control over, or responsibility for, any third-party websites referred to or in this book. All internet addresses given in this book were correct at the time of going to press. The author and publisher regret any inconvenience caused if addresses have changed or sites have ceased to exist, but can accept no responsibility for any such changes.

Library of Congress Cataloging-in-Publication Data
Names: Lopoukhine, Juliana, editor. | Regard, Frédéric, editor. | Wallart, Kerry-Jane, editor.
Title: Transnational Jean Rhys : lines of transmission, lines of flight / edited by Juliana Lopoukhine, Frédéric Regard and Kerry-Jane Wallart.
Description: New York : Bloomsbury Academic, 2020. | The essays and interviews included in this work were developed from the International Jean Rhys Conference: Transmission Lines / Lignes de transmission, held 21-22-23 June 2018, Paris Sorbonne University. | Includes bibliographical references and index.
Identifiers: LCCN 2020022412 | ISBN 9781501361296 (hardback) | ISBN 9781501371653 (paperback) | ISBN 9781501361302 (epub) | ISBN 9781501361319 (pdf)
Subjects: LCSH: Rhys, Jean–Criticism and interpretation. | Rhys, Jean–Influence. | Transnationalism in literature. | Modernism (Literature).
Classification: LCC PR6035.H96 Z93 2020 | DDC 823/.912–dc23
LC record available at https://lccn.loc.gov/2020022412

ISBN:	HB:	9781-5013-6129-6
	PB:	9781-5013-7165-3
	ePDF:	9781-5013-6131-9
	eBook:	9781-5013-6130-2

Typeset by Integra Software Services Pvt. Ltd.

To find out more about our authors and books visit www.bloomsbury.com and sign up for our newsletters.

Contents

Notes on Contributors   vii
Foreword *Judith Raiskin*   xi
Acknowledgements   xiii
List of Abbreviations   xiv

Introduction: On reading Rhys transnationally *Juliana Lopoukhine, Frédéric Regard and Kerry-Jane Wallart*   1

Part One   Lines of transmission: Rhys's continental transculturalism

1   The white Creole in Paris: Joséphine, Colette and Jean Rhys's *Quartet* and *Good Morning, Midnight* *Elaine Savory*   15

2   Strange defeat: *Good Morning, Midnight* and Marc Bloch's *L'Étrange Défaite* *Scott McCracken*   35

3   'Also I do like the moderns': Reading Rhys's reading *Andrew Thacker*   51

4   'Parler de soi': Jean Rhys and the uses of life writing *Simon Cooke*   65

5   Jean Rhys and Indonesia: A lineage and alienage *Christopher GoGwilt*   81

Part Two   Lines of flight: Rhys's transnational legacy

6   Jean Rhys in Australian neo-Victorian and Great House imaginaries *Sue Thomas*   95

7   Twisted lines in Caribbean postcolonial Modernism: Jean Rhys and Edward Kamau Brathwaite *Françoise Clary*   109

8   Dressing and addressing the self: Jean Rhys, Jamaica Kincaid and the cultural politics of self-fashioning *Denise deCaires Narain*   127

9   'Competing conversations': Voice and identity in Caryl Phillips's *A View of the Empire at Sunset* *Kathie Birat*   143

10 'A journey into the familiar underworld': Revisiting Jean Rhys in
    Caryl Phillips's *A View of the Empire at Sunset* Catherine Lanone   159

11 'The small things that they've not been able to talk about':
    An interview with Caryl Phillips about his novel
    A View of the Empire at Sunset (2018) Kerry-Jane Wallart   177

Bibliography   187
Index   203

Contributors

Kathie Birat is Emeritus Professor of American, Afro-American and Caribbean Literature at the Université de Lorraine, France. She has published articles on writers from the English-speaking Caribbean with special emphasis on the work of Caryl Phillips, Fred D'Aguiar and David Dabydeen. She edited a special edition of *Commonwealth Essays and Studies* devoted to Caryl Phillips (2017). Her most recent research involves questions of voice and orality; an article on David Dabydeen, '"Talk prappa": Voice, Orality and Absence in David Dabydeen's *Slave Song*' was published in *Sillages Critiques* (2018) and her study of Sam Selvon, 'Making Sense of Memory in the Writings of the Caribbean Diaspora: Sam Selvon's London Calypso' is forthcoming in *The Journal of Postcolonial Writing*.

Françoise Clary is Emeritus Professor of American Literature and Civilization at the Université de Rouen, France. She is the author of the prize winner *Violence et sexualité dans le roman afro-américain de Chester Himes à Hal Bennett* (1988); *Black American Stories* (1991); *Jean Toomer and the Harlem Renaissance* (1998); and of *Ernest J. Gaines: The Autobiography of Miss Jane Pittman* (2006). She has published various articles on pan-Africanism, Afro-Caribbean poetry and Edward Kamau Brathwaite, including 'Sonia Sanchez's Political Writing' in *An Anthology of Sonia Sanchez*, edited by Jamie Walker (2014). She is a member of the Advisory Board of *The Journal of Contemporary Communication*. She has also authored *Ben Okri: The Famished Road* (2013).

Simon Cooke is Lecturer in Modern and Contemporary Literature in the Department of English at the University of Edinburgh, UK. He is the author of *Travellers' Tales of Wonder: Chatwin, Naipaul, Sebald* (2013), and is currently working on two monographs – *'Life and Work': Modernity and the Literary Life* and *Forms of Secrecy: Modernism and Espionage* – as well as a memoir of reading, *Gathering Gifts*. He is a convenor of the Edinburgh Research Group in Life-Writing, and a co-director of Edinburgh Spy Week.

Denise deCaires Narain is Reader in Postcolonial Literatures at the University of Sussex, UK. She teaches courses on postcolonial women's writing and postcolonial feminisms, including a course on Jean Rhys and Jamaica Kincaid. She has published widely on Caribbean women's writing, including two monographs, *Caribbean Women's Poetry: Making Style* (2001) and a study of the Jamaican writer, *Olive Senior* (2011). She is currently working on a monograph on the relationship between 'maids and madams', *Strange Intimacies: Representing the Servant in Postcolonial Women's Texts*. She is Editor for *Contemporary Women's Writing*, and sits on the editorial board of several journals. She is co-editor, with Andrea Quaid and Gina Wisker, for the Palgrave Series, *Contemporary Women's Writing*.

Christopher Gogwilt is Professor of English and Comparative Literature at Fordham University, New York, USA. He is the author of *The Passage of Literature: Genealogies of Modernism in Conrad, Rhys, and Pramoedya* (2011), winner of the Modernist Studies Association book prize for 2012, *The Fiction of Geopolitics: Afterimages of Culture from Wilkie Collins to Alfred Hitchcock* (2000) and *The Invention of the West: Joseph Conrad and the Double-Mapping of Europe and Empire* (1995). He is the co-editor with Melanie D. Holm of *Mocking Bird Technologies: The Poetics of Parroting, Mimicry, and Other Starling Tropes* (2018).

Catherine Lanone is Professor of English Literature at the Université Sorbonne Nouvelle-Paris 3, France. She is the author of *E.M. Forster, Odyssée d'une écriture* (1998), Wuthering Heights *d'Emily Brontë: un vent de sorcière* (2000) and Howards End *(E. M. Forster, J. Ivory): Beyond Heritage*, with Laurent Mellet (2019), and has published many articles on nineteenth- and twentieth-century literature, including the Brontës, Hardy, Forster, Woolf and Phillips.

Juliana Lopoukhine is Senior Lecturer in English Literature at the Sorbonne. She wrote her doctoral dissertation under the supervision of Chantal Delourme and Scott McCracken and received her PhD from the Université de Paris-Nanterre and Keele University. She has published various chapters and articles on women modernist writers (Virginia Woolf, Jean Rhys, Rose Macaulay), a critical edition of *Mrs Dalloway* (2013), and co-edited three issues of *L'Atelier* (2016, 2019, 2020).

Scott McCracken is Professor of Twentieth-Century Literature at Queen Mary, University of London, UK. He is General Editor of the Oxford Edition of Dorothy Richardson, the first volume of which will appear in 2020. His books include *Masculinities, Modernist Fiction, and the Urban Public Sphere* (2007), *Pulp: Reading Popular Fiction* (1998) and, as co-author, *Benjamin's Arcades: An Unguided Tour* (2006). He is co-editor with David Glover of *The Cambridge*

Companion to Popular Fiction (2012) and with Sally Ledger of *Cultural Politics at the* Fin de Siècle (1995). He is currently working on a monograph, provisionally titled, *Thinking Through Defeat: Literary Responses to Political Failure from the Paris Commune to the Berlin Wall*.

Caryl Phillips is a major novelist, essayist and playwright. He grew up in Leeds and read English Literature at The Queen's College, Oxford, UK. His first play, *Strange Fruit*, was first performed in 1980 and his first novel, *The Final Passage*, was published in 1985. He received the James Tait Black Memorial Prize for *Crossing the River* (1993) and the Commonwealth Writers' Prize for *A Distant Shore* (2003). *Dancing in the Dark* (2005) received the PEN Open Book Award. His latest novel, entitled *A View of the Empire at Sunset*, is loosely based on the last years of childhood and the first years of adulthood of Gwendolyn Rees Williams; it ends with Jean Rhys's journey back to her Caribbean island of Dominica in 1936. In full resonance with the rest of his work, this novel explores the causes and consequences of exile, uprootedness and statelessness, both for the individual and the community, on a number of levels. His portrayal of the writer has succeeded in catching the combination of bewilderment and hunger for form which traverse Rhys's textual practices. Having held prestigious positions at Amherst College and Barnard College, Caryl Phillips is currently Professor of English at Yale University, USA. He is a Fellow of the Royal Society of Literature and Royal Society of the Arts.

Judith Raiskin is Associate Professor of Women's, Gender and Sexuality Studies at the University of Oregon, USA. Her publications on Jean Rhys include *Snow on the Cane Fields: Women Writers and Creole Subjectivity* (1996), and she is the editor of the Norton Critical Edition of Jean Rhys's *Wide Sargasso Sea* (1999). Judith Raiskin received her PhD from Stanford University, USA, her MA from the University of Chicago, USA, and her BA from UC Berkeley, USA.

Frédéric Regard studied under the supervision of Hélène Cixous and is Professor of English Literature at the Sorbonne, Paris. He is the author of books on 'feminine writing' in the English novel, Virginia Woolf, Josephine Butler, William Golding and George Orwell. He also edited collections of essays on life-writing and exploration narratives. His latest work bears on gender issues in the genesis of the detective novel as a genre (*Le Détective était une femme*, 2018).

Elaine Savory is Chair of Environmental Studies at New School University in New York, USA. She has published widely on Caribbean and African literature. She wrote *Jean Rhys* (1999) in the Cambridge series on African and Caribbean writers, and *The Cambridge Introduction to Jean Rhys* (2009) and served as Editor of *The Jean Rhys Review* for some years. *Out of the Kumbla: Women and Caribbean Literature*, which she co-edited with Carole Boyce Davies (1990), marked a key moment in the evolution of feminist/gender-centred criticism of Caribbean literature. She has returned to writing poetry, and is presently working on a new collection, *The Miranda Journals*, as well as an eco-critical reading of Caribbean literature, and a memoir.

Andrew Thacker is Professor of Twentieth-Century Literature at Nottingham Trent University, UK. He is the author or editor of several books on Modernism, including the three volumes of *The Oxford Critical and Cultural History of Modernist Magazines* (2009–2013) and, most recently, *Modernism, Space and the City* (2019). He was a founder member and the first Chair of the British Association for Modernist Studies. He is currently working on two projects: a cultural history of the modern bookshop, and a new series of volumes for Oxford University Press on global modernist magazines.

Sue Thomas is Emeritus Professor of English at La Trobe University, Melbourne, Australia. A Fellow of the Australian Academy of the Humanities, she has published extensively on nineteenth- and twentieth-century women's writing and colonial and postcolonial literatures. Her books include *The Worlding of Jean Rhys* (1999), *England in Twentieth-Century Fiction through Colonial Eyes*, with Ann Blake and Leela Gandhi (2001), *Imperialism, Reform and the Making of Englishness in* Jane Eyre (2008), and *Telling West Indian Lives: Plantation Slavery and the Reform of Plantation Slavery Cultures 1804–1834* (2014).

Kerry-Jane Wallart is a Full Professor in Black Atlantic Studies and decolonial literatures at the University of Orléans. Her Alma Mater is the Ecole Normale Supérieure Ulm and she has been a Procter Fellow at Princeton University. She has published over forty book chapters and articles, co-edited an issue of *Sillages Critiques* (2019), an issue of *Revue de Littérature Comparée* (2017), a volume on Jamaica Kincaid, published by Wagadu in 2018, and edited three issues of *Commonwealth Essays and Studies* (2019, 2012 and 2009).

Foreword

Judith Raiskin
University of Oregon

The first Jean Rhys conference ever held in France took place in 2018, surprisingly overdue given that Paris is the city where Ella Williams Lenglet became the author 'Jean Rhys' and where so many of her stories and novels are set. Following conferences in London and New York City that celebrated the fiftieth anniversary of the publication of *Wide Sargasso Sea*, Juliana Lopoukhine, Frédéric Regard and Kerry-Jane Wallart invited scholars from around the world to the Sorbonne to explore Rhys's internationalism beyond the contested and overdetermined binary of her Caribbean and British identities. The essays and interviews developed from this conference and collected in *Transnational Jean Rhys: Lines of Transmission, Lines of Flight* examine Rhys's other international connections, either in her own lifetime or through her far-reaching literary influences. Critics have often noted that Rhys's fiction anticipates by many decades later theoretical perspectives ranging from postcolonial theory to the #MeToo movement. This volume of essays asks us to rethink what Rhys's exploration of foreignness, statelessness and displacement offers us as we confront the current global crises of mass migration and climate change that have been centuries in the making.

The iconic 1972 *Blue Marble* photograph of earth from space propelled humans into an awareness of ourselves as global beings, achingly alone and vulnerable in the endless dark universe. The photograph reminds us that the national boundaries and colors on our maps are fictions that cannot contain the flow of water, the circulation of wind, the spread of fire, nor the migration of animals, people or viruses. Jean Rhys would have us think about connections between these environmental and human movements and how they affect some people more than others. Her cryptic title invoking the mysterious currents of the Sargasso Sea gestures to the history of colonialism, slavery and international capitalism that led a sixteen-year-old girl from Dominica to wrongly imagine another island over 4,000 miles away as 'home' and to embark on a journey that would leave her feeling homeless the rest of her life.

This volume of worldly articles starts by exploring Rhys's French connections and expands to investigate an even larger, cosmopolitan, transnational Rhys. Each piece builds on the title's metaphors of transmission and flight, highlighting the international connections and influences of Rhys's writing. The metaphor of electrical currents carried by these 'transmission lines' evokes Rhys's own interest in oceanic currents and other mediums of circulation and exchange (such as money and sex). These essays acknowledge Rhys's ambivalence about connection but also focus on the way her work continues to connect (with) readers and writers who are vastly different from herself and from each other. Similarly, the guiding metaphor of 'taking flight' references Rhys's and her characters' international passages motivated by fear or despair but also signals the way her work has 'taken flight', influencing writers and other artists around the world almost a century after the publication of Rhys's first book, *The Left Bank and Other Stories*. Fortunately, the recent Left Bank gathering of scholars and writers interested in Jean Rhys resulted in this stimulating collection that will certainly inspire new circuits of thought about Rhys's transnationalism and the global challenges we now face.

Acknowledgements

The editors would particularly like to thank Dr Ellen Ruth Moerman, Jean Rhys's granddaughter, for her kind encouragements and benevolent attitude towards the project, starting with her continuous presence throughout the three-day conference held in June 2018 in Paris – 'Jean Rhys: Transmission Lines' – during which some of the papers that now compose the chapters of this book were delivered. The editors are also very grateful to Sorbonne Université and the Research Institute VALE (Voix Anglophones Littérature et Esthétique) for supporting the organization of the conference; to the École Normale Supérieure Ulm, King's College London, Queen Mary University of London, the Société d'Études Modernistes, the Université de Liège, the Université Jean Monnet Saint-Etienne and the Université Lumière Lyon 2 for their contribution to the funding of the conference. We would like finally to thank Bénédicte Ledent (Université de Liège) for inviting Caryl Phillips to the conference, and Judith Raiskin (University of Oregon) for supporting the project and authoring the foreword to the volume. For permission to quote from manuscripts, our thanks go to the University of Tulsa, McFarlin Library. Last but not least, the editors would like to thank Katherine De Chant from Bloomsbury for her detailed editorial assistance and patient replies to our queries.

Abbreviations

ALM   *After Leaving Mr Mackenzie*

CSS   *The Collected Short Stories*

GMM   *Good Morning, Midnight*

L   *Jean Rhys's Letters*

Q   *Quartet*

SP   *Smile Please, An Unfinished Autobiography*

VD   *Voyage in the Dark*

View *A View of the Empire at Sunset*

WSS   *Wide Sargasso Sea*

Introduction: On reading Rhys transnationally

Juliana Lopoukhine, Frédéric Regard and
Kerry-Jane Wallart

The Hills – have a way – then –
That puts the Heart – abroad –
          —'Good Morning, Midnight', Emily Dickinson (2016: 203)

On the threshold of their own recent critical reassessment of Jean Rhys's writing, Johnson and Wilson ask, 'which Rhys, exactly, are we talking about?' (2013a: 1). They go on to remark that 'she remained significantly difficult to place' (2) and conclude to a possible 'renewed Anglicization of Rhys and her work', although they advocate 'a method for reading Rhys that would resist any urge' of the sort (17). The issue is certainly not new and it has kept readers and academics busy for a few decades now. Rhys is tangential to a number of spaces: the modernist Parisian and Londoner scenes of cosmopolitan expatriates, her native Caribbean Sea, the marginal positionality of interwar bohemian female *déclassées*. Beyond these loci, she is a writer whose recognition as such followed famously sinuous paths and whose current canonicity still remains problematic, 'ghostly' and even 'haunting', as Erica Johnson and Patricia Moran have called it in the introduction to *Jean Rhys: Twenty-First-Century Approaches* (2015: 4). Even as they establish a useful panorama of Rhysian criticism they also argue in favour of reading Rhys 'from across the critical spectrum' (14) to better seize 'the complexity of her work and the ways in which it troubles the very categories through which she is read' (2). We wish to confront the same author in another series of categories, and to 'trouble' them: transnationalism, transculturalism and diasporic cultural trajectories.

The current volume builds upon the hypothesis that 'placing' Jean Rhys might not only be impossible but also simply beside the point. If any grid could apply to Rhys's writerly achievements, the concept of 'diasporic writing' might be the most apt to approach her texts from up close. The 'strangeness' which emerges from the novels and short stories, and which is, Mary Lou Emery writes, 'what really matters' about Rhys (Emery 2013: 3) has been analysed as a mark of alienation by a first generation of critics but is now taken up by such fields as 'affect studies'[1] and 'happiness studies'. Yet this strangeness is not primarily intimate but entails her bewilderment at having to live among, if not always with, others. Rhys's structural unbelonging, a characteristic she shared with such other 'colonial' writers as Katherine Mansfield (Smith 2015: 142), we contend, is a harbinger of the migratory existence which now extends to all artistic forms in a world gone global. This statement is not new either; Anna Snaith, for instance, already opened her chapter on Rhys in *Modernist Voyages: Colonial Women Writers in London, 1890-1945* with the following redefinition of her peculiar brand of Modernism: 'The work of the Dominican writer Jean Rhys (1890-1979) is particularly well served by the move towards transnational, or global, modernism' (2014: 133). Snaith goes on to suggest that the recent forays of diasporic studies had been a necessary practice for some years in the analysis of such texts as *Voyage in the Dark* or the short stories: 'In fact, one could argue that in responding to her emphasis on the spaces between, or those exiled from, nation states, criticism of Rhys has long anticipated such paradigmatic shifts' (133).

Alongside this line of investigation one could reread Maudie's alluding to Anna Morgan's remote place of birth, 'she was born in the West Indies or somewhere' (*VD* 12), and understand the phrasing 'or somewhere' not so much as a dismissive gesture towards a derisory periphery but as an acknowledgement of the interconnectedness of all peripheries, Rhys/izomatically so. 'Somewhere' could be Katherine Mansfield's Wellington, Francis Carco's Nouméa, Dickinson's Amherst, it could also be Aimé Césaire's Fort-de-France, Maryvonne and Ruth's Indonesia or the Williams's Welsh church at Gyfylliog, it could be Joyce's Dublin, it could even be Conrad's Berdychiv and Kraków. It could be the Bombay/Mumbai of Kipling, whose *Kim* is redeemed from destruction in 'The Day they Burned the Books' (*CSS* 149). From a transnational point of view, somewhere is not elsewhere: it is everywhere European colonialism has imposed its law, order and power relations. It is every where. And it is 'anywhere', as one of the chapters in *After Leaving Mr Mackenzie* suggests (*ALM* 109).

The perspective of *Transnational Jean Rhys* is both aligned with recent excavations of the fundamentally and previously neglected transcultural dimension of Modernism, high and low, and with the transcultural (Ortiz 1940; Coronil 1995; Berg and Ní Éigeartaigh 2010; McLeod 2011; Rønning 2011) and transnational (Giles 2010; Jay 2013) theories which now allow us to read Rhys as a diasporic visionary and not only as a modernist type. Such a transcultural approach has recently been put to the fore in the case of Mansfield, in *Katherine Mansfield and Continental Europe* (Kascakova and Kimber 2015). The volume emblematically displays Mansfield's passport on its cover and testifies to the emergence of a new critical stance by focusing on the transnational influences of Rhys's 'sister colonial' (Johnson and Moran 2015: 6), who had previously been read chiefly through her polarized relationship with England and New Zealand. Instead, the chapters are dedicated to her connections with Italy, Hungary, Czechoslovakia, Poland, and Germany, with foreign authors who were influences or whom she has influenced – and with Jean Rhys herself.[2] In a similar fashion, and because the biographical fact is never far with Rhys, we too choose to emphasize not the drinking, the depressed solitude or the rogue men, but Jean Rhys's stays in Saint Lucia, in Paris and Vienna, her trips to Amsterdam, her knowledge of French and, to a lesser extent, of Dutch, her letters to her family in Indonesia, 'offering analyses of previously untrodden paths and dark corners' (Kascakova and Kimber 2015: 4) of her life as a person and as a writer.

Rhys's first known translation is, in all likelihood, that of Francis Carco's *Perversité*. Throughout her life she enjoyed reading French and read the French translations of her own works with a very appreciative eye.[3] The debate over whether she is more English, or more Caribbean, is relevant to some extent but might have been too narrow. Like Joyce's, her Europe is larger than the borders of England or even of the British Isles; Dominica somehow becomes a template for Americanness at large, as can be seen in the story 'Pioneers, Oh Pioneers' (*CSS* 264–73). Borrowed from Walt Whitman, this is the title of a short story looking at the delusions of the New World Dream in Dominica, with the Imperial Road an avatar of the Yankee belief in going west.[4] This scaling up of Rhys's scope is no way of eschewing the culture wars which have been raging around her texts, but instead, an attempt at widening the geographical horizons which her critique of imperialism included. In the current geopolitical context where the tendency seems to be an ever more rigid entrenchment behind national frontiers, starting with the impending Brexit and the desire expressed by some to 'make America great again', reading and discussing authors who have kept escaping and defeating all categories, national and otherwise, has become more urgent than ever.

There is no denying that the Caribbean figures prominently in the novels, especially *Voyage in the Dark* and *Wide Sargasso Sea*, as well as in a number of short stories, not to mention the unfinished autobiography *Smile Please*. The very fact that Rhys's positionality as a Caribbean author should have been first and crucially spotted by Wally Look Lai (1968), Kenneth Ramchand (1970), V. S. Naipaul (1972) and John Hearne (1974) speaks volumes of her Caribbeanness, as all four critics and writers share a tangential relation to the then Afro-dominant interpretation of what 'creolization' and 'creoleness' might mean. However, as Catherine Lanone suggests in this volume, E. M. Forster's advice to 'only connect' (Forster [1910] 2012: iii, 159) could have been taken up by Jean Rhys as a creative and authorial motto.[5] Her representation of colonial oppression allows her narrators and protagonists to see reverberations of power relations at the centre of other empires in their various situations and stages of collapse: London, Paris, Amsterdam, Vienna and even Tokyo[6] – whose 1945 demise was going to lead to the creation of Indonesia, a country focused upon by Chris GoGwilt in a chapter concerned with the Indonesian background to Rhys's family universe. René the gigolo who did a stint in Morocco with the Légion Etrangère in *Good Morning, Midnight*; the anonymous but nonetheless eponymous Sidi in the Santé prison in the short story 'The Sidi' (*CSS* 65–9); the Russian refugees in *Good Morning, Midnight*, who have fled a generous ideology which was only going to reinvent empire under new forms for the twentieth and twenty-first centuries; the Hungarian peasant at Lake Balaton in 'Vienne' (112) – all these figures are representatives of the defeated to imperialism – and to its fundamental backdrop: world capitalism. This 'scattered collective of the lost', or 'legion of strangers' as Scott McCracken calls them in Chapter 2, belong nowhere, but they belong with one another. Their interconnectedness is correlated to an immense horizon of possible transcultural passages.

In Dominica Jean Rhys grew up in the isolation resulting from the size of a small Caribbean island, but she was also connected with the whole empire through her father, who had sailed in and out of its various harbours before taking a position as government doctor in Roseau. In the chapter entitled 'My Father' in *Smile Please*, Rhys records 'one of [h]er last memories of him' (*SP* 72). He is engaged in a conversation with 'a woman who had spent most of her life in India' and she mentions Nirvana. Rhys's father objects: 'He said: "But Nirvana is not nothingness. Nirvana is ….." I've forgotten how he explained Nirvana' (73). The line is interrupted by memory loss but is already registering an imagination sent across cultures. The author's recollection of absolute bliss, while poor, lost to the world and pregnant, smiling at strangers on the Champs-Elysées, could be an illustration of Nirvana as a *contre-coup* (146–7).

We wish to argue against the relative isolationism that is sometimes associated with Rhys's writing through a double demonstration: that she was influenced by French authors in major and often overlooked ways, and that her influence was in turn disseminated in a myriad of directions, an array of which are outlined in the second section of the volume. *Transnational Jean Rhys* charts new territories into the influences on/of an author known for her dislike of literary coteries (see Andrew Thacker in Chapter 3), but whose literary reticularity has been underestimated – perhaps because those influences were never intentional, or testamentary, and were therefore more discrete and discreet.[7] While *Wide Sargasso Sea* displays overt forms of literary influences, Jean Rhys's fiction is so fraught with connections to other texts and textual practices that her classification as a modernist writer must be nuanced. Her playful use of a crowd of cultural references anticipates postmodernism and postcolonial rewritings, but also diasporic and/or migration writing.[8]

One might argue, with very good reason, that these questions of spatial scale hinge on the strategic choice of corpus. The critical 'renewed Anglicization' of Jean Rhys at stake in the analysis of Wilson and Johnson (2013a: 17) will emerge most visibly in the texts of Rhys's so called 'modernist' period, such as *Quartet, After Leaving Mr MacKenzie* or *Good Morning, Midnight*, while her Caribbeanness and cosmopolitanism are visible in *Voyage in the Dark* or *Wide Sargasso Sea* but also in some short stories, especially the later ones. In 'Temps Perdi' (*CSS* 246–63), for instance, a story which falls into three sections, various forms of non-literary art (photography, popular music performance, dance) are identified as a metafictional source of inspiration and stem from all corners of the globe. Situated in the English countryside, in Rolvenden, the narrator convokes 'a performer in a Havana circus which was touring the smaller Caribbean islands' (248), 'photographs of Greek temples' (250), photographs of Japanese women 'wearing European clothes' (251), evening papers turned into Oriental origami, a song entitled 'Dardanella', a Japanese song (252), 'Viennese clothes' (253). In view of these ever-expanding horizons, it seems that the opposition between an English or a Caribbean Rhys narrows the lens through which one may look at her short stories and her novels.

The present volume neither ignores nor disregards the long-standing issue of Rhys's status as a Caribbean writer, or the question of her Creoleness (Brathwaite 1974; Hulme 1994): a 'prominent and long abiding' divide, in J. Dillon Brown's words (2010: 568). We suggest, however, that Creoleness, or *créolité*, are not merely regional features apt at describing the Caribbean. *Créolité* becomes an ability to absorb and translate, through whose practice Jean Rhys may be one of the first truly diasporic writers of our postmodernity. To go back to the short story 'Temps Perdi', it is striking to see how the ultimate key to understanding the peculiar structure of the text might be the act of translation which is connected to its title, and which, if read against the Russian formalist concept of 'estrangement', can also be seen as the 'wasted time' of translation and interpretation. Rhys writes, '"Temps Perdi" is Creole patois and does not mean, poetically, lost or forgotten time, but, matter-of-factly, wasted time, lost labour' (*CSS* 257). Indeed, the distance that pervades Jean Rhys's writing blocks all forms of automatic interpretation, or translation: the way she holds herself at a distance, describes the world at a distance, puts her life at a distance, forces us, in turn, to face the duration of the process of interpretation. Viktor Shklovsky writes that 'by "estranging" objects and complicating form, the device of art makes perception long and "laborious"' ([1917] 1991: 7). In 'Temps Perdi', the narrative is slowed down by a fragmented temporality that defeats any form of readymade interpretation and transmits the process of travelling between different languages and cultures: the narrator's stay in Vienna among a group of interpreters prepares the beginning of the third section and, more precisely, this moment of translationability. The author is leading her reader towards linguistic passages that far outreach the geographical location of the Caribbean and Europe. What is initiated here is a connection between languages and cultures that, it seems to us, must be emphasized.

Transnational Jean Rhys comes after a raging debate over a reconsideration of Modernism as including traits of postcolonialism, as has been recently posited again by Peter Childs: '[M]odernist writing itself is to a large degree a literature of outsiders, in terms of ethnicity, nationality, gender, sexuality or class. […] [M]any modernist writers were in their different ways hybrids, mongrel selves moved by both the voyage out and the voyage in' (2007: 63). Modernism is a singularly shape-shifting movement and the authors usually labelled modernist have all deployed a fair amount of multi-scalar, transcultural, translinguistic aesthetics. What we suggest here is that the recent and striking rediscovery of Jean Rhys's texts goes beyond, and comes long after, her rediscovery in the 1970s.

The reason why scholars from both the global South and the global North are turning to Rhys decades into a new millenium is because she has anticipated our days of fluid identities, with all the misconstructions, misdirections, and misfires that these will entail.

The subtitle of the volume, 'Lines of transmission, lines of flight', takes up the famous Deleuzean metaphor which 'has to do with surveying, mapping, even realms that are yet to come' (Deleuze and Guattari 1987: 5) or, as Chris GoGwilt writes in Chapter 5, 'a history yet to be written'. Indeed, the authors of this volume offer a reassessment of Rhys's texts in terms of cosmopolitanism but also transnationalism and diasporic studies. Taken together, the eleven contributions make for a new investigation into the frames of recognition which can be applied today to our reading Jean Rhys. The first section of the present volume constitutes forays into Jean Rhys's French connections, and the second one offers essays looking at similar lines of transmission radiating outwards, worldwide, at 'movements of deterritorialization and destratification' (Deleuze and Guattari 1987: 5). The volume will contribute further to connecting *Wide Sargasso Sea* with the rest of her work and foreground Rhys as a migrant writer who experienced and expressed the tension between impossible belonging and possible creative affiliations.

If Gwendolyn Rees first started filling notebooks in London shortly during the First World War (*SP* 128–30), it is in Paris that the same notebooks caught the interest of a Mrs Adam and then of Ford Madox Ford – it is only there that she became Jean Rhys. This first part is no attempt at foregrounding the bohemian anecdotes in the Parisian existence of a woman whose sensational life has garnered often irrelevant attention: 'all of a writer that matters is in the book or books. It is idiotic to be curious about the person' (*SP* 168). Or, in a letter to Francis Wyndham in 1960, 'I've always hated personal publicity. (*Why Necessary?* Only the writing matters.)' (*L* 190). Such words ring in tune with Proust's own forceful distinction between the man and the artist, as expressed in *Contre Sainte-Beuve*, posthumously published in 1954. The first four chapters focus instead on the influences to which Jean Rhys has been exposed while in Paris, a place where, by her own admission, she met more writers than she ever did in England (*SP* 168). Helen Carr writes that '[p]erhaps one reason English critics were slow to recognize the extensive intertextuality within her writing was lack of knowledge of her French sources' (Carr [1996] 2012: 10). Her own contribution did enlighten the intertextual presence of Maupassant, especially of the novel entitled *Fort comme la mort* (40–5), a connection emphasized by

Simon Cooke in this volume.⁹ Carr also contends that Rhys was influenced by 'the French precursors of Modernism (Flaubert, Maupassant, Baudelaire, Rimbaud, etc.)' (9), which would be one more reason to refrain from trying to force her back into the canon of English or even British Modernism.

Starting with French as a model for transcultural passages is a way to understand how such passages have been practiced by Rhys over and over again. We believe that the French language, literature and cultural experiences which traversed Jean Rhys's formative years must be understood not as a fixity but as a matrix for fluctuating identities. In Paris, Sasha Jensen is 'l'étrangère' (*GMM* 59): this paradigmatic inability to fit in has to do with class and gender, as has been amply shown, leading to the classification of the 'Rhys woman', but also with borders that the characters in Rhys's fiction never fully acknowledge and resist through minimal yet tangible modes. The creative malleability of these transcultural passages is the object of *Transnational Jean Rhys*, a critical engagement which follows such studies as Ileana Rodriguez's, who reads Rhys alongside de Beauvoir, Doris Lessing and Toni Morrison, or Erica Johnson's, who reads her alongside Marguerite Duras and Erminia Dell'Oro. Helen Carr insightfully brings in the concept of 'undecidables' coined by Zygmunt Bauman and she connects Rhys and Kafka ([1996] 2012: 28); perhaps such 'undecidability' is what the five chapters of the first part follow elsewhere – which is also Anna Morgan's 'somewhere'.

Elaine Savory's chapter explores Rhys's representation of sexual experiences with reference to the fiction of Colette, so often represented as frank with regard to sexuality, as well as to the figure of Josephine de Beauharnais, another white Creole whose sexuality was the object of gossip and control.

In the following chapter, Scott McCracken reads Jean Rhys's *Good Morning, Midnight* against the historian Marc Bloch's *L'Étrange Défaite*, his memoir and historical reflection on the fall of France in 1940. Starting from an analysis of the unfamiliarity of modernist texts, McCracken suggests that more than a victim, the 'Rhys woman' ought to be considered as vanquished – of her own will, and in full awareness. Playing with the border between fiction and non-fiction in ways that compare Rhys to a historian, no longer to an autobiographical witness, he contends that Rhys's narratives, and none more so than *Good Morning, Midnight*, are essentially narratives of the disruptive experience of defeat.

With '"Also I do like the moderns": Reading Rhys reading', Andrew Thacker delivers a fine piece of literary investigation as he follows the archival paths of Rhys towards and from Sylvia Beach's Shakespeare and Company bookshop.

In so doing he probes the puzzling and relative absence of Jean Rhys among the modernist, interwar artistic crowd in Paris, and by extension, her marginal (or 'ghostly', as he terms it) position in relation to literary recognition and canonicity.[10] This is the occasion of a thought-provoking re-placing of Rhys not only among other expatriates, such as Joyce and Hemingway, but among the French as well.

Simon Cooke addresses the thorny issue of the autobiographical nature of Rhys's texts from a renewed, transnational perspective. Starting from a letter where she states that "*parler de soi*" [speaking about oneself] is not supposed to be the proper thing to do [, n]ot in England. And not now', he excavates the French influences that might have been neglected around such an enterprise, from Flaubert's disguises ('Madame Bovary, c'est moi'), Verlaine and Rimbaud's scandalous personal lives, and Proust's conviction that the author and the person be two entirely distinct entities (*Contre Saint-Beuve*). The chapter stresses the ways in which Rhys's writing, in its formal strategies, invites but also frustrates identification between author and protagonist, and traces these strategies back to a number of French influences from her, and the previous, generation.

In a fifth chapter, Chris GoGwilt explores the relevance of Indonesia for Jean Rhys's work. Letters to her daughter, Maryvonne Moerman, reveal Rhys's interest in events in Indonesia from the moment her daughter's family moved to Indonesia in the mid-1950s until after they were compelled to leave in the late 1950s, suggesting a number of fascinating parallel lines linking those interests with the lineages of colonial and postcolonial identity that are woven into *Wide Sargasso Sea*. As with so many of the material cultural references in Rhys's work, these may be more consequential than merely indexical features of narrative form. Their material historical references may be all the more revealing about what constitutes form and structure in Rhys's work and literary Modernism more generally. The general scope of the chapter embraces the extent to which Rhys's work reveals an Indonesian lineage underwriting her own 'European' Modernism.

The second part of the volume outlines lines of transmission radiating from Rhys, rather than leading to her, all the way to Caryl Phillips's 2018 novel *A View of the Empire at Sunset*. Sue Thomas looks at the ways in which Rhys's critical engagement with Charlotte Brontë's *Jane Eyre* in *Wide Sargasso Sea* has inspired writers of neo-Victorian fiction, and influenced adaptors of *Jane Eyre* for opera, the stage, television, and cinema, with a particular emphasis on Barbara Hanrahan's *The Albatross Muff* (1977), Amanda Lohrey's 'Jane Eyre'

(1995), Jennifer Livett's *Wild Island* (2016), and Willoh S. Weiland and Halcyon Macleod's *Crawl Me Blood* (2018). The affiliative poetics of *Crawl Me Blood* routes Rhys's influence through shared Caribbean diasporic location rather than the logic of imperial centre and periphery.

In the next chapter, Françoise Clary revisits the positionality of Rhys with regards to the Barbadian writer Edward Kamau Brathwaite – a notoriously contested line of literary filiation. She probes Brathwaite's adaptation of Rhys's modernist strategies to forge his own discrepant postcolonial Modernism; the chapter examines the overlapping concerns and complementary strategies of Jean Rhys and E.K. Brathwaite to construct a Self that has a contradictory identity, being both particular and part of the collective in the postcolonial imagination. Clary focuses on Rhys's *Wide Sargasso Sea* and Brathwaite's early works *The Arrivants*, *Mother Poem*, *Sun Poem* and *X/Self*, and such later works as *The Zea Mexican Diary*, *Barabajan Poems* and *Dream Stories*.

Denise deCaires Narain's chapter questions the way Rhys's interest in clothes, her longing for them, her self-consciousness about them, to the extent of almost believing in their 'magic', 'talismanic' power, becomes a way of 'fashioning' her own identity as a writer. This chapter examines the unfinished autobiography *Smile Please* and her short stories. The parallel with Jamaica Kincaid's similar attention to dressing, in *Talk Stories*, emphasizes the importance for both writers of the sociopolitical value of clothing and posing, as they both record narratives of their respective pictures being taken as children, not only as a way of defining themselves as women Creole writers but also as a way of redefining, in turn, 'Caribbean-ness' and femininity.

Kathie Birat then shows in Chapter 9 how Caryl Phillips creates zones of narrative indeterminacy through which the hierarchies of voice and perspective usually associated with both biography and fiction are disturbed. *A View of the Empire at Sunset* problematizes the notion of narrative voice in ways that blur the boundaries between self and other, colonized and colonizer, actor and spectator. This chapter explores how Phillips, in a manner that runs counter to the practice of other writers from the Caribbean, disrupts the expectations surrounding voice as a source of individual and collective identity.

Chapter 10 focuses on the capacity of Caryl Phillips's 2018 novel to prompt Rhys's readers to discard the personal fallacy and read Rhys with a fresh eye, as aesthetic projects rather than autobiographical projections. Catherine Lanone analyses the manner in which the journey to Dominica taking place at the end of *A View of the Empire at Sunset* traces the discovery of an exotic but (un)familiar underworld, and explores one of Caryl Phillips's key themes: the fact that there is no return, ever.

Caryl Phillips had already included a passage from *Smile Please* in *Extravagant Strangers* and has long dialogued with such Rhysian texts as *Voyage in the Dark*. In 2018, he published *A View of the Empire at Sunset*, based on the personal life of Gwendoly/en Rees Williams. The final chapter – an interview with Phillips – discusses Rhys's existence as both insider and outsider, and her fated quest for, but also rebellion against, belonging. Phillips lays the emphasis on Rhys's commentary on the constructedness of Englishness and evokes his own journeys to Dominica as key to understanding how the particular Caribbean landscape has shaped her, and his, writing. Phillips brings to life an interstitial writerly position which he shares to some extent; the dialogue into which his novel enters with *Smile Please* makes for a renewed take on the autobiographical nature of Rhys's writing and suggests that the only autobiography there can ever be is in fact profoundly fictional.

The first ten chapters contained in this volume are drawn from papers given at a three-day international conference entitled 'Jean Rhys: Transmission Lines' held in June 2018 at the Sorbonne, in Paris, gathering over thirty-five participants from all around the globe – a fair tribute to a 'transnational Jean Rhys', in the city where she had lived and written, and which she had loved.

Notes

1 See the 2020 issue of *Women: A Cultural Review* 31 (2) entitled *Jean Rhys: Writing Precariously* (Lopoukhine, Regard and Wallart 2020). The essays in this issue are drawn from papers given at a conference held at the Sorbonne in Paris in June 2018.
2 On Rhys and Mansfield, see Chapter 3 in this volume. See also Sue Thomas's comparative study (Thomas 2015a: 21–39).
3 It is of note that Carco was born to Corsican parents in New Caledonia: his French identity is just as centrifugal, and fluid, as Rhys's British one. To our knowledge, no critic has remarked upon the fact that Carco's *nom de plume*, Jean d'Aiguières, might be the origin of Gwendolyn Williams's own choice for a pen name: according to Carole Angier, it was Ford who gave her that pen name, and it is also he who asked her to translate Carco's novel (Angier [1990] 1992: 38).
4 The North American connection is tackled only tangentially in the present volume but has been traced by a number of critics, a few examples being: Hawthorn

comparing Rhys and Faulkner, Kloepfer looking at Rhys alongside H.D., or Lorna Sage dealing with Rhys but also Tillie Olsen.
5 The links between Forster and Rhys are convincingly explored by Lanone in Chapter 10 in this volume.
6 Her first husband Jean Lenglet had been hired as a diplomatic secretary to the Japanese delegation in Vienna, from early 1920 to mid-1921, and he took Jean Rhys, then Gwendolyn Lenglet, with him there.
7 Erica Johnson writes about Rhys's 'ironic ability to create such community' (Johnson and Moran 2015: vi).
8 Current critical work testifies to the widening of the scope of Rhys's influence beyond the cultural categories, as in the volume edited by Erica Johnson and Elaine Savory, Wide Sargasso Sea *at 50* (2020), which explores her influence in fashion, visual art and the theatre.
9 For the influence of Maupassant, see also *L* 99 and 105.
10 An oxymoron coined by Johnson and Moran in the introduction to *Jean Rhys: Twenty-First-Century Approaches*, entitled 'The Haunting of Jean Rhys' (Johnson and Moran 2015: 4).

Part One

Lines of transmission: Rhys's continental transculturalism

1

The white Creole in Paris: Joséphine, Colette and Jean Rhys's *Quartet* and *Good Morning, Midnight*

Elaine Savory

Ron Eyerman explains that cultural trauma theory emphasizes collective memory as a means of survival and strengthening both identity and lasting witness: 'the notion of cultural trauma implies that direct experience of an event is not a necessary condition for its inclusion in the trauma process' (2001: 12). Descendants of victims of the Holocaust and the Middle Passage inherit cultural trauma via collective memory. Eyerman notes here a marked 'difference between black and white in social and historical understanding' (17). Speaking of the United States, and the aftermath of the Civil War, he says: 'Whites, regardless of whether chance had placed them in the North or South, shared a European cultural heritage, what would soon be identified as part of Western civilization' (17). This white supremacy evades responsibility for causing cultural trauma.

Still, it may be argued that Rhys records personal and fictional trauma for white women, through sexual experience. She herself felt permanently an outsider to white communities and even when young longed to belong to the black world.[1] She often felt isolation and alienation. The colonial elite into which she was born in colonial Dominica, in 1890, certainly tried to co-opt her but she never fitted in.[2] She was even uncomfortable with her physical self as the palest of the children of her white Creole family, with blue eyes: no wonder, for she heard her mother say 'black babies were prettier than white ones' (*SP* 42). This memory, in her unfinished autobiography ([1979] 1990), is relevant to her self-exile. She suffered early sexual trauma, as indicated in her journal account of Mr Howard: it seems very likely this was not a fictive entry, but recorded an actual experience (Angier [1990] 1992: 26–9).[3] Young white Creole girls in Dominica in Rhys's time found their sexuality constrained within strict codes. Carole Angier, in her biography *Jean Rhys*, refers to an attempt by Rhys's brother

Owen to write a story about a character with some similarity to Rhys, who had an affair with a young man of colour in the island.[4]

But if interracial love was forbidden, as recorded in her notebook, an elderly child abuser was allowed access to the young Rhys by her mother. This molester spun stories that seem to contain faint echoes of the pornographic and sadomasochistic side of the Marquis de Sade's fiction (though Sade is seen by some as a philosopher, his work clearly has the potential to inspire and justify abusive male sexual behaviour in those who read for the story). Rhys's notes reveal the sexual, racial and class pathology in which she grew up in Dominica. It was a place in which a young girl could feel both a victim of history as a woman and, at the same time, part of a culpable racial and class elite. There was further trauma Rhys endured as a young woman. At sixteen, she left Dominica to finish secondary school in Britain, then briefly attended Tree's Drama School in London (from where, the story goes, she was dismissed for her West Indian accent).[5] She then defied her family and class expectations and became a chorus girl, thereby losing her class status. Even her race became somewhat indeterminate, as she was an exotic foreigner, despite her blue eyes.[6] Her relationship with Lancelot Grey Hugh Smith, exploitative, rich and emotionally damaged, hurt her lastingly at and after its end. Her marriage to French-Belgian Jean Lenglet failed, in Paris, a city she loved. Her home, her shelter from trauma, was really in writing itself, the place which never failed her. This essay reads the sexual experience of two Rhys protagonists in Paris, fabled city of love: Marya in *Quartet* and Sasha in *Good Morning, Midnight*, in the context of mythologies and experience of the white Creole woman in Europe.

Paris was not outside Rhys's linguistic or cultural space. French was in her history. As a result of European colonialism, both English and French are spoken in Dominica. In Rhys's childhood, English-speaking whites looked back to ancestry in Britain, French-speaking to both an educated mixed-race group (the so-called 'Mulatto Supremacy'[7]) descended from refugees from the Haitian Revolution and the poor majority, who spoke a local French Creole. Rhys could claim both languages quite naturally as part of her childhood experience. In *Smile Please*, she points out that mountains ('Mornes' in Dominica) have French names such as 'Morne Diablotin', and that the island was once French (*SP* 21). Francine, a 'Negro girl' Rhys played with as a child, always began a story with an exchange between teller and audience in French (31). Rhys thought the black community in Dominica (which spoke French Creole) was warmer and more fun than the white (50–1). In the chapter of her autobiography titled 'My Mother', a memory comes with two lines of French poetry (44). In the chapter 'Poetry' French poetry is quoted twice (including Victor Hugo's 'Un peu de musique') and she says she was 'assaulted' by both French and English poetry at school (59). We also know Jean Rhys kept French poetry by her side throughout her writing life, and that Ford Madox Ford told her when in doubt about something she had written, to translate it into French and back to English again (Angier [1990] 1992: 134). Though just being married to Jean Lenglet, her first husband, who was French-Belgian, would not have bestowed skills in French, the relationship certainly would not have separated her from immersion in the language once she moved to France. Diana Athill, in her introduction to *Smile Please*, reminds us that Rhys translated two books from French to English (Athill 1979: 14–15).

There is certainly plenty of evidence to think of her work as in conversation with French writers and French cultural figures. Sometimes she references these in her texts. Specifically, this chapter argues, she is writing back to Colette, the Marquis de Sade and Joséphine de Beauharnais, implicitly or explicitly.

Contributing to a myth?: Joséphine de Beauharnais

Andrea Stuart's biography of the woman she calls, with good reason, Josephine (without the accent) includes many details relevant to thinking about elements of the reputation of white Creoles in Paris.[8] Joséphine, Napoleon's first wife, was born Marie-Josèphe-Rose-de Tascher de La Pagerie (Stuart 2003: 4). Her birthplace, L'Habitation de La Pagerie, a plantation in Martinique, was and is a place of exceptional natural beauty to which her family was very much attached (5). Stuart says Martiniquan Creoles were 'seen as coarse, clannish, impatient – and according to one observer "violently attached to their pleasures"' and that she was 'in many ways an exemplary Creole', meaning she had sensuality and willfulness (19). Stuart also connects the 'sensory splendor' of Martinique to Joséphine's evidently sensuous nature: 'it was a world that had to be apprehended through the body, not the intellect' (12). It was a world of violence. Violence was commonplace. White men declared their supremacy by sexual predation and other violence to those in their power, and duelled among themselves to test their place in the white male hierarchy. As for the white Creole girl, she was expected to accept a future as mother of white heirs to family wealth, the main support of white supremacy. She grew up at first playing with other children (including enslaved children) but before puberty, her training to be a planter's wife had to involve not just admonitions but careful scrutiny. Stuart quotes a visitor to Martinique on young white Creole girls: 'she is a bird in a cage who vaguely aspires to liberty but without suspecting the perils of that liberty once it happens' (27).

Like Rhys in the early twentieth century, Joséphine left for Europe in her midteens, to become a wife in Paris. Stuart records that at this stage, Joséphine was not physically appealing, though she would eventually become 'an essential pillar of [...] Creole mythology' (35), a leader of fashion in post-Revolution Paris, in a small and well-known group of women which included a Mme Hamelin, whom Stuart describes as a 'witty and wild young Creole' (155).[9]

Stuart does not think that she was in love with Napoleon, who boasted that he hurried sex with his mistresses and who, in Stuart's words, was 'never the most sensual of men' (177). Stuart also argues that, much like Colette and Rhys, 'Rose had learned through bitter experience the difference between passion and love' (177). Stuart's representation of Rose as a person of strength of will however makes it easy to think that becoming Napoleon's Joséphine must have suited her. He eventually divorced her because he needed a son to carry on his line. So it is clear that even the most romantic and successful of white Creoles in Paris had come to a sad end with regards to a man she had trusted. Martinique is close to Dominica and it is likely Rhys would have heard of Joséphine. Rhys often indicates, in her fiction, the ways such a woman in Europe was thought exotic, different.

Ford Madox Ford played into this stereotype in his lurid portrayal of Lola Porter in *When the Wicked Man* ([1931] 2012). This was his revenge on Rhys for her negative portrait of him as a fat, pompous sexual predator in *Quartet*. It is one of his weakest novels.[10] Ford gives Lola Porter 'fiery Creole ancestry' and upbringing (192) and a birth in Martinique. His narrator notes that 'Creoles are as noted for their indolence as for their passion' (192). The anger is certainly there in Lola, who is said to sometimes 'let the tiger peep out from beneath her Creole nonchalance' (197). Stella Bowen, Ford's long-suffering partner, referenced this idea of the Creole woman when she said Rhys was 'a doomed soul, violent and demoralized' (Bowen [1941] 1984: 116).

Colette's sensuous woman and the white Creole

The French writer Colette (Sidonie-Gabrielle Colette, subsequently Madame Henry Gauthier-Villars, 1873–1954) might also have had Creole ancestry. From her mother, she heard her grandfather, Henry Landoy, was called 'The Gorilla' for his African blood. Judith Thurman, Colette's biographer, writes that at 'the end of her life, in a passing phrase, Colette described her mother's antecedents as "cocoa harvesters" from the colonies, "colored by island blood", with frizzy hair and purple fingernails' (Thurman 1999: 6).[11] She also said her ancestors 'came from a warm island [...]. There! I have a stain of black in my blood. Does that disgust you?' and described her father, Henry Landoy, as a 'quadroon' (7). Whether or not this can be proven, there is a consciousness of race inherent in this statement, similar to that in the Caribbean. It is also present in something else Colette says in 'Music-Hall Sidelights' (*My Apprenticeships*), when she speaks of a chorus girl called 'Misfit' (this is also the title of a short story). 'Misfit' dislikes summer audiences because they have a lot of foreigners, 'rough teutonic beards, oriental hard blue-black hair pads and oily skins, and impenetrable negro smiles' (Colette 1967: 207).

Like Joséphine, Colette contributed to the construction of the idea of the French woman as sexually open and passionate, with her definite hint of something offshore, less constricted by mores of class, church and state: though had she been raised in the Caribbean, her sexuality could not have been so open and free and she could not have so openly challenged the idea of male sexual supremacy. Colette broke the rules in both life and art. She had a famous affair with her second husband's son, Bertrand de Jouvenel, when she was forty-seven and he was sixteen. She fictionalized such love more than once, perhaps most famously in *Chéri* (1920). There were, as Thurman points out, numerous examples of sexual relationships between older women and younger men in French literature and life, but in Colette's fiction, there is great sensuality: a sort of textual equivalent of Josephine's elegant, unrestrained muslin.[12]

In Colette's texts, women have orgasms, draw attention to their passion by making cries, notice more or less skilled ways of male kissing. In the story 'The Victim', a woman speaks about a man who loves her but whom she cannot love: 'I'll die without knowing whether he kisses good or bad, if he makes love good or bad. When he kisses me, my mouth becomes like ... like ... nothing. It's dead, it doesn't feel anything. My body either' (1991d: 193). In *Le Pur et l'impur* (*The Pure and the Impure*), a kind of creative non-fiction discourse on sex and love, Colette is wonderfully direct and detailed about physical sensations: 'she turned her head from side to side on the white cushion, her lips parted, like a woman threatened with a paroxysm of pleasure' (Colette 1968: 35); in the original text, 'Elle tournait de côté et d'autre sa tête sur le coussin blanc, agitée, la bouche entrouverte, comme une femme que le plaisir menace' (Colette [1941] 2004: 25).

The French phrase 'comme une femme que le plaisir menace' is far more powerful than this English translation 'threatened with a paroxysm of pleasure'.

She represents a man who has had many female lovers being utterly dismissive, even rude about them all, saying they did not spare him a single embrace (and calling them 'bitches'), but Colette's narrator adds: 'he did not say embrace, but used a blunter term that refers to the terrible paroxysm of male sexual satisfaction' (Colette 1968: 38); in the original text, 'Il n'usa point de ce dernier mot, mais d'un autre plus bref, et qui se rapporte au terrible traumatisme du plaisir viril' (Colette [1941] 2004: 28). There is something important in the French delivery of the idea of male climax as the specific trauma of 'manly pleasure' (*plaisir viril*). For if there is such a thing, there is certainly female pleasure also, and that is experienced internally, out of sight, without the outward appearance of conquering anyone.

But men who want to believe in conquest might dislike being reduced to spent creatures after sex is done. Colette's narrator goes on: in the translation by Herma Briffault, 'rarely have I encountered in a woman the kind of hostility with which a man regards the mistresses who have exploited him sexually. The woman, on the contrary, knows herself to be an almost inexhaustible store of plenty for the man' (Colette 1968: 38). In the French, this reads, 'grenier d'abondance de l'homme, la femme se sait à peu près inépuisable' (1932 as *Ces Plaisirs*. 1941 as *Le Pur et l'impur*; [1941] 2004: 28), which gives a better sense of the extent of female resources. One promiscuous man the narrator knows says of women, 'they allow us to be their master in the sex act, but never their equal. That is what I cannot forgive them' (Colette 1968: 58); in the original, 'Être leur maître dans le plaisir, mais jamais leur égal. Voilà ce que je ne leur pardonne pas' ([1941] 2004: 48). Colette's literal words 'to be their master in the pleasure but never their equal' may refer to male and/or female pleasure but is definitely about the sexual act as inherently about power or loss of it.

Reading Colette and Rhys together

Both Colette and Rhys tackled the difficult question of how to write honestly and boldly about female sexuality, in societies where women (including their readers) are contained in social restrictions.[13] What first brings them together is the freemasonry of the woman writer. There are distinct parallels between them in their accounts of the beginning of their craft. Colette talks about the role of writing in *Mes apprentissages*:

For I had just recovered from a long and very serious illness that had left me sluggish in mind and body. But having found and bought, at a local paper shop, a number of copy-books similar to those I had used at school, I set to work. The heavy grey-ruled pages, the vertical red line of the margins, the black cover and its inset medallion and ornamental title, *Le Calligraphe*, re-awakened the urge, a sort of itch in my fingers, to do an 'imposition', to fulfill a prescribed task. A well-remembered water-mark in the thick, laid paper, took me back six years. Diligently, with complete indifference, perched at the corner of the desk, with the window behind me, one shoulder hunched and my knees crossed, I wrote.

(Colette 1967: 22)

There is a passage in Rhys's autobiography, *Smile Please* ([1979] 1990), which is strikingly similar in tone and content, another version of a woman's entry into writing as identity:

After lunch I walked along looking into shop windows. […] I passed a stationer's shop where quill pens were displayed in the window, a lot of them, red, blue, green, yellow. Some of them would be all right in a glass, to cheer up my table. I went into the shop and bought about a dozen. Then I noticed some black exercise books on the counter. They were not at all like exercise books are now. They were twice the thickness, the stiff black covers were shiny, the spine and the edges were red, and the pages were ruled. I bought several of those, I didn't know why, just because I liked the look of them. […] It was after supper that night – as usual a glass of milk and some bread and cheese – that it happened. My fingers tingled, and the palms of my hands. I pulled a chair up to the table, opened an exercise book, and wrote, *This is my Diary*. […] I wrote on until late into the night, till I was so tired that I couldn't go on, and I fell into bed and slept.

(*SP* 128–9)

The next day, she wakes determined to continue all day. The act of writing, as described in these passages, is as much physical and emotional as mental exertion.

Also Rhys and Colette were both chorus girls for a while, and wrote about the chorus girl life. A woman who has expressed herself on stage through the body-language of acting or dancing, has that memory of the intelligence of the body to draw on for her representation of experience. Perhaps this is why both of them write so innovatively about what it is to live in a female corporeal awareness. This, for Rhys at least, recalls Stuart's remark about Caribbean landscape having to be apprehended physically (Stuart 2003: 12).

Colette's stories often reference the physicality of her characters. Colette's chorus girl 'Bastienne', weak with hunger when dancing, chooses to explain the cause as a lover who has exhausted her ('A Bad Morning'; 1991a: 112). When, in 'Bastienne's Child', she is five months pregnant, she is a 'radiant beauty, tall' (1991b: 147). When her baby needs feeding, 'without waiting to sit down or to unfasten her low-cut bodice, she uses both hands to free from its pressure a swollen breast, blue in color from its generous veins' (149). Judith Thurman writes that Colette's prose is 'both detached and voluptuous, minutely observant of those pleasures and irritants of the flesh which are lost on grosser human senses' (Thurman 1999: 397). Thurman has noticed how closely the consciousness of Colette's narrators attends to details of bodily sensation.

Renée, in Colette's *The Vagabond* (*La Vagabonde*), is able to account for her sexual experience in a way which conveys all its elements, physical sensation, emotional openness and mental insight:

> I move my head imperceptibly, because of his moustache which brushes against my nostrils with a scent of vanilla and honeyed tobacco. Oh! ... suddenly my mouth, in spite of itself, lets itself be opened, opens of itself as irresistibly as a ripe plum splits in the sun. And once again there is born that exacting pain that spread from my lips, all down my flanks as far as my knees, that swelling as of a wound that wants to open once more and overflow – the voluptuous pleasure that I had forgotten. [...]
>
> His mouth tastes of mine now, and has the faint scent of my powder. Experienced as it is, I can feel that it is trying to invent something new [...]. [A]lready I am bold enough to indicate my preference for a long, drowsy kiss that is almost motionless – the slow crushing, one against the other, of two flowers in which nothing vibrates but the palpitation of two coupled pistols.
>
> (Colette 1982: 126–127)

This is a woman in control, even in the experience of sexual passion. She achieves this not by restraining sensation but by encouraging the man to do what pleases her. Colette, in her casual but emphatic self-connection to the Antilles and her richly sexual writing, can be said to have subtly reinforced the idea of connection between ancestry in the Caribbean and a female sensuous, open, intelligent sexuality, which understands the importance of allowing sexuality to be freely and deeply understood as well as experienced. A likely fiction but an important one in her work.

As we shall see in close reading two of Rhys's novels shortly, her writing is far less sensual, in the sense of enjoyable sensation. Her heroines experience more violence than pleasure, more withdrawal than engagement. Whilst it is true, as we have seen in the exploration of translations of Colette's work, the

French language can offer some opportunities to the sensuous writer which are harder to come by in English, that is not the whole explanation for the difference between the two writers.

Women: Sex and class

In their embrace of chorus girl life, and writing as a profession, both Colette and Rhys were in effect *déclassées*, necessarily a French term, beyond the strictures of the English class system. This describes the odd position of the theatrical young woman, earning a living by representing staged fictions in dance, song and spoken word. Working-class women in European culture are allowed earthier desires, but also considered easy prey by elite men (though actually many working-class girls were brought up to be sexually prudish). Rhys and Colette both knew the way chorus girls in their own times (a separate category of working girls) were thought, by elite men, to be easier to exploit sexually than women of their own class, guarded as they were for the purpose of appropriate marriage by which they became the property of their husbands.

A male-authored fiction about an educated woman who rebels against the sexual constraints on women in Victorian Britain, Grant Allen's *The Woman Who Did* (1895) received a lot of attention after its publication as somewhat daring female-centred fiction. Yet the story represents a woman's sexuality in exceedingly male-centred terms – as when Herminia, the protagonist, 'was woman enough by nature to like being led' (Allen [1895] 1995: 51). Herminia is a paradox; she is quintessentially pure, 'her cheek was aglow with virginal shrinking as she opened the door and welcomed Alan in' (61). Alan coming to her for sex is her 'espousal'. But she proves passionate, not just in the beginning, when she 'thrilled to the delicate fingertips' (63). Herminia is convinced that "tis the wear and tear of too close a daily intercourse which turns unawares the lover into the husband', and so she works hard as a lover (perhaps, the reader might sceptically think) because the lack of marriage means she has to maintain his interest at the level of the beginning of their relationship. 'Herminia had planned it so of set purpose' (63). After all, as is revealed later, 'it is a woman's ancestral past to look up to the man; she is happiest in doing it, and must long remain so; and Herminia was not sorry to find herself in this so much a woman' (77). In short, this tale (which ends with the rejection of Herminia by her daughter and Herminia's suicide) is at root anything but supportive of women's right to choose their own path in life.

Likewise, the idea that working-class women are inevitably less principled than women with more economic resources is a male fantasy. Françoise Barret-Ducrocq's *Love in the Time of Victoria* (1991) constitutes an analysis of working-class sexuality in Victorian London, largely through examining the archives of the Foundling Hospital. Barret-Ducrocq concludes: 'the alleged anarchic sexual behaviour of the labouring classes, denounced so violently and insistently by Victorian and Edwardian observers, is nowhere perceptible in the actual comportment of these young people and their families' (176). There is of course faithlessness and the use of sexual favours by women to try to get a better standard of living, but not wholesale lack of scruples across the board. At the end of her study, Barret-Ducroq says: 'few would deny that the Western world in the last century developed a civilization which was deeply biased against working-class women' (184).[14]

Colette and Rhys both write about women of indeterminate class status who take matters into their own hands, sometimes with great risk to themselves, sometimes with foolish or immature indifference to the consequences of their action. That Rhys (who belonged to the upper class in Dominica as a child and teenager) experienced life as an economically working-class, young chorus girl in London is important; she understood that sexual freedom as practised by talented and hopeful young women in economic need was particularly fraught and difficult. But whilst Colette's work represents ways women can evade or reconfigure power structures which confine their sexuality, whilst affirming sexuality as joyous, Rhys's protagonists are miserable being poor or short of money for the material supports (clothes, for example) of femininity. White they may be, but they have lost caste in Europe, and find it impossible to regain it through either work or relationships with men. Rhys's white Creoles have dropped out of their elite world and find the new one hard to live in. In addition, their experience of sex is mostly dismal.

Quartet and *Good Morning, Midnight*

Rhys's protagonists are, like their creator, *déclassées* women. *Quartet* (published in Britain as *Postures* in 1928) and *Good Morning, Midnight* (1939) are centrally located in Paris, as are some of the stories in *The Left Bank* (1927). Her protagonists experience a good deal of sexual experience as Rhys explores the underlying complexities which result from expecting Paris to be the city of love.[15] Rhys provides a great many details so the reader may understand that a woman down on her luck, in the economic power of an older man, is entirely in charge of her sexual responsiveness. When Marya (*Quartet*) sits on a terrace in Paris, having drinks and coffee one evening with her new acquaintances Mr and Mrs Heidler, she suddenly feels a hand on her knee: far from stirring her desire, it feels 'heavy as lead' ([1928] 2000: 13), and after she makes 'a cautious but decided movement' he withdraws it.

Marya had a history as a chorus girl in Britain, where not only the towns her company toured were a 'vague procession all exactly alike' but so were the men (15). She is also married, and we learn a disturbing detail about this marriage: that 'Napoleon's sabre' once lay unsheathed on the couple's bed, a definite echo of the mythological sword lying between illicit lovers trying to remain celibate (19). It does seem significant that this treasure has an association with Napoleon, and that the inscription offers submission to Napoleon from one of the powerful he conquered. Her husband Stephan has lost his freedom over illegal art dealing in the chaos following the First World War. This sabre seems a metonym, standing for all the ways Marya has never truly found passionate sexual experience with anyone.

Stefan is said to be 'a very gentle and expert lover', who makes his wife 'the petted, cherished child, the desired mistress, the worshipped, perfumed goddess' (20). All of these terms imply that the man is doing something to and for the woman, with her consent, but there is no hint of responsiveness from her to him. Marya is often referred to as a child (by Heidler's wife and Heidler) and disturbingly with Heidler sexually she has 'the fright of a child shut up in a dark room' (32, 71, 94). This might well be reminiscent of Jane Eyre's punishment, being shut in a room as a child.[16] When Heidler tells Marya that he is 'tortured with desire' for her, she only stares at him, silent (57). When he later says he wants to comfort her and 'hold her tight', she just says, 'H.J., don't' and puts her hand over her mouth to block his access (62). When she allows him to take her in his arms, she thinks: 'I was lost before I knew him.' She feels he shelters her, but then her response to his declaration of love is to shiver, smile and shut her eyes (66). What is between them is not healthy, nor even honest.

Marya's sexual withdrawal is in tune with her response to Parisian cultural sexual suggestiveness, 'naked girls' dancing in a music hall, which leave her cold (67–8), perhaps a reference to such dancers as Josephine Baker, who arrived in Paris in 1925. Her hotel bedroom seems haunted by 'departed and ephemeral loves', like 'stale scent' (87). The wallpaper here is horrible, 'vaguely erotic', with huge, lurid mauve, green and yellow flowers. Marya can only think of the 'petites femmes' who have stretched out on the bed in 'carefully thought out pink or mauve chemises' (87). Even Cri-Cri, a 'girl dressed in red' in the restaurant where Marya meets the Heidlers, and who provocatively sits with her 'legs widely apart', seems in her man-spreading pose, like a mixture of courtesy and aggression in the description 'hardy cavalier'. Furthermore, since she is strikingly and particularly made up, she is not to be touched (33). Heidler is explicitly described as a terrible lover:

> He didn't really like women. She had known that as soon as he touched her. His hands were inexpert, clumsy at caresses; his mouth was hard when he kissed. No, not a lover of women, he could say what he liked.
>
> He despised love. He thought of it grossly, to amuse himself, and then with ferocious contempt. Not that that mattered. [...]
>
> What mattered was that, despising, almost disliking, love, he was forcing her to be nothing but the little woman who lived in the Hôtel du Bosphore for the express purpose of being made love to. A *petite femme*.
>
> (92)

Her lips dry, her body aches and his heaviness crushes her (93). Afterwards, she lies on the bed and smells a stale scent, thinking of all the other women who have been where she is, and for the same purpose. In a confrontation with Heidler, she asks "'Didn't you say that sex was a ferocious thing?'" (101). Then she thinks (and speaks) of strangling Heidler's wife, only to be replaced once more by her return to a child's 'little voice' (102). When he kisses her, her lips are cold and she ends up being 'quivering and abject in his arms, like some unfortunate dog abashing itself before its master' (102). Marya is no different with her husband, Stefan, when she is reunited with him. Though his body trembles, he feels like a stranger to her (103). She stiffens when he touches her, and avoids sex (110).

Stefan leaves Paris, she tries to return to Heidler, unsuccessfully, and then 'like a sleep-walker' impulsively goes to a strange young man's room. She takes risks continuously. She finds Stefan 'greedy' (129). She even calls Heidler's name under her breath when with him. When in his disgust and sense of betrayal, Stefan still tries to take her in his arms, she shrinks away and he declares a jealous rage against Heidler, even showing he has a gun and intends to go to hurt him. To this, she responds that she loves Heidler and she blocks Stefan's exit through the door. As he tries to pull her aside, she falls and hits her head on the edge of the table, becoming unconscious. Thus instead of sexual reconciliation, there is physical conflict followed by her abandonment by him. The novel ends with the apparently warm and sexually indiscriminate Mselle Chardin and Stefan going away in a taxi.

Marya is not the only Rhys protagonist to have trouble with sexual passion, or who engages in unwanted sex just as potentially self-destructive as these passages suggest. This behavior also demonstrates an element of stereotypical Creole impetuosity which can get them into danger. Veronica Gregg saw that:

> Jean Rhys's writing demonstrates that the 'identity' of the Creole is made of the sociohistorical, discursive fabric of the colonial West Indies. The articulation of the Creole subjectivity is at once and the same time a discursive self-destruction articulated within the historical specificity of racialized slavery in the Caribbean.
>
> (1995: 38)

In a distanced but important way, Marya has both the necessity of submission required of a white girl in the colonial West Indies, in a society built on the violent exploitation of millions of people, and a resentment of it. That Marya's story takes place in France is also a complicated matter, as Paris is construed as a place where, as we have already considered, the white Creole had made herself known to be sexually appealing, though also capable of determining her own sexual destiny. Marya subverts the script in her own way, even though this proves self-destructive.

In the background of all of Rhys's texts lurks the shadow of plantation slavery and its facilitator, racism, a shadow much closer to Rhys's life, chronologically and geographically, than to Colette's. Sue Thomas, in her detailed discussion of sexual behaviour *in Good Morning, Midnight* in *The Worlding of Jean Rhys* (1999) points out that Serge's story of the mulatto woman who wants him to make love to her in *Good Morning, Midnight* suggests he finds her blackness a sign of promiscuity. Lurking in the background of this story is race, Sasha says that the instinct of men to either fill a woman with wine or to stop her drinking is 'racial' (*GMM* 150).

Sex begins here as absence: 'the small bedroom is in case you don't feel like me, or in case you meet somebody you like better and come in late' (29). The language of sex and love is French. Sex is the work of the lithe 'mauvais garçon' (62), René the gigolo. So it is important that he approaches the protagonist, Sasha, with a declaration that he is not after money. Rather he wants comfort and trust 'to put my head on your breast [...] and tell you everything' (64). René also thinks he is with 'a child' when he walks with Sasha, even though she is older than he is – this is reminiscent of Heidler thinking Marya is a child. This, of course, has implications for the way sexual connection can happen. But Sasha could feel sensuous and fully alive once, long ago:

> I am tuned up to top pitch. Everything is smooth, soft and tender. Making love. The colours of the pictures. The sunsets. Tender, north colours when the sun sets – pink, mauve, green and blue. And the wind very fresh and cold and the lights in the canals like gold caterpillars and the seagulls swooping over the water. Tuned up to top pitch.
>
> (98)

But when she and Enno, her husband at that time, are short of money, she gets a hundred dollars from a man from her past, who then kisses her: 'I am hating him [...], yet I feel my mouth go soft under his, and my arms go limp' (100). This is a disturbing moment of anger and surrender, in one. Then Enno complains she is sexually too passive (107). By the present time in the novel, an ageing Sasha can be extraordinarily funny about sex (her drawers drop off whilst she is at the bus stop with a man she has turned off in bed, and she just rolls them up and puts them into her handbag; 114). When René thinks of trying to make money by having sex with English women, Sasha thinks:

> Love is a stern virtue in England. (Usually a matter of hygiene, my dear. The indecent necessity – and who would spend money or thought or time on the indecent necessity? ... We have our ration of rose-leaves, but only because rose-leaves are a gentle laxative.)
>
> (132)

She has some memories of kind touching, as when she remembers a girl she saw once, who inspired her to think of putting her arms around her, kissing her eyes and comforting her – but again this is hardly sexual passion (135). An image in Sasha's head is of a 'little grimacing devil' wearing a '*cache-sexe*'. He sings a sentimental song which replaces sexuality with drab pantomime (146). Perhaps this is explained in part by Sasha's fantasy (memory? dream?) of being in sexual servitude to a man who ill-treats and betrays her: 'He often brings home other women and I have to wait on them.' But she still is 'not unhappy. If he were to die I should kill myself' (147) Yet this is not masochism. there is no charge, no excitement, no transgressive energy. Of course she is drunk. Reading this alongside the Marquis de Sade's texts however shows the brilliance of Rhys's exposure of the tragic consequences of male reduction of both women and themselves to mechanical sex toys: the popular reading of Sade is the one Rhys appears to be answering, in which such behaviour is offered as thrilling and provocative. It is easy to find scenes of male-centred power in Sade's work, in which victims are simply dismissed in their attempts to appeal to pity or empathy on the part of their abusers. In *Justine*, Clément, the abusive monk, theorizes the kind of desire in men which was clearly made fact by slave masters on Caribbean plantations: 'Does not tyranny give a much stronger boost to pride than beneficence? In short, is not the man who dominates much more obviously the master than the man who shares' (Sade [1791] 2012: 138). We should recall that Napoleon had Sade arrested on the assumption that he had written *Zoloé et ses deux acolytes* (anonymous, 1800).[17] Napoleon objected to what he saw as the fictionalizing of Joséphine's sexual life before her marriage to him. It is tempting to read some aspects of Rhys's fiction, especially in *Good Morning, Midnight*, in relation to the popular interpretation of Sade as the creator of toxic fantasies. Certainly in Rhys's work, there is a striking representation of loveless sex as deeply traumatizing.

It is in the conclusion of *Good Morning, Midnight* where we see this most disturbingly. Sasha's reunion with René seems at first to bring back 'love, youth, spring, happiness' (*GMM* 148). They kiss 'fervently' (148), but she feels that 'something has gone wrong' (148). She blames her withdrawal on being out of practice (150). She orders him to go. '"I don't like it," he says, "that voice that gives orders"' (151). Sasha thinks that she does not 'always' like that sort of voice either. They enter a physical battle for dominance because they both remember what it is to be dominated and want no part of it again:

> And there we are – struggling on the small bed. My idea is not so much to struggle as to make it a silent struggle. Nobody must hear us. At the end, he is lying on me, holding down my two spread arms. I can't move. My dress is torn open at the neck. But I have my knees firmly clamped together.
>
> (151)

Perhaps to distract herself from the violence of this, she turns again to her bitter humour which so informs this novel: they are on the wrong bed, with all their clothes on, 'just like English people' (152).

Furthering the turn from cynicism to violence, René describes something 'in Morocco' where four comrades help a man have a woman and each take their turn (152), which seems another direct writing back to Sade, as well as a referencing of colonialism and representations of women as sexually dominated.[18] Though Sasha claims she is strong, he asks, why has she closed her eyes? Then he threatens: 'Je te ferai mal' (I will hurt you). He thinks it is her fault. His hard knee is between her knees and she says: 'my mouth hurts, my breasts hurt, because it hurts, when you have been dead, to come alive' (153). But she does not 'come alive'. Instead, after the sex, she insults him by offering him money. He leaves, and Sasha, realizing her mouth is swollen and still bleeding where he bit it, grieves her own behaviour, wills him back and then, believing he will come, prepares for him to return, leaving the door open. But instead, the strange man, the *commis*, comes in and looks at her with mean eyes. What she says is an ironic version of Molly Bloom's earthly joy at the end of Joyce's *Ulysses:* 'and yes I said yes I will yes' (Joyce [1922] 1971: 703). Sasha says simply 'Yes-yes-yes.' Not that she will do anything, but that she accepts something. She is not going to 'despise another poor devil of a human being' ever again. She is not going to be a victim, and neither is the man she embraces.

The ending of *Good Morning, Midnight* is generally read as a simple degradation and even potential annihilation of Sasha as the *commis* enters her room. Shari Benstock argues: 'in embracing this salesman, Sasha opens her arms to the slow numbing of human responses that will end in death' (Benstock [1987] 1994: 440). But there may be another possibility – the ironical echo of Molly Bloom inverts the cliché roles of female and male. Sasha is in charge, of a world in which sex is just another inequitable space of human activity, but one that, in her drunken state, she is willing to enter into on her own terms. Of course, she risks more than just an impersonal sexual encounter in allowing a strange man to come to her with not so much as a word spoken. But she makes her reader identify with this wounded daughter of the two European cultures which coexisted tensely in her childhood Dominica.

Rhys thus reminds us, in the idealized city of love, that power in the present takes its patterns from power in the past, and that for some people, like her protagonists, that means ultimately making a stand for who you are, or happen to be, and taking energy from that. This also recalls Joséphine, who also had a complicated, not entirely successful life in some terms, but who we remember as being herself. Paris is a complicated space for Sasha. Rhys's childhood in Dominica was also complicated, not just by family but by history, as Louis James points out, with regard to the polarization of the French and English in Dominica as a result of Napoleon's wars.[19] The ending of this novel has Sasha making a declaration, an acceptance of where she is and what she is doing. In the shadow of the plantation, Sasha claims a very wounded freedom, cognizant of the place white Creole women occupy in the world when they do not live by the rules – but nevertheless, full of energy, not of defeat – and at least it faces all the brutal truths which have haunted her. As we face a world in which it is clear powerful men have continued to violate basic human rights with regard to women and sex, even after political victories for gender justice and equality, Rhys reminds us that every woman needs to be true to herself, to engage with the world in public and private, on her own terms. What is very evident is not only how honestly and exquisitely she wrote, but how much she *knew*.

Notes

1   Kamau Brathwaite pointed to white Creole alienation in 1974 in a much misunderstood statement, 'White creoles in the English and French West Indies have separated themselves by too wide a gulf and have contributed too little culturally, as a group, to give credence to the notion that they can, given the present structure, meaningfully identify or be identified, with the spiritual world on this side of the Sargasso Sea' (1974: 38). But he has never rejected Rhys as a Caribbean writer. He was speaking here of a comment by a critic of Rhys with whom he was disagreeing. My first book on Rhys appeared in the Cambridge series on African and Caribbean writers (Savory 1998). It was by no means an accepted idea in Rhys criticism that Rhys is a Caribbean writer, though Caribbean writers such as Olive Senior, Lorna Goodison, Jamaica Kincaid, Caryl Phillips, Robert Antoni and many others have never had doubts. We continue to see how Rhys inspires new Caribbean writers, and how now we know how much we need to go to the Caribbean to read her fully – not as an exclusive approach but as a necessary one.
2   This oligarchy, even in the English community in Dominica, was not all Anglo-Saxon: Rhys's family included ancestry from Scotland on her mother's side and Wales on her father's – the Caribbean has many stories of people of Irish, Scottish or Welsh descent who migrated to the Caribbean and adopted privileged 'white' positions, erasing their own people's long struggles against English power.
3   The 'Mr Howard' story is a draft or diary entry in 'The Black Notebook' and is also fictionalized in the story 'Goodbye Marcus, Goodbye Rose' (*CSS*) discussed by several critics, including Sue Thomas (1999). Rhys's fiction collectively explores the evolution of female responses to sexual or emotional abuse and domination (even at times becoming aggressive themselves). It is a very different world from that of Sade because Rhys understands women complexly: reading her texts beside his helps make the reader more aware of the originality and power of her work.
4   Though Carole Angier's biography is weakened by taking reportage and Rhys's own fiction as biographical fact, her discussion of Owen's manuscript is an intriguing suggestion of ways the Rees-Williams children imagined transgressions of race and sex in their segregated world. Owen certainly had mixed-race children, whom Rhys visited in 1936 on her return to Dominica. There is also Sandi, the character

in *Wide Sargasso Sea*, the one Antoinette loves, and from whom she is taken away (Angier [1990] 1992: 31). Angier quotes Rhys on a white girl with a lover of color, 'in those days *a terrible* thing for a white girl to do. Not to be forgiven. The men did as they liked. The women – *never*' (33; emphases in the original).

5 Angier quotes the letter from the Administrator of Tree's School: 'although she is painstaking, we consider her accent will stand very much in her way in stage work' (Angier [1990] 1992: 49).

6 In *Voyage in the Dark*, the white Creole Anna is called 'the Hottentot' by her fellow chorus girls in Britain, and when Walter Jeffries, soon to be her lover, asks why, there is no answer (*VD* 12).

7 See Honeychurch [1975] 1984. Dominica had 'the Mulatto Ascendency', and was the only island in the British West Indies where white rule was successfully challenged – by this group of mixed-race and moneyed people (a result of migration after the first, middle-class Haitian revolution failed). Perhaps this made the small English white community more defensive.

8 Andrea Stuart, being Barbadian, is fully conversant with the Caribbean and has also written an excellent family history, *The Sugar in the Blood: A Family's Story of Slavery and Empire* (2013). She begins: 'My family is just one of millions across the globe that were forged by sugar and slavery' (vxii). She is the ideal biographer for Joséphine: she omits the accent on the name, pointing out that this name was given to her by Napoleon, after his eldest brother Joseph (2003: 178). Because this essay was delivered as a talk at the Sorbonne, the accent has remained here for all but the first Stuart reference, in the main text, out of respect for French linguistic and cultural norms.

9 Stuart asks if Joséphine was a courtesan, and points out that she freely chose her partners. A good many women after the Revolution turned to using their sexuality in the search for a more secure financial future. Divorce was legally allowed after 1793, to the extent that there were many more single women available (also single men) (see Stuart 2013: 160–1).

10 Ironically, in a relationship in which Ford had all the power – material resources, and success as a writer and publisher, older man – Ford's biographer Alan Judd remarks that what Ford 'taught her was not so much how to write, though there was some of that, as that she was a writer' (1991: 358). In short, he gave her the confidence to defeat her social fragility with her talent, a talent which in her first novel was strong enough to reveal Ford's *When the Wicked Man* as the poor writerly job it is.

11 Thurman tells the story of how some of Colette's ancestors went to Martinique because as Protestants they suffered persecution in France in the seventeenth century, and they were slave owners. They had children of mixed race, some of whom returned to France (1999: 6–7).

12 Thurman points out that 'most of the great fin de siècle cocottes had at one time kept much younger men' (1999: 283), clearly a manifestation of a certain kind of female power, even if supported by economic provision for the younger man.
13 Helen Carr points out that an early essay on Rhys by Judith Kegan Gardner indicates reference to Colette in *Good Morning, Midnight* (Carr 1996: 9).
14 The French nationality of the author of this study gives a stronger meaning to her comment about the Western world, showing she does not see Victorian London as unique with regard to the mores of working-class women.
15 Rhys's first collection of stories is remarkably reticent about sexual passion, written in the leanest of prose.
16 'Take her away to the red room and lock her in there' (Brontë [1847] 1985: 43).
17 I am indebted to Kerry-Jane Wallart for reminding me of this uncanny connection between the perversity of Sade's male fantasies and the realities of the white Creole woman in Paris.
18 Morocco is clearly a metonym, for France has colonial control of Morocco from 1912 to 1956.
19 James says, of her feeling about Dominica, 'Jean identified more strongly with the French side – Roman Catholic, cosmopolitan and with a greater acceptance of life – than with the more Puritan English tradition' (1978: 15).

2

Strange defeat: *Good Morning, Midnight* and Marc Bloch's *L'Étrange Défaite*

Scott McCracken

I cry for a long time – for myself, for the old woman with the bald head, for all the sadness of this damned world, for all the fools and all the defeated.
—Jean Rhys, *Good Morning, Midnight* ([1939] 2000)

Nous venons de subir une incroyable défaite.
—Marc Bloch, *L'Étrange Défaite* ([1946] 1992)

What would happen if we were to read *Good Morning, Midnight* against the historian Marc Bloch's memoir of the fall of France: *L'Étrange Défaite: témoignage écrit en 1940* (*The Strange Defeat: A Statement of Evidence*)? Bloch's title alone provokes a comparison. Critics such as Helen Carr ([1996] 2012) and Mary Lou Emery (1990) have highlighted the strangeness of Rhys's fiction. In her introduction to *Good Morning, Midnight*, A. L. Kennedy describes Rhys's fiction as 'both strange and unnervingly familiar' (2000: v). The French word, *étrange*, with its derivations, *l'étrangeté*, *l'étranger*, translates into English as strange, strangeness, the stranger/the foreigner or sometimes, as with the British translation of Albert Camus's *L'Étranger*, the outsider. The strange, the foreign, outsider status, these are all ideas critics have associated with Rhys's work. *Good Morning, Midnight*'s borrowed title (from Emily Dickinson's poem 'Good Morning – Midnight') performs the encounter with strangeness that so often lies at the heart of Rhys's texts. It has the force of one of Walter Benjamin's dialectical images – 'dialectics at a standstill', as Rolf Tiedemann described them (1999). Two opposing concepts are held together, light and dark, day and night, and though these contradictory states and temporalities pull apart, the explosive force of their opposition is yet to be released by the messianic force of history. As for defeat, Sasha comments early in the novel: 'Today, this day, this hour, this minute, I am utterly defeated' (*GMM* 25). Reading the Rhysian subject as defeated counteracts the danger of seeing victimhood as inevitable or worse, unalterable, as in Walter Allen's 1967 review of *Wide Sargasso Sea*, in which he described the 'Rhys woman' as 'hopelessly and helplessly at sea [...] a passive victim doomed to destruction' (1967: 5; for an excellent overview of the tendency in early Rhys criticism to emphasize the powerlessness of her characters, see Johnson and Wilson 2013a). According to Reinhart Koselleck, the defeated are always better historians than victors:

> [The victors'] history has a short-term perspective and is focused on those series of events that, through their own efforts, brought them victory [...]. The historian who is on the side of the victor is prone to interpret short-term successes from the perspective of a continuous, long-term teleology ex post facto.
>
> This does not apply to the vanquished. Their first primary experience is that everything happened differently from how it was planned or hoped. If they reflect methodologically at all they face a greater burden of proof to explain why something happened in this and not the anticipated way [...]. If history is made in the short run by the victors, historical gains in knowledge stem in the long run from the vanquished.
>
> (2002: 76)

Those critics who read Rhys's novels as historical rather than psychological are less liable to describe her heroines as victims (Helen Carr reads Rhys's fiction in relation to histories of colonialism and fascism: [1996] 2012; Jess Issacharoff in relation to the growth of fascism and anti-Semitism in the 1930s: 2013; Anna Snaith in relation to the history of the imperial metropolis: 2014). Helen Carr writes of *Good Morning, Midnight*:

> The colonial-bred Rhys's 'terrified consciousness' must certainly have sensitized her to the violence and fear behind European respectability, but the paranoia she evokes is not just [...] that of a 'psychological type', but of an epoch. She is describing the febrile nightmarish world of Europe on the eve of the Second World War, with its anti-Semitism, its racism, its class-machinery, its nationalistic posturing.
>
> ([1996] 2012: 53)

As narratives of defeat, *Good Morning, Midnight* and *L'Étrange Défaite* trouble one another. Comparing Rhys with Bloch allows a rereading of both texts: *L'Étrange Défaite* as modernist, and *Good Morning, Midnight* as historical, without losing the generic qualities of either. Reading the Rhysian subject as defeated turns the novelist into a historian. Reading Bloch's historical account as modernist highlights the ways in which the strange temporality of defeat pushes the historian towards literary form.

Rhys and Bloch were from very different backgrounds, but they were of the same generation and each was already middle-aged when *Good Morning, Midnight* and *L'Étrange Défaite* were published. Bloch was born in 1886 in Lyon, Rhys in 1890 on the island of Dominica in the British West Indies. Rhys was forty-nine when *Good Morning, Midnight* was published, Bloch was fifty-four when he wrote *L'Étrange Défaite*. Moreover, both carried markers of outsider status: Rhys's Caribbean accent announced her Dominican origins; and Bloch's name revealed his Jewish heritage, which put him in mortal danger in occupied France:

> Je suis Juif, sinon par la religion, que je ne pratique point, non plus que nulle autre, du moins par la naissance. Je n'en tire ni orgueil ni honte, étant, je l'espère, assez bon historien pour n'ignorer point que les prédispositions raciales sont un mythe et la notion même de race pure une absurdité particulièrement flagrante, lorsqu'elle prétend s'appliquer, comme ici, à ce qui fut, en réalité, un groupe de croyants, recrutés, jadis, dans tout le monde méditerranéen, turco-khazar et slave. Je ne revendique jamais mon origine que dans un cas: en face d'un antisémite. Mais peut-être les personnes qui s'opposeront à mon témoignage chercheront à le ruiner en me traitant de 'métèque'.
>
> (Bloch [1946] 1992: 31)

> I am Jewish, if not in religion, which I no longer practise, then at least by birth. I draw no pride or shame from it, being I hope a good enough historian to know that racial predispositions are a myth and the notion of racial purity itself a particularly flagrant absurdity when applied to those who are, in reality, a group of believers, recruited throughout the Mediterranean, Turko-Khazar and Slavic worlds. I never make an issue of my origins except when faced with an anti-Semite. But perhaps those who will contest my testimony will look to wreck it by calling me a 'métèque'.
>
> (Bloch 1949: 3)

By the outbreak of the Second World War, Bloch was an established historian. One of the original founders of the Annales school in France, he was best known for his studies of feudalism, notably *Les Rois thaumaturges* (*The Royal Touch*, [1924] 2015), about the magical healing abilities attributed to monarchs. He had fought and been decorated in the First World War, and in 1939 he left his job at the Sorbonne to join up again aged fifty-three. When the German forces overwhelmed the Allies in the spring of 1940, he was evacuated from Dunkirk to England, and then transported to Normandy, where the French army was supposed to regroup. But instead of arriving in a war zone, he had the strange experience of watching German troops entering French towns unopposed. He chose to discard his uniform, stay in France, and join the Resistance. In 1944, he was captured by the Vichy police, handed over to the Gestapo, tortured and shot, ten days after D-Day. Written in 1940, *L'Étrange Défaite* was Bloch's immediate response to defeat. After the war it became a classic text of the Resistance. But *L'Étrange Défaite* was only retrospectively a heroic text. It was written as a document of defeat at a time when victory felt distant and uncertain, when the Sorbonne professor had become a 'métèque', an untranslatable racial slur used to describe someone of mixed 'race' or ethnicity – in other words, a stranger in his own land.

Étrange/Strange

Raymond Williams famously described the modernist city as the city of strangers (1989: 34). Williams does not include gender in his definition of strangeness, but many women writers of the period saw their position as strange. In the first two chapter-volumes of Dorothy Richardson's *Pilgrimage* (2020), *Pointed Roofs* (1915) and *Backwater* (1916), the words 'strange', 'stranger' or 'strangely' are used 132 times. In *Pointed Roofs* the epithet is applied mainly to Miriam Henderson's experience of Germany, where she has gone to work as a seventeen-year-old pupil-teacher in a school in Hanover. As an *émigrée* in a foreign land, Miriam is forced to recalibrate the familiar categories of class, religion and gender that made sense of the world in England. At first this makes her anxious, but she finds strangeness can also be a joyful experience: German, French and English are all part of everyday discourse in the school's polyglot culture, often fusing into creative hybrid constructions, a new international language. In contrast, when Miriam returns to England, she feels cut off, stranded in a school in North London. Strangeness there is not joyful but rather a *malaise*, a strangeness from self. Miriam does not fit. None of the available feminine identities – suburban wife, *femme fatale*, old maid – can be reconciled with her desires. In 1890s London Miriam is strange. She is the stranger. The *émigrée* has become the internal exile.

In the novels of Jean Rhys the dialectic is the same, but the starting point is different. Rhys's protagonists in many of her novels and short stories begin as outsiders, arriving from the colony, only to find themselves as strangers in the imperial cities of London or Paris. Her narratives seem to be stories of isolation, but they show similar, repeated patterns. Rhys's short stories, particularly the handful that represent the experience of colonial exile, focus on a singularity that symbolizes the sense of being out of place: the hidden dresses in 'Illusion'; the pallid artist in 'Tout Montparnasse and a Lady'; the artist who refuses to sell his art in 'Tea with an Artist'; the starving woman in 'Hunger'; the Caribbean family in Paris in 'Trio' (*CSS*). Though Sasha's story of homelessness acts as its organizing narrative, *Good Morning, Midnight* resembles Rhys's oeuvre as a whole in the sense that it is a collection of story fragments, which are closer to anecdotes told by a scattered collective of the lost than fully-fledged narratives. The stories of the people Sasha meets narrate the experience of homelessness as a consequence of defeat. Sasha herself says: 'I have no pride – no pride, no face, no country. I don't belong anywhere' (*GMM* 38). René, the hapless gigolo, says he has come from Morocco, where he was a member of the Foreign Legion (*la Légion étrangère*). The Russians, perhaps Russian-Jews, seem to be refugees, in exile from perhaps the Soviet Union or perhaps Germany. They speak a language strange to Sasha, perhaps Russian, perhaps not, which she cannot understand. These characters tell anecdotes about themselves or others like them.

For example, one of the 'Russians', who gives his name as Serge Rubin, tells a story about a woman from Martinique, whom he found drunk outside his door, when he was living in Notting Hill in London. The woman has been made into a stranger by the hostility of her English hosts: 'She said every time [the other people living in the house] looked at her she could see how they hated her, and the people in the streets looked at her the same way' (*GMM* 80). This woman has a close relationship to, and may even be the same character as, the protagonist in Rhys's short story, 'Let Them Call it Jazz', Selina Davis, a Caribbean exile living in London, who is reported to the police by her neighbours for singing (*CSS* 150–67). Both characters, and the exiled Serge himself, connect Sasha's experience to the experience of exile and defeat (Issacharoff 2013: 112).

These figures, who are scattered across Rhys's fiction, comprise an unconstituted and unachieved assembly, what one might call not so much *une Légion étrangère*, a foreign legion, as *une légion d'étrangers*, a legion of strangers. Sasha is one of them and she also tells anecdotes, such as the story about the old, bald woman who comes into the shop where Sasha briefly finds a job. The woman is looking for something to wear on her head, but her attempts to present a brave face in a city that has no time for older women collapses in the face of her daughter's embarrassment and hostility. Sasha sympathizes with the woman: 'why not buy her a wig, several decent dresses, as much champagne as she can drink, all the things she likes to eat and oughtn't to, a gigolo if she wants one' (*GMM* 20). Sasha's isolation and precariousness make her, like the bald woman, subject to derision or worse – the verbal and sexual violence of the men in the hotel where she lives. I will return to the relationship between Sasha's narrative and the anecdotes of those she meets; but for a better understanding of their condition not as one of victimhood but of defeat, we need to return to Bloch's *L'Étrange Défaite*.

L'Étrange Défaite

Bloch's memoir is divided into three chapters that move from the personal to the political. In the first, 'Présentation du témoin' (Presentation of the Witness), Bloch tells his personal experience of the Battle for France. In the second chapter, 'La déposition d'un vaincu' (The Testimony of One of the Defeated), Bloch makes the transition from personal witness to forensic historian: 'Nous venons de subir une incroyable défaite. À qui la faute?' (Bloch [1946] 1992: 54); 'We have just suffered an unbelievable defeat. Whose fault was it?' (Bloch 1949: 25; translation modified). The English translation of the chapter title is 'One of the Vanquished Gives Evidence'. It is perhaps an ironic consequence of Britain's history that English doesn't offer an exact translation of *un vaincu*: 'one vanquished' is too formal, 'one of the defeated' too awkward, 'a loser' too pejorative. After a necessarily brief military analysis, because he does not feel he has sufficient access to the relevant documents to write a proper history of the campaign, Bloch turns in the third chapter, 'Examen de conscience d'un Français' ('Examination of the Conscience of a Frenchman', translation modified), to the question of 'mentalité', one of the key concepts of the Annales school. He argues that 'the triumph of the Germans was, essentially, an intellectual victory and it is perhaps this in itself that makes it more serious' (66; translation modified); 'le triomphe des Allemands fut, essentiellement, une victoire intellectuelle et c'est peut-être là ce qu'il y a eu en lui de plus grave' (36). And it is in Bloch's pursuit of the origin of France's defeat in the pre-war mentality of the 1930s, that *L'Étrange Défaite* meets *Good Morning, Midnight*, transforming the novel from a psychological study of a single mind into a history of an epoch, and the work of history into a work of the imagination.

The defeated historian, in hiding and separated from the archive, is forced into a literary mode. Consider the opening lines of Bloch's text:

> Ces pages seront-elles jamais publiées ? Je ne sais. Il est probable, en tout cas, que, de longtemps, elles ne pourront être connues, sinon sous le manteau, en dehors de mon entourage immédiat. Je me suis cependant décidé à les écrire. L'effort sera rude: combien il me semblerait plus commode de céder aux conseils de la fatigue et du découragement!
>
> (Bloch [1946] 1992: 29)

> Will these pages ever be published? I don't know. In any case it is likely that for a long time they will be unknown, except clandestinely in my immediate circle. However, I have decided to write them. It will be hard. How much easier it would be to succumb to fatigue and discouragement!
>
> (Bloch 1949: 1; translation modified)

These lines exceed the bleak reality of the author's situation. There are echoes of the French Romantic tradition – Victor Hugo and Alexandre Dumas – but also, in the proleptic gesture to an unknown future, a gesture to the play of temporalities in modernist texts. However dire his circumstances, Bloch was an experienced writer. He knew what he was doing: creating a text for a future that would know what he could not. The strangeness for the reader of holding this text, written in secret, hidden from the enemy, now in our hands, is anticipated by a historian who knows the sense of wonder when the past gives up its secrets. In retrospect, after 1946, the published text was not just about the defeat of France, but the defeat and death of its author. The narrative of *L'Étrange Défaite* anticipates and incorporates that likely future. This uncanny premonition is a starting point for the text's examination of the strange temporality of defeat.

Bloch's primary metaphors for the temporality of defeat are slowness and reversal. In the Nazi invasion of France, German speed, *Blitzkrieg* (lightning war), reveals French slowness:

> Les Allemands ont fait une guerre d'aujourd'hui, sous le signe de la vitesse. Nous n'avons pas seulement tenté de faire, pour notre part, une guerre de la veille ou de l'avant-veille. Au moment même où nous voyions les Allemands mener la leur, nous n'avons pas su ou pas voulu en comprendre le rythme, accordé aux vibrations accélérées d'une ère nouvelle. Ce furent deux adversaires appartenant chacun à un âge différent de l'humanité qui se heurtèrent sur nos champs de bataille. Nous

avons en somme renouvelé les combats, familiers à notre histoire coloniale, de la sagaie contre le fusil. Mais c'est nous, cette fois, qui jouions les primitifs.

(Bloch [1946] 1992: 67)

The Germans conducted a war of today, a war of speed. We fought a war of yesterday or the day before. From the very moment we saw their method, we neither knew nor wanted to understand the rhythm matching the accelerated pulse of a new era. It was as if the two adversaries who met on the battlefield each belonged to a different age of humanity. We repeated the familiar combat of our colonial history: spear against rifle. But this time it was us who played the primitives.

(Bloch 1949: 37; translation modified)

If France is defeated by speed, deceleration is the consequence of defeat. After occupation, Bloch describes the village in which he is living as having gone back in time to an earlier, slower period:

Car les privations, issues de la guerre ou de la défaite, ont agi sur l'Europe comme une machine à remonter le temps et c'est aux genres de vie d'un passé, hier encore considéré comme à jamais disparu, qu'elles nous ont brusquement ramenés [...]. Cette année, où il nous faut, pour les personnes les plus ingambes, nous contenter de bicyclettes et, pour les matières pondéreuses, de la voiture à âne, chaque départ vers le bourg prend les allures d'une expédition. Comme il y a trente ou quarante ans!

(Bloch [1946] 1992: 66)

For the privations resulting from the war or the defeat acted on Europe like a time machine in reverse. We have been plunged suddenly into a way of life, considered only recently to have disappeared for ever [...]. This year, when the fittest have to content themselves with bicycles, and for heavy loads, carts pulled by donkeys, each trip to town feels like a major expedition. Like thirty or forty years ago!

(Bloch 1949: 37; translation modified)

In defeat, time slows down to the point of reversal: the victors become the vanquished, the occupiers become the occupied, and the colonizers become the colonized. To borrow a verb from the title of Walter Rodney's classic anti-colonial text *How Europe Underdeveloped Africa*, France is 'underdeveloped' by its invaders. As Rodney writes: 'To mark time, or even to move slowly while others leap ahead is virtually equivalent to going backward' ([1972] 2018: 271). For Bloch as for Rodney, underdevelopment is the result of defeat, a process, not a state of being. Invasion sends France backwards, but the historian Bloch sees France's backwardness not just as one of the effects but also as a cause of defeat, the roots of which lie in the mentality of the pre-war. Its origins are not military or technological, but intellectual and social. They lie in the internal collapse of French society in the 1930s, above all the abdication of its ruling class: 'une crise de la moralité collective, dans certaines couches de la nation' (Bloch [1946] 1992: 138 n.1; footnote added July 1942); 'a crisis of collective morality in certain strata of the nation' (Bloch 1949: 105–6 n.1; translation modified):

> À dire vrai, ce mot de classes dirigeantes ne va pas sans équivoque. Dans la France de 1939, la haute bourgeoisie se plaignait volontiers d'avoir perdu tout pouvoir. Elle exagérait beaucoup. Appuyé sur la finance et la presse, le régime des 'notables' n'était pas si 'fini' que cela. Mais il est certain que les maîtres d'antan avaient cessé de détenir le monopole des leviers de commande. À côté d'eux, sinon les salariés en masse, du moins les chefs des principaux syndicats comptaient parmi les puissances de la République.
> (Bloch [1946] 1992: 168)

> But this very question of the 'ruling class' raises questions which need very careful consideration. In the France of 1939, the members of the upper middle class were never sick of declaring that they had lost all power. This was an exaggeration. Solidly backed by the banks and the Press, the régime of the *élite* was not, to that extent, finished. But it *is* true that the great industrialists no longer held a monopoly on the levers of power. Next to them, the leaders of the principal trade unions, in contrast to the mass of wage-earners at least, had risen to a position of power in the affairs of the Republic.
> (Bloch 1949: 134–5; translation modified; emphasis in the original)

The temporality of defeat is experienced as a deceleration to the point where time itself is reversed. But for Bloch the historian, reversal provokes a recognition that these processes are not just the consequences of defeat: they were already there. In bringing the origins of defeat to light, *L'Étrange Défaite* not only describes but also deploys the temporal disruptions inflicted by defeat to disrupt the logic of the victor's narrative. What has quickly come to seem inevitable, even natural, is analysed in terms of an already existing state of mind, not least the predisposition of certain strata of French society towards fascism (a predisposition that existed in all European states). This mentality led to particular decisions, both passive and active, before, during and after occupation; but it is the historian's job to show that the outcome was not inevitable. Things could have been otherwise; and if the past could have been otherwise, then so might the future.

Sasha's strange defeat

Sasha's predicament can seem as inevitable as the fall of France. A common reading of *Good Morning, Midnight* is that it describes not history but a pathology, specifically the pathology of alcoholism, where each day starts with the inevitability of drinking again. The being drunk of midnight is already there in the hung-over start of the morning; but reading the novel against Bloch suggests that it represents not a pathology but an analysis of the mentality of an epoch.

A much commented upon episode in *Good Morning, Midnight* lends itself to such a reading. When Sasha is working in the shop, her English employer, a man she calls 'Mr Blank', asks her to take a letter to the 'kise', a word Mr Blank compresses to the point where Sasha doesn't understand it. She sets off nonetheless, and quickly gets lost. The layout of the building, made up of two houses, is unnavigable. At first Sasha is too embarrassed to ask the way, and when she does ask another employee, she is told, 'Connais pas' (Don't know): 'After this it becomes a nightmare. I walk up stairs, past doors, along passages – all different, all exactly alike. There is something very urgent I must do. But I don't meet a soul and all the doors are shut' (*GMM* 23). In what seems to be an apt figure for her slow spiral downwards, Sasha returns to where she started, Mr Blank's office, humiliated. Mr Blank and his assistant, Salvatini, insult and ridicule her, telling her too late, that the 'kise' is 'la caisse', the cashier's office.

This incident is one of the few examples in the novel of Sasha engaging with the social apparatus, but it is typical of *Good Morning, Midnight*'s narrative structure in that the paradoxical effect of Mr Blank's linguistic *Blitzkrieg* is one of deceleration. In this respect it resembles Franz Kafka's narratives: the confusing layout of the building echoes the labyrinthine architecture found in Kafka's *The Trial* and *The Castle*. As with Kafka's frustrated characters, Sasha finds it impossible to make progress (Carr [1996] 2012: 33–5). That Sasha's experience is again told in the form of anecdote is important. When Walter Benjamin tries to explain Kafka's technique in his essay written on the tenth anniversary of Kafka's death, he also resorts to an anecdote (apparently borrowed from Pushkin) about Shuvalkin, an 'unimportant little clerk', in the court of Catherine the Great.

The story begins when Potemkin, Catherine's all-powerful minister, is suffering from a prolonged bout of depression, which has brought the business of the state to a halt (Benjamin 1999b: 794). Documents requiring Potemkin's signature pile up, driving the Empress's high officials to distraction. Entering a room in the midst of the crisis, Shuvalkin naively offers to take the documents to Potemkin's bedroom. Finding him on his bed in the darkened chamber, Shuvalkin thrusts the papers into Potemkin's hand, then watches with satisfaction as the minister signs every one. Shuvalkin then returns in triumph to the high officials only to watch them react with horror as they examine the documents. Only now does he read the signatures: 'One document after another was signed Shuvalkin ... Shuvalkin ... Shuvalkin ....' Benjamin describes this story as follows:

> Like a herald of Kafka's work, storming two hundred years ahead of it. The enigma which beclouds this story is Kafka's enigma. The world of offices and registries, of musty, shabby, dark rooms, is Kafka's world [...]. Potemkin [...] is an ancestor of those holders of power in Kafka's works who live in the attics as judges or in the castle as secretaries. No matter how highly placed they may be, they are always fallen or falling men, although even the lowest and seediest of them, the doorkeepers and the decrepit officials, may abruptly and strikingly appear in the fullness of their power.
>
> (795)

Just as Kafka's 'holders of power' are the heirs to Potemkin, so Jean Rhys's Mr Blank is heir to Kafka's 'fallen or falling men'. Even though his business is going bust, Mr Blank still has power over Sasha and that power manifests itself in a disorientating slowing down, which seems to contradict the apparent acceleration of capitalist modernity, but which is integral to it. We might compare the experience of the worker on the factory production line, where, as in Chaplin's *Modern Times*, the line goes too fast, but the clock slows down, so that minutes stretch out into hours of boredom. For Sasha, life is passing her by with demoralizing speed. She seems older than she is – hence her fixation on the old bald woman as her own future already come to pass – but her daily experience, particularly after she loses her job, is the opposite: slow, purposeless, an unending empty time (on temporality and Rhys's fiction, see Flynn 2013): 'This damned room – it's saturated with the past. ... It's all the rooms I've ever slept in, all the streets I've ever walked in. Rooms, streets, streets, rooms' (*GMM* 91). And later in the novel:

> Eat. Drink. Walk. March. Back to the hotel. Back to the hotel. To the Hotel of Arrival, the Hotel of Departure, the Hotel of the Future, the Hotel of Martinique and the Universe. ... Back to the hotel without a name in the street without a name [...]. This is the Hotel Without-a-name in the Street Without-a-Name and

the clients have no names, no faces. You go up the stairs. Always the same stairs, always the same room.

(120)

Equally, the atmosphere in Mr Blank's firm can be compared with the garrison mentality Marc Bloch describes as both typical of the French Army and as representative of pre-war French society: 'les états-majors ressemblaient à une maison d'affaires [...] pourvue au sommet de chefs de service – représentés ici par les officiers' (Bloch [1946] 1992: 90); 'the army staffs resembled business houses with departmental managers – represented by the officers' (Bloch 1949: 59; translation modified). In both *L'Étrange Défaite* and *Good Morning, Midnight* defeat is ensured by power structures, guarded by place-men and officials, who block and slow time, ensuring that the battle is lost even before it has begun.

Anecdote

In both Bloch and Rhys, the anecdote acts as a counter to the process of deceleration. The anecdote is one of the few narrative forms available to the defeated, who in their condition of homelessness, have been separated from the narrative structures, whether historical or literary, that might otherwise sustain them. Its importance was recognized by Benjamin. Allusions to the anecdote are scattered throughout his writings and his use of the Shuvalkin anecdote to introduce his essay on Kafka is more than a convenient point of comparison. For Benjamin, the anecdote is a fragment that works like a key to unlock the fragmentary, incoherent experience of urban modernity. In his essay, 'The Storyteller', Benjamin describes how the bond of experience shared by the oral teller of tales and their audience has been lost in the twentieth century: 'For never has experience been more thoroughly belied than strategic experience was belied by tactical warfare, economic experience by inflation, bodily experience by mechanical warfare, moral experience by those in power' (2002: 144).

The modern short story writer has to sacrifice the satisfying plenitude of the 'tale' for fragments of experience. Though Benjamin does not introduce the concept of the anecdote in 'The Storyteller', it figures in *The Arcades Project* as one of the lost or detached objects (such as collar studs that have lost their collar) one can find in the Parisian arcades, that might be given new meaning if rearranged into a new constellation:

The true method of making things present is to represent them in our space (not to represent ourselves in their space). (The collector does this and so does the anecdote.) Thus represented, the things allow no mediating construction from out of 'large contexts'. The same method applies, in essence to the consideration of great things from the past [...]. We don't displace our being into theirs; they step into our life. [H2, 3]

(1999a: 206)

In *Good Morning, Midnight*, Sasha's anecdote about Mr Blank is just such a fragment, one that allows her briefly to make sense of her situation, reconfiguring her experience into social critique:

You who represent Society, have the right to pay me four hundred francs a month. That's my market value [...]. [T]o lodge me in a small dark room, to clothe me shabbily, to harass me with worry and monotony and unsatisfied longings till you get me to the point when I blush at a look, cry at a word. [...] Some must cry so that others may be able to laugh more heartily [...]. You must be able to despise the people you exploit. But I wish you a lot of trouble Mr Blank and just to start off with, your damned shop's going bust. Alleluia!

(*GMM* 25-6)

This insight does not help Sasha. In fact, it sharpens her sense of defeat prompting her to say: 'I cry for a long time – for myself, for the old woman with the bald head, for all the sadness of the damned world, for all the fools and all the defeated' (25). Yet to see that social order in terms of defeat is at least to register a battle lost. In that recognition, as in Bloch's recognition of defeat, there is an implicit acknowledgement that things could have been (and still could be) otherwise. Unlike Marc Bloch, Sasha does not fight back: 'Did I say all this, of course I didn't. I didn't even think it' (26). The conflict is registered, not acted upon, but that registration is nonetheless a significant act.

Bloch also uses anecdotes, examples from his experience of defeat, but his personal anecdotes are given in lieu of a history deferred, when all the evidence can be assembled together. Rhys's narratives are less hopeful that a future history might make sense of the fragmented experience she represents. Where Bloch moves from the temporal disruptions experienced by the defeated subject to the strange reversals of history, Rhys's narrative of dislocated subjects refuses the historian's attempt to make sense of defeat through a reinstatement of before and after, cause and effect. This is because where Bloch believes victory is possible, if unlikely, in *Good Morning, Midnight* it seems impossible. Sasha, René, the 'Russians', the bald woman, the woman from Martinique are all scattered, isolated from one another. Yet reading *Good Morning, Midnight* as a collection of anecdotes told by the defeated posits, if not a collective resistance, then, at least an unarticulated collective subject. It is a connection Sasha makes herself, her sadness is the sadness shared by all the defeated. What Benjamin describes in *The Arcades Project*, as the 'street insurgence of the anecdote' plays a crucial part in this potential. Drawing on the same family of garrison metaphors as that used by Bloch, he writes:

> The constructions of history are comparable to military orders that discipline the true life and confine it to barracks. On the other hand: the street insurgence of the anecdote. The anecdote brings things near to us spatially, lets them enter our life. It represents the strict antithesis to the sort of history which demands 'empathy', which makes everything abstract. [S1a, 3]
>
> (1999a: 545)

What Benjamin does not make explicit is that the anecdote is the form taken by the counter-history of the defeated, the scattered, the lost and the homeless. As Robert S. Lehman argues, the anecdote represents a form of counter-history, which can bring events close in time and space without succumbing to the illusion that we can actually relive another's experience (2016: 145–70). It turns the strangeness of defeat into narrative form, bringing it nearer to us, without explanation or reconciliation. In *Good Morning, Midnight* multiple anecdotes are organized into a collection in such a way that the connections between narratives can be drawn. It is worth reflecting on the collective subject – 'all the fools and all the defeated' – posited in Sasha's acceptance of defeat. This collective might be taken to encompass all the apparently isolated characters in her fictions. Yet where Bloch, the historian, believes it should be possible to go back to the point before the defeat and to analyse its origins, Rhys is not so convinced that this is possible, because the temporalities of the defeated – 'the Hotel of Arrival, the Hotel of Departure, the Hotel of the Future, the Hotel of Martinique and the Universe' (*GMM* 120) – are not outside but already inside the imperial metropolis embodied in the non-community of scattered exiles that collect there.

If the acknowledgement of defeat means the acknowledgement of a struggle, does it also for Rhys mean an implicit acknowledgement that things might have been (and might yet be) otherwise? If this is the case, the lack of collective purpose among the defeated need not be their final state. Just as the novel brings their narratives together, they too might be brought together. Before she succumbs in the final pages of the novel, Sasha travels through Paris in a taxi with René:

I say: 'Whistle that tune, will you? The one you said is the march of the Legion.'
He whistles it very softly. And I watch the streets through the window.
À l'Hôtel de l'Espérance ....

(147)

Strangeness does not presuppose defeat, even if all defeats are strange, but if the future is dark, it is also open: midnight, but also morning. *Espérance* in French means hope, promise, expectation (and also concealed in its Latin root, *sperare*, the idea of waiting). For Rhys's legion of strangers, hope beckons, but is not expected soon.

Thinking through defeat allows a different perspective on Rhys's scattered and homeless army. It allows us to see the vanquished, not just as victims but as losers in a conflict which may have turned out otherwise – and may even yet resume with a different outcome in the future. An understanding of Sasha Jansen as defeated reverses victimhood as inevitable or worse, unalterable. It historicizes her predicament. Even as the image of midnight as morning holds history's potential in stasis, it leaves us waiting but expectant. As Emily Dickinson, the source of Rhys's title, puts it,

> Sunshine was a sweet place –
> I liked to stay –
> But Morn — didn't want me — now –

(2016: 203)

Morn does not want us now and perhaps will never want us, so we are left waiting with Rhys's defeated exiles, hoping for the future midnight's victory would deny us.

3

'Also I do like the moderns': Reading Rhys's reading

Andrew Thacker

This chapter begins with two very Rhysian themes: a textual ghost and a case of mistaken identity in the streets of Paris. These themes will offer a way into a consideration of what Jean Rhys read and why her reading matter is of importance in her writings. We begin in a rather well-known bookshop in Paris in the 1920s.

A ghost in the bookshop

Shakespeare and Company was opened in 1919 by the American Sylvia Beach and located in Rue de l'Odéon between 1921 and 1941. The bookshop was a quintessential site in the geography of European Modernism, a cultural institution that disseminated the great works of modernist literary experimentation and which served also as a place for writers and artists to gather and meet.[1] Shakespeare and Company famously published the first edition of *Ulysses*, but also operated a lending library, available to patrons for a small fee. While working on the Sylvia Beach archive in Princeton, I consulted a set of index cards for the books available to borrow and another set of cards recording the borrowers from the library, for the customers known by Beach as her 'bunnies' (French for subscriber, *abonné*). The borrower's cards for Shakespeare and Company (now the subject of a digital humanities project),[2] offer us a tantalizing glimpse into the reading habits of many key modernists and intellectuals in Paris in the 1920s and 1930s, from familiar Anglophone *habitués* such as Ernest Hemingway, James Joyce and Katherine Mansfield to young student intellectuals such as Simone de Beauvoir, Aimé Césaire and Jacques Lacan. Mansfield's card, for example, offers but the briefest peep into what she was reading towards the end of her life, borrowing copies of *Three Lives* by Gertrude Stein and four books by Sherwood Anderson in October 1922.[3] Some 5,000 library index cards (kept in a freestyle format that would alarm any self-respecting professional librarian) also offer us a fascinating glimpse into the range of material it was possible to borrow from the bookshop, and how the compositional practices of writers may have been influenced by their reading. For example, the French author Nathalie Sarraute joined the library in 1926 and proceeded to borrow a volume of tales by Edgar Allan Poe, along with Conrad's *Lord Jim*. In March 1939 she borrowed *Pointed Roofs* by Dorothy Richardson, *Dubliners* by Joyce and *The Aspen Papers* by Henry James. Soon after this Sarraute began work on one of her most acclaimed experimental novels, *Portrait d'un inconnu* (*Portrait of a Man Unknown* [1946] 1990). From Djuna Barnes to Gertrude Stein, the library stocked most Anglophone modernist writers, along with many other European authors, as well as selections from earlier classic authors (Tolstoy, Thackeray, Trollope, Shakespeare) and works on topics such as psychology, relativity, philology, art, architecture and drama. There was also a good collection of detective fiction: for example, eleven books by Dorothy L. Sayers were available for borrowing.

The sojourns of writers such as Mansfield or Hemingway in Paris are now well documented. However, Rhys's stay in the only city she 'really loved' and which forms the setting for several of her novels and short stories is much more obscure and difficult to date precisely (Angier [1990] 1992: 107). Carole Angier's biography, for example, remarks upon the difficulties of tracking her movements in the city in the early 1920s (122–5). Rhys has sometimes, even in Shari Benstock's pioneering *Women of the Left Bank*, seemed to drop off the map of expatriate female writers in Paris, and her connections to the modernist networks existing in the city, such as those centred upon Beach's bookshop, have always appeared tenuous. This absence from the cultural geography of expatriate Anglophone Modernism in Paris has always represented something of a puzzle for scholars of Rhys, particularly given her early connections with Ford and the precise mapping of the city from the stories in her first collection, *The Left Bank* (1927), onwards. Indeed, in the second story in *The Left Bank*, 'A Spiritualist', a character describes visiting a woman who lived in Place de l'Odéon, at the top of the road from Shakespeare and Company.[4] Ford was a borrower from Beach's library, and the bookshop also stocked the modernist magazine he edited while in Paris, *Transatlantic Review*, which was, of course, the place in which Rhys was first published, with the story 'Vienne' in the last issue of the magazine in December 1924.⁵ That Rhys read at least some of the contents of the magazine is demonstrated by the fact that the epigram she uses in her first novel, *Quartet* ([1928] 2000), is from a poem by R.C. Dunning, titled 'The Hermit', and which was published in the *Transatlantic Review* the previous month.⁶ The poem, with its warning to beware of 'good Samaritans' and to 'hide thee by the roadside out of sight' when they appear, is thus Rhys's acerbic comment upon 'L'Affaire Ford' and her feelings towards his initial literary patronage of her.⁷ In quoting from this poem Rhys textually turns Ford's *Transatlantic Review* against him, cleverly suggesting that her published appearance within its pages was something more than the act of a literary Samaritan.

When considering Rhys and her ghostly presence amidst these literary networks in Paris it was, therefore, intriguing to find that in her Black Exercise Book Rhys refers to 'One day in Sylvia Beach's bookshop': 'in Paris rue de l'Odeon I think it is or was I wanted a book on psychoanalysis' and she picked one up (probably Freud given the references to particular case histories) and read about women who 'imagined/fantasised' when they were young that they were seduced by older men.⁸ Rhys then continues that she read,

> something like this not the words but the sense .... 'Women of this type will invariably say that they were seduced when very young by an elderly man. In *every* case the story is ficticious [*sic*] [...]. They will relate a detailed story which in every case is entirely ficticious' [...]. No honey I thought it is not ficticious in every case. By no means. Anyhow how do you know.⁹

Here Rhys appears to be recalling her own 'seduction' by Mr Howard when a young girl in Dominica, an incident that she fictionalized several times in her work, perhaps most directly in the short story 'Goodbye Marcus, Goodbye Rose', written in 1976 and first published in *Sleep it Off Lady* in 1979.¹⁰ It is also interesting to note her acquaintance with at least some of the ideas of psychoanalysis, a feature rarely noted in work upon Rhys, but one that is also confirmed by the brief reference to the works of Freud and Adler in *Good Morning, Midnight* (141).

Finding this reference to Beach's bookshop made me wonder whether there was a library borrower's card for Rhys in the Shakespeare and Company archive. Upon further scrutiny there was indeed a card for several periods between 1920 and 1925, which identifies a Rhys as a borrower, and one which used a significant address for the subscriber – Quai des Grands Augustins – the location of the 'hotel on the quay' at the start of *After Leaving Mr Mackenzie* (7).¹¹ The card lists a fascinating collection of books borrowed, including Joyce's *Exiles*, Stein's *Tender Buttons*, Conrad's *Typhoon*, a *Georgian Poetry* anthology and Ford's *Critical Attitudes*. Even more intriguing is George Moore's *Esther Walters* (1894), which charts the fortunes of a 'fallen women' with Zolaesque naturalism, perhaps a model for many of the protagonists of Rhys's early novels. In 1953, Rhys wrote that she had just reread *Esther Waters* for the sixtieth time and that it has 'this magic effect on me': 'It is a book I keep for very bad days, and it never fails me,' she added (*L* 103).¹² The borrowing of another Moore novel, *A Mummer's Wife* (1885), is also interesting. This was the novel attacked and banned by Mudie's circulating library and which led to Moore's famous anti-censorship pamphlet, *Literature at Nurse* (1885). The story of that novel, concerning a bored housewife in the English Midlands who undertakes a disastrous affair with a travelling actor, might well have appealed to Rhys with her own background as a travelling thespian in Edwardian England. The censorship of Moore's text also echoes the way that the initial ending of *Voyage in the Dark* was rejected by Rhys's publisher. The borrower's card also listed two novels by Aldous Huxley, *Those Barren Leaves* (1925) and *Antic Hay* (1923), the latter of which contains a fictionalization of Philip Heseltine, the composer and music critic (Smith 1996). Rhys had met Heseltine in 1915 through her friendship with the painter, Adrian Allinson, associated with the Camden Town Group and a fringe member of the Bloomsbury Group (Angier [1990] 1992: 88–92; and 1993: 2, 14), and in her later short story, 'Till September, Petronella', Heseltine appears as the character Julian Oakes.

However, pondering this card repeatedly, something seemed wrong. The dates did not quite tally with those offered by Angier for Rhys's stay in Paris (was she not in Vienna for most of 1920 to 1921?); and why was the name on the card given as 'Mr Rhys'? Was this because her husband, Jean Lenglet, had paid the small membership fee for the library? But then why not give the name as Mrs Lenglet? Then I realized this was a case of mistaken identity: for this was not the card of Jean Rhys, as I originally believed, but of Mr *Ernest Rhys*, the Welsh author and critic, who was best known as the editor of the Dent book series Everyman (E. Rhys 1931; and Roberts 1983).

Why did I want it to be the card of Jean Rhys? A case of academic wish fulfillment? Probably. But also because it would help reposition Rhys from a ghostly presence on the fringes of literary networks around Beach's bookshop to a more consecrated status within Modernism, to use Pierre Bourdieu's terms, thus adding to her cultural capital as a writer (Bourdieu 1983). A more obvious factor behind my desire to locate Jean Rhys's borrower's card would be because it would reveal further what Rhys was reading, and as literary critics we are of course trained to look for intertextual allusions, patterns of influence, and connections to other intellectual trends and figures. It is, however, worth pausing to consider this investment in discovering what Rhys, or indeed any writer, read. One reason is to trace how a writer forges their own voice by engaging with predecessors, an approach articulated by influential critics such as T.S. Eliot, in his essay 'Tradition and the Individual Talent' ([1919] 1975), and later by Harold Bloom in *The Anxiety of Influence* (1973).[13] However, what would it mean to try to fit a Caribbean female writer such as Rhys into the patriarchal thesis of the 'anxiety of influence' or Eliot's Eurocentric notion of 'tradition' as the 'mind of Europe' ([1919] 1975: 39)?

In contrast to these models of literary influence, Rhys was a writer whose mind was often resolutely set upon elsewhere in the world, never feeling quite at home in Europe and, particularly, in England. Tracing patterns of literary influence through Rhys's reading thus needs to take full account of how her 'individual talent' was forged in the complex colonial modernity of the Caribbean. Rhys was an outsider to the European 'tradition' proposed by Eliot and was thus a resistant reader of that tradition.[14] This, of course, is the premise and motivation of *Wide Sargasso Sea*, formed through Rhys's resistant reading of *Jane Eyre* over the course of many decades, as emphasized by Judith Raiskin (1991). Or as she put in a letter to Selma Vaz Dias in 1958: 'Take a look at Jane Eyre. That unfortunate death of a Creole! I'm fighting mad to write *her* story' (*L* 157).

One of the most fascinating aspects of Rhys's work is thus this very resistance to becoming incorporated into conventional networks of authority and literary tradition, a feature that also marks her uncertain position within the cultural networks around Beach's bookshop. However, although there was no lending library card from Shakespeare and Company for Jean Rhys, there was a record of a subscriber in 1924 named Mlle Lenglet.[15] So, along with the mention in the Black Exercise Book of consulting a book on psychoanalysis in Beach's bookshop, it appears that Rhys's ghostly presence in Shakespeare and Company was thus confirmed, even if 'Mlle Lenglet' proves to be another case of mistaken identity. However, for detailed evidence on what Rhys read in this period, and later, we have to look elsewhere.

Readers and critics

In a letter Rhys wrote to Peggy Kirkaldy in July 1946 she discussed her 'half finished' novel (which was to become *Wide Sargasso Sea*, some twenty years later) and her attempts to collect together a volume of short stories (*L* 44). After detailing these difficulties, Rhys compares Kirkaldy to a character in Brinsley Sheridan's eighteenth-century play, *The School for Scandal*, only to then compare herself to a literary figure from the nineteenth century. Rhys then offers a fascinating set of comments upon her reading and listening habits. All winter she has only been able to read poetry as it was 'the only thing that kept me from cracking up' (44); she prefers Keats to Shelley, Shakespeare is the best, then Milton, along with other seventeenth-century writers she reads in 'many anthologies' (44). However, Rhys then notes that she has been unable to read her favourite French authors: 'I couldn't *look* at Rimbaud whom I thought so great or Mallarmé or Baudelaire (I haven't got Verlaine) without a horrible pain – I don't know why' (45; emphasis in the original). She then discusses the music she prefers: 'As to music dearie I really am 19th century. French school. Also I do like the moderns' (45). Here I want to explore some examples of the 'moderns', in literature rather than music, that appealed to Rhys, focusing in particular upon her strategies as a resistant reader of these texts.

The published letters of Rhys, covering the period between 1931 and 1966, not only point to her extensive reading, from Stevie Smith (*Novel on Yellow Paper* was 'a great favourite of mine') to Jean-Paul Sartre ('I like [his plays] better than his novels'), but also to her connections at various points in her life to other cultural networks beyond Paris in the 1920s (*L* 122, 98). There are, for example, scattered instances that indicate Rhys knew many key figures within some of the most significant literary networks in Britain in the 1930s. In 1936, for example, she forwarded a poem by the radical American poet Lola Ridge for possible publication by Geoffrey Grigson in his influential anthology *New Writing*; the editor and critic Frank Swinnerton in 1932 recommended that she send a manuscript for consideration to the Woolfs' Hogarth Press; while in the same year novelist and critic Rebecca West wrote to her, saying 'I do hope we are going to have another book from you soon.'[16] West was closely linked to the feminist magazine, *Time and Tide*, and may have been responsible for Rhys publishing the short story 'The Christmas Presents of Mynheer Van Rooz' in the journal in 1931 (1360–2). Rhys also knew John Lehmann in this period, before he edited the *London Magazine* and published her work after the Second World War, and was friendly too with his sister, the novelist Rosamond Lehmann, who once wrote to Rhys: 'You don't seem to realize you are a writer – and there are hardly any true writers. You've got a lot of admirers that you don't know about, I think it's time you met some of them.'[17] In some ways, these tentative connections to British literary culture in the 1930s might be expected, given that Rhys had three of her five novels published in the decade, and that her husband in this period, Leslie Tilden Smith, had operated a literary agency (unsuccessfully) and then worked as a freelance reader for various publishers (Angier [1990] 1992: 279–96). However, until recently, Rhys has often been omitted from literary accounts of the decade.[18]

Despite the evidence of these literary connections the notion that Rhys's reading informed her texts, particularly those of the 1920s and 1930s, has been somewhat neglected. Coral Ann Howells, for example, in her introduction to Rhys in Bonnie Kime Scott's first *Gender of Modernism* anthology, wrote that Rhys's use of Emily Dickinson for the title of *Good Morning, Midnight* and the revisions of *Jane Eyre* for *Wide Sargasso Sea* indicated that in 'an unstated and nontheoretical way, Rhys appears to be situating her fiction in a female writing tradition' and that 'her letters' show a 'rather unsystematic reading of contemporary fiction by women, including Eliot Bliss, Elizabeth Jenkins, Katherine Mansfield, and Stevie Smith. Rhys always saw herself as an isolated figure' (Howells 1990: 376). 'Isolated' seems too strong a term here, for a writer who in the 1930s was writing to figures such as the Lehmanns or Grigson. Rhys, as the letter to Kirkaldy demonstrates, read widely, and read other modern authors too, even if she did not borrow them from Shakespeare and Company – but the dominant image of her as a seemingly uneducated *naïve* in the cultural milieu of the modern metropolis seems to persist. Helen Carr points out that even Angier's biography states that the 'completely modern' quality to her novels was a paradox given that '*she knew so little*, and wrote only about herself' (Angier [1990] 1992: 218; emphasis added). Carr comments that this 'image of Jean Rhys, the inward-looking chronicler of private pathos, ignorant of literary culture [...] has clung as closely as that of the passive victim, in spite of the overwhelming evidence to the contrary' (Carr [1996] 2012: 9). Judith Gardiner, many years ago, pointed out the references to Keats, Rimbaud, Verlaine, Wilde and Colette in *Good Morning, Midnight* and argued that the conclusion to the novel parodies the ending of *Ulysses* (Gardiner 1982–3: 233–51).[19]

Joyce and Hemingway are two of the key modernist figures in the mythology of Beach's bookshop, so it is interesting to see how they appear in Rhys's works. Rhys seems to have suggested to Diana Athill that she had once met Joyce at a party, and in *Quartet* Marya is invited to a literary gathering at the Café Lavenue, where the writers 'Rolls and Boyes' will be present, names that echo that of Joyce (*Q* 34).[20] In a 1964 letter to Francis Wyndham when completing *Wide Sargasso Sea*, Rhys noted that she had the idea of making the last chapter of the book 'partly "poetry" – partly prose – songs'. She then expresses a concern that this was a not a new technique, adding, 'James Joyce tried to make sound I know like Anna Livia Plurabelle – but this is of course lighter, different – a musical comedy compared to grand opera' (*L* 278). Here Rhys not only acknowledges an understanding of Joyce's *Finnegans Wake*, extracts from which as *Work in Progress* were also published in the *Transatlantic Review* in April 1924, but positions her own text as 'different'. It is a self-deprecating, yet profoundly odd, way to describe the finale of *Wide Sargasso Sea* as 'musical comedy', which is perhaps an attempt to avoid closer comparisons with Joyce's practice, or place herself as somewhat eccentric to the experimental 'grand operas' of European Modernism.

Hemingway was another figure closely linked to the *Transatlantic Review*, acting as co-editor for a while.[21] Immediately preceding Rhys's 'Vienne' in the December 1924 issue we find Hemingway's story 'Cross Country Snow', later revised for his important collection, *In Our Time*. Rhys freely acknowledged that she admired Hemingway's writing, praising his stories 'Hills Like White Elephants' and 'A Way You'll Never Be', and then writing in 1965: 'I am a Hemingway fan. I knew him by sight, though not personally, but I liked what I saw. I remember, at a dance, watching him and thinking that he danced as if he were gay and loved life' (*L* 100, 291).[22] Some critics have tried to trace the stylistic links between the two writers, particularly in terms of a preponderance of short paragraphs, use of dialogue, and a precision of vocabulary, though Rhys is much keener on the use of commas than Hemingway (Brown 1986: 2–12).

The point of these brief comparisons to Joyce and Hemingway is thus not to validate Rhys by association with highly 'consecrated' modernists but at least to suggest there is more complexity in Rhys's reading than she is often given credit for – this is far from Angier's judgement that 'she knew so little'. It is also meant to suggest that her engagement with canonical male Modernism is from the position of a resistant colonial woman writer, as shown in the parodic ending of *Good Morning, Midnight* analysed by Gardiner.

French connections

A key aspect of this strategy of resistant colonial reading relates to Rhys's engagement with French authors, drawing upon the divided linguistic heritage of her native Dominica. As well as Rhys's citing of French authors in the letter to Kirkaldy discussed above, both Gardiner and Carr point to the many echoes and allusions to French modernist authors in Rhys's fiction, citing figures such as Baudelaire, Flaubert, Rimbaud, Verlaine and Zola. Here, for example, is Anna Morgan early on in the novel, *Voyage in the Dark*:

> I was lying on the sofa, reading *Nana*. It was a paper-covered book with a coloured picture of a stout, dark woman brandishing a wine-glass. She was sitting on the knee of a bald-headed man in evening dress.
>
> (*VD* 9)

Zola's novel of a French courtesan chimes with the themes of prostitution and commodification also explored in *Voyage in the Dark*. It also perhaps recalls the book that Rhys picked up in Beach's bookshop, with its reference to Freud's controversial seduction theory. In the novel, Anna's friend, Maudie, comments that *Nana* is a 'dirty book' and then adds, 'I know; it's about a tart. I think it's disgusting. I bet you a man writing a book about a tart tells a lot of lies one way and another. Besides, all books are like that – just someone stuffing you up' (*VD* 9). Anna's story is thus framed from the beginning as a rejoinder to this particular narrative, as we see Rhys – in the guise of Maudie – as a resistant reader, proposing that while Zola's vision of a 'tart' may be rooted in the tradition of naturalism, it is still full of falsehoods and ultimately just a way of 'stuffing you up' as a woman.

Allusions to other modern French authors occur elsewhere in Rhys. Hardly any of her own poetry has been published, but the poems in her archive demonstrate how her reading of figures such as Verlaine and Rimbaud influenced her own verse. In her archive one set of typed poems has a cover page on which are placed quotations from poems by Jean Richepin and from Rimbaud's prose poem, 'Matinée d'Ivresse' (Drunken Morning), published in his *Illuminations* (1886):

> O *mon* Bien ! O *mon* Beau ! Fanfare atroce où je ne trébuche point ! Chevalet féerique ! Hourra pour l'œuvre inouïe et pour le corps merveilleux, pour la première fois ! [...] Nous avons foi au poison. Nous savons donner notre vie tout entière tous les jours.

(O *my* Good! O *my* Beauty! Atrocious fan fare in which I never falter! Enchanted easel! Hurrah for the unknown work and for the marvellous body, for the first time! [...] We have faith in poison. We know how to give our whole life every day.)
(Rimbaud 1964: 154–5; my translation; emphases in the original)

It would be too easy to read this biographically in the light of Rhys's own issues with alcohol (she described herself as 'Le Bateau Ivre' [The Drunken Boat], another Rimbaud reference, in a letter [*L* 276]), but there seems to be something more to her engagement with a writer she thought 'so great'. Rhys may have been attracted to Rimbaud for his image as a rebellious outsider figure, infamous for his support for the French Commune of 1871, for his homosexuality and for his work as a trafficker in Africa. A writer whose commitment to 'giving one's whole life everyday' marks a particular intensity of experience that Rhys often found lacking in much of polite English or what she termed 'Anglo-Saxon' society, where 'it is a crime to feel intensely about anything in England'.[23] As Kristin Ross notes of Rimbaud's 'Matinée d'Ivresse', it is a poem whose 'violently transformed body' demands 'more than' what existing capitalist society will currently allow, and which imagines a future for a 'marvellous body, for the first time' (Ross 1988: 120–1). In addition, we might wonder whether the experimental prose poem form of Rimbaud's *Illuminations* also appealed to Rhys, as shown by her comments (discussed above) about the prose-poetry style she considered for the final part of *Wide Sargasso Sea*.

If one aspect of Rhys's enthusiasm for the excesses of Rimbaud can be understood as part of her rejection of Englishness, a moment in *Good Morning, Midnight* reveals a more complex attitude to him and his fellow outsider, Verlaine, in a section of the novel exploring notions of belonging. The passage occurs early in the novel when Sasha Jensen suddenly decides she must find another hotel to live in, as the one in which she is currently staying starts to overwhelm her with its odours and she feels 'ill and giddy' (*GMM* 31). She tries to find a room she likes in another hotel but fails, as the room she is offered is not a 'light room' but a 'dark one'; she is also put off when she hears the receptionist in the new hotel complain of another guest, 'foreigners, foreigners, my God' (32). Rejecting the new hotel, Sasha muses: 'All rooms are the same [...]. A room is a place where you hide from the wolves outside and that's all any room is. Why should I worry about changing my room?' (33). When she returns to her original hotel, Sasha overhears a conversation about Rimbaud and Verlaine in the hallway:

Somebody's *Times Literary Supplement* peeps coyly from the letter-rack. A white-haired American lady and a girl who looks like her daughter are talking in the hall.

'Look here, look at this. Here's a portrait of Rimbaud. Rimbaud lived here, it says.'
'And here's Verlaine .... Did he live here too?'
'Yes, he lived here too. They both lived here. They both lived here together. Well now, isn't that interesting?'

(33–4)

Sasha then returns to her original room, which speaks to her: "'There you are,' it says. "You didn't go off, then?" "No, no. I thought better of it. Here I belong and here I'll stay"' (34). The reference here to Rimbaud and Verlaine at first seems puzzling, occurring as it does between two moments which interrogate the familiar Rhysian theme of the difficulty faced by a single woman in locating a place to belong in the modern metropolis.[24] However, both Rimbaud and Verlaine lived peripatetic lives, sometimes together, and Rimbaud in particular celebrated the notion of being a vagabond, drifting for many years between various locations across France and Europe, before a final period working in Africa.[25] Is Rhys here thus identifying with this aspect of the poets' lives, aware that she too cannot readily settle in any European location, a condition for which a change of hotel room can never suffice? Possibly, but Sasha only overhears the conversation and does not comment upon it, as if she is somewhat detached from these two poets, even though she is temporarily staying at an address that they too, temporarily, inhabited. The image of the *Times Literary Supplement* seems significant here, as it points cryptically to a sense of a literary tradition to which Rhys felt she never really belonged; even Rimbaud and Verlaine, notorious *poètes maudits* in their time, were by the 1930s acclaimed establishment figures in French Modernism. Rimbaud and Verlaine may have challenged literary norms, but it is figures such as Sasha and Rhys that remain outsiders or 'foreigners, foreigners, my God', in the words of the hotel receptionist. The incident also demonstrates Rhys's uncertain position between English and French literary traditions – the *TLS* or *poètes maudits* – with Sasha's final words, 'Here I belong and here I'll stay', something of a statement of defiance by Rhys, a resistant reader-turned-writer trying to stake a claim to be acknowledged by one tradition or the other.

A final aspect of Rhys's reading discussed briefly here is her practice as a translator, a practice that also relates to notions of belonging. To translate, one must first read and inhabit the foreign text, before reworking that text into the other language, trying to make it belong there. Rhys acknowledged that a key part of her apprenticeship as a writer derived from the practice of translating French writers such as Colette, Maupassant and Flaubert into English: 'I think

French books helped me an awful lot there. They had clarity. Ford insisted – if you weren't sure of a paragraph or statement, translate it into another language. And if it looks utterly silly, get rid of it. Anglo-Saxon is rather messy, don't you think?'[26] Sometime in the early 1920s Ford arranged for Rhys to provide a translation of one of Francis Carco's novels, *Perversité/Perversity*. Rhys referred to Carco's work as a chronicler of French bohemia in an early story, 'Tout Montparnasse and a Lady', when a female American fashion artist arrives in Paris 'to be thrilled' after having read the *Trilby* of Du Maurier and 'the novels of Francis Carco, which tell of the lives of the apaches of to-day' (*CSS* 17).[27] *Perversity* is a lurid novel of the Parisian *demi-monde*, concerning a Parisian prostitute, Irma, and her brother, Emile, and concludes with Emile killing his sister. However, when the English translation appeared in 1928, it was Ford's name on the cover, not that of Rhys. Though the error was that of the publisher, Pascal Covici, rather than Ford's himself, Rhys always believed that it was Ford's doing, after he had finished the affair with her (Angier [1990] 1992: 164). Some of her anger at this perceived slight (and the rejection by Ford overall) clearly fuelled the bitter mood that suffuses *Quartet*.

In a brilliant analysis of this text Juliette Taylor-Batty has argued persuasively that Rhys's translation of Carco's novel 'bears the marks of an interlingual and intertextual struggle and conflict, of the translator's visible labour with languages' (Taylor-Batty 2013: 90). Although it might not be judged a 'good' translation, Taylor-Batty suggests that it 'bears the traces of creolising linguistic processes that are fundamental to Rhys's fiction, and to Rhys's development of a specifically Caribbean modernism' (92). This is another aspect of Rhys's resistant reading, we might argue, articulating her own Creole identity through a creative reworking of a French text into an English one, implanting the 'clarity' of French within 'messy' Anglo-Saxon words: as Taylor-Batty concludes, Rhys 'leaves her visible mark upon the text' (93). A similar strategy can be found in Rhys's later translation of her husband Jean Lenglet's novel *Barred* (1932), published under the name Edward de Nève.[28] Martien Kappers-den Hollander has shown how Rhys's translation of this work represented a drastic revision of the source text: some 7,000 words were cut, tenses and syntax altered, with virtually no paragraphs left untouched. The result, argues Kappers-den Hollander, is a 'text that strikes us as more economical and consistent' and appears in a style 'more like her own' than that of her husband (1987: 21).[29] The work of translation is here a simultaneous reading and rewriting, with the ghostly translator a more active presence in the final text.[30] The impact upon Rhys's own identity as a writer of these acts of translation was profound. In the 1960s she wrote to Francis Wyndham, coyly describing *Barred* as a book which 'I read which helped me when I was very down' and which was written by a 'poet manqué [...] who knew me well'. The book, Rhys comments to Wyndham, 'would show you that for a long time, for years, I escaped from an exclusively Anglo-Saxon influence and have never returned to it' (*L* 281).

If Rhys's presence within the consecrated modernist space of Shakespeare and Company remains somewhat ghostly, it is important to remember that within her written work there are often traces of the authors she read, traces that tell of how she also resisted aspects of what she read, escaping, for instance, the 'exclusively Anglo-Saxon' (*L* 281). As readers we can follow these ghostly voices of the authors Rhys read but, as with the art of translation, we should always remember that they are shaped and remade as her own particular words, written acts of cultural defiance and literary belonging.

Notes

1 The most detailed account of Beach remains Noel Riley Fitch's *Sylvia Beach and the Lost Generation: A History of Literary Paris in the Twenties and Thirties* (1983). The current Shakespeare and Company bookshop in Paris, located on rue de la Bûcherie, is a different commercial entity, started by George Whitman in 1951.
2 For information on the project, see Mapping Expatriate Paris n.d.
3 For a brief discussion of Mansfield in the bookshop and a comparison with Rhys, see Thacker 2019a.
4 See Armstrong 2013: 175.
5 Jean Rhys, 'Vienne', published in the *Transatlantic Review* (1924: 639–45) was a much different, and shorter, version of the story of the same title published in *The Left Bank*.
6 'The Hermit' was one of twelve poems by Dunning published in the *Transatlantic Review*.
7 'L'Affaire Ford' is an unpublished typescript in the Jean Rhys Archive.
8 Black Exercise Book, Archive, Tulsa, Series 1, Box 1, folder 1, p. 11. I am grateful to the McFarlin Library for permission to quote from this source.
9 *Ibid*.
10 For discussion of this incident, see Savory 1998: 61–3, 160–2; and Thomas 1994–5: 65–84. Leah Rosenberg reads this comment as Rhys's critique of psychoanalysis (1999: 5–33).

11 Interestingly the location is used as the title for the French edition of the novel.
12 For a discussion of Rhys and Moore, see Berry 1996: 17–25.
13 For an overview of theories of influence and intertextuality, see the essays in Clayton and Rothstein 1991. For a feminist critique of Bloom's thesis, see Kolodny 1986: 46–62.
14 I am here adapting Judith Fetterley's (1978) notion of the 'resistant reader' to indicate how Rhys's own reading practices demonstrate acts of resistance.
15 Joshua Kotin of Princeton University confirmed that there is a subscriber's record for a Mlle Lenglet (email to author, 18 June 2018).
16 Rebecca West to Jean Rhys (8 April 1932), British Library, RP6206.
17 Rosamond Lehmann to Jean Rhys (n.d.), British Library, RP6206.
18 For a recent collection on the 1930s that does discuss Rhys, see the chapter by Emma Zimmerman, 'Uncanny Cities: Urban Geographies and Metropolitan Life' (2019).
19 Carr also lists a number of the writers mentioned by Rhys ([1996] 2012: 91 n.18).
20 The reference to meeting Joyce occurs in correspondence between Diana Athill and *The Economist*, referenced in the Rhys Archive, Tulsa.
21 For the fullest history of the magazine see Poli 1967.
22 The character Cairn in *Quartet* is sometimes said to be a portrait of Hemingway, though Angier provides a strong counter to such interpretations; see Angier [1990] 1992: 136.
23 See her remarks on how 'anglo-saxons' treat women writers (*L* 32); Rhys writes about the 'crime' of feeling in 'The Bible is Modern' (cited by Savory 1998: 28). Rhys's unpublished 'Essay on England' continues the critique.
24 For more on this topic see the discussion in Andrew Thacker's *Modernism, Space and the City: Outsiders and Affect in Paris, Vienna, Berlin and London* (2019b: 45–58).
25 For Rimbaud and vagabondage, see Ross 1988: 55–9.
26 Rhys cited in Pierrette M. Frickey (1990: 24).
27 A later story, 'Night Out 1925', opens: 'It had been raining and the green and red reflections of the lights in the wet streets made Suzy think of Francis Carco's books' (*CSS* 335).
28 The novel was published in the original French one year later, with the title, *Sous les verrous*.
29 See also Taylor-Batty's excellent analysis of this translation (2013: 93–9).
30 Rhys's name as a translator did not appear on the cover or in the text. She is only acknowledged by her first name in the author's preface, but only vaguely for her help with the manuscript and its publication.

4

'Parler de soi': Jean Rhys and the uses of life writing

Simon Cooke

Prefacing Rhys

In the postscript to a letter of 1953 to the English novelist Morchard Bishop, Jean Rhys responded to her reading of George Bernanos's *Journal d'un curé de campagne*. 'Just as I was deciding I wasn't in the mood for it,' she wrote, 'I read this':

> '*Il faudrait parler de soi avec une rigeur* [sic] *inflexible. Et au premier effort pour se saisir, d'où viennent cette pitié, ce relâchement de toutes les fibres de l'âme et cette envie de pleurer?*'[1]
>
> So one is caught, nothing to do but read on. I know that 'parler de soi' is not supposed to be the proper thing to do. Not in England. And not now in 1953.
> I feel so fiercely about that. No one knows anything but himself or herself. And that badly.
> Don't you think so? Other people are seen and heard and felt. Known? Not on your life.
>
> (*L* 103–4; emphasis in original)

Rhys's letter speaks powerfully to that most prominent of motifs in her own reception: a reading of Rhys as a writer who 'talks about herself' in her writing, and the controversy over whether this is 'proper'. That all Rhys's writings 'relate closely to her own experience' (Athill 2017: xii) has been at issue in such diverse responses as Ford Madox Ford's stung reaction to *Quartet* as a *roman à clef*, Carole Angier's use of the fiction to flesh out the gaps in her biographical subject's life, and the critical figure of the 'Rhys Woman' – as well as, more implicitly, in postcolonial excavations of Caribbean hinterlands for the 'European' fictions and psychoanalytically oriented feminist readings. Indeed, to an unusual extent, an emphasis on the transmission lines between Rhys's life and work has operated as a threshold as well as a supplement: few writers have been so consistently prefaced (and as it were 'pre-faced'), often in such a way as to invite a biographical reading, from Ford's chaperoning of *The Left Bank* with 'Rive Gauche', to Francis Wyndham's 'Introduction' to *Wide Sargasso Sea* and the 'Publisher's Note' to the subsequent reissues of the interwar novels that followed, both telling the now legendary story of Rhys's 'disappearance' and 're-discovery'. In Diana Athill's edition of the *The Complete Novels* we encounter *Voyage in the Dark* first, not third, in part because its 'central figure' was 'created out of experiences which her author underwent within a few years of coming to school in England in 1907' (Athill 1985: ix). A biographical chronology is privileged over the creative.

As Rhys's letter already illustrates, this reception finds both a source and a challenging critique in her own writings. Where Rhys supplies the vocabulary for the view that she 'knew so little, and wrote only about herself' (Angier [1990] 1992: 218), we find a 'fierce' conviction that such a limit is an irreducible condition for everyone. As Helen Carr observes, while Rhys articulates 'a profound truth [...], and one often stressed by modernists, [...] it has been interpreted as a symptom of Rhys's personal egoism' ([1996] 2012: n. 9, 139), indicative of an entrenched misogynist double standard. Equally, what 'caught' Rhys in Bernanos, and what she adds emphasis to, was his expression of the 'inflexible rigour' demanded by literary 'talk of the self' in its tension with the affective – the 'desire to cry' – as much as any cathartic 'therapeutic function' (Athill 1979: 10) promised by the act of writing. And in stressing that attitudes to the propriety of 'parler de soi' are bound up with specific places and times – England, 1953 – Rhys unsettles any moral stance we might take. Rhys's response to Bernanos's novel signals not only the importance of specifically French writing to Rhys, but also the way this engagement contributes to a decidedly transnational perspective that relativizes precisely the views on the autobiographical that have swirled so persistently around her work.

While both Rhys's 'French connection' (Carr [1996] 2012: 45–51) and her innovations in auto/biographical[2] practice have been the subject of vital scholarship on Rhys, an emphasis on this transnationalism in her understanding of 'parler de soi' offers one way to sound afresh the question of the autobiographical in her writings. As Rhys told Mary Cantwell when asked about how she brought shape to autobiographical material: 'French books helped [...] an awful lot there. They had clarity'; she 'loved Maupassant,

Anatole France, Flaubert' (Cantwell 1990: 24). This prizing of 'clarity' itself echoes France's verdict that Maupassant 'possesses the three great qualities of the French writer, first, clearness, then again, clearness, and lastly, clearness' (1923: 46–7); and while a conviction that the human condition is irreducibly subjective is certainly widespread among an international range of modernist writers and intellectuals, Rhys's emphasis chimes particularly with France's view that 'we are shut up in our personality as if in a perpetual prison', and that 'the best thing for us [...] is to admit this frightful condition with good grace, and to confess that we speak of ourselves every time we have not the strength to remain silent' (viii). The forms of Rhys's first-person auto-narrations, too, invite comparison with French autobiographical fiction – preeminently Proust's *À la recherche du temps perdu* (*In Search of Lost Time*, [1913] 2002), later volumes of which were being published while Rhys was in Paris – as well as looking ahead to what Serge Doubrovsky termed 'autofiction' (1977). To do so is not to accommodate Rhys to a national-cultural tradition, but rather to highlight the ways in which her innovation is expressed in part through her transnational alertness to the culturally specific inflections in writing the self.

Rhys's insistence on the personal coexists with an equally pronounced resistance to the biographical. As Wyndham reports, Rhys wished that 'no biography should be written of her unless authorized within her lifetime' (*L* 9). She expresses the objection emphatically in the 'From a Diary' section in *Smile Please*: 'I have not met other writers often. A few in Paris. Ford of course. Even fewer in England. That does not matter at all, for all of a writer that matters is in the book or books. It is idiotic to be curious about the person' (*SP* 168). This too has a strong French dimension. While controversy over the pertinence of biographical approaches is prominent in much criticism and theory of the long twentieth century – from T.S. Eliot's doctrine of 'impersonality', to Wimsatt and Beardsley's censure of the 'intentional fallacy', or indeed to the French theoretical interventions of Barthes and Foucault – such critical views find a touchstone in the letters of one of the French writers Rhys professed to love, Flaubert. Her valorization of the work sounds close to his declaration that 'the man is nothing, the work everything!' (1982: 227). And her sense that the writer is 'in' the work resonates again with Proust, in his rejection of Sainte-Beuve's method of seeking out 'every possible piece of information about a writer' as a means of interpreting the work. To do so, Proust argued, 'ignores what a very slight degree of self-acquaintance teaches us: that a book is the product of a different *self* from the self we manifest in our habits, in our social life, in our vices', while the books are the product of 'the innermost self [*moi profond*] which one can only recover by putting aside the world and the self that frequents the world' (1984: 99–100; emphasis in original). Like Proust, Rhys is not quite denying a connection between the writer's life and work: indeed, what matters of the writer for Rhys as for Proust is within the work. As this indicates, and as scholarship has increasingly stressed,[3] while Modernism and its legacies have often been characterized in terms of a reaction against a nineteenth-century investment in biography, it also involves a preoccupation with the relationship of the writer's life and work, and a proliferation of formal experimentation and inquiries into life writing – the 'New Biography' of Woolf and Strachey, Maurois's explorations of the ways in which modern auto/biography contends with a sense that the 'human being is a more complex amalgam than was ever believed before' (1929: 25).

My principal aim in what follows is to approach Rhys less as a case study and more as a vital contributor to these debates and practices: to attend to the scope and acuity of the perspectives Rhys herself opens up on the uses of life writing,[4] drawing attention to the critically underemphasized role played in this by her engagement with French literary culture. *Good Morning, Midnight* is the main focal point. Along with *Voyage in the Dark*, it is a sustained performance of fictional auto-narration, whatever our view of the extent to which it represents autobiographical fiction, and it has attracted a particularly rich vein of critical commentary as a challenge to 'the premises and promises of post-Enlightenment autobiography, in particular the premise of a stable and triumphant sovereign self who narrates his autobiography and the promise of personal growth and social advancement culminating in insight and self-assured reflection' (Wittman 2014: 195). The only novel in which Rhys's protagonist is presented explicitly – if far from straightforwardly – as a professional writer, it also brings the uses of writing to the fore, while as one of Rhys's Parisian novels, it is suffused with the French literature and culture in focus here. The stakes of talking and writing about ourselves and others are centrally at issue in the novel, and the subtlety with which Rhys crafts fictional autobiography requires we reconsider the terms by which her work can be understood as autobiographical fiction. In asking whether and with what implications Rhys made use of her life (and the lives of others) in her writing, we might turn first to her own contributions, discursive and performative, to debates and practices which Rhys, with an 'inflexible rigour' alive to the affective in all 'parler de soi', responds to, critiques, anticipates.

'Name So-and-so, nationality So-and-so': Exposures and evasions

To borrow Rhys's own term in her thinking on 'parler de soi', we know both more and less than might be considered 'proper' about the first person of *Good Morning, Midnight*. The 'catastrophe' in the opening pages – which becomes one of the novel's leitmotifs – is to have cried in public, and to have been judged harshly because she 'let everybody see' (*GMM* 10). As readers, against decorum, we accompany the narrator into private places – the lavabos, the bed, the ward – and are privy through the form to much she does not 'let everybody see': to what she conceals, attempts to conceal or finds herself unable to express in public. But while the first person is disconcertingly exposed, we do not really know the first things about her. Akin to a keyhole biography, the novel gravitates around a short period of the protagonist's life – a fortnight or so revisiting Paris, from London, in 'late October, 1937' (78) – but the keyhole offers only partial, uncertain glimpses into the architecture of her backstory. If it is immediately clear that the narrative cannot be classified as autobiography as defined by Philippe Lejeune in what has become the benchmark in discussions of the genre – Rhys subscribes to no 'autobiographical pact' requiring that the 'author, narrator, and the protagonist must be identical' (Lejeune 1989: 5) – it is equally the case that, as fiction, it frustrates the autobiographical model of a 'retrospective prose narrative written by a real person concerning his own existence, where the focus is his individual life, in particular the story of his personality' (4). It is a narrative of exposures and evasions, which excavates and validates the obscure, marginalized and suppressed, while obscuring the socially codified. The biographical processes by which one might attempt to probe and describe Rhys's own life as a foundation on which the novel might be based are acutely questioned within the novel itself.

The 'proper name' with which the novel, as fictional auto-narration, might be 'undersigned' (Lejeune 1989: 11), is itself indeterminable. The narrator recalls that she 'started calling [her]self Sasha', but when is uncertain (either in '1923 or 1924', or else 'in 1926 or 1927') (*GMM* 11). Later we learn that her given name was Sophia – but this is brought into question as it is noted, through a memory of being put out when someone called her 'Sophia, full and grand' instead of 'Sasha, or even Sophie' (37). Sasha/Sophie/Sophia recalls being addressed, in her earlier life in Paris, as 'Mrs Jansen' (*GMM* 17), but it is most likely that this was the name she took on through marriage, since ended, to Enno. Her nationality is equally enigmatic. While we hear that she travelled to Paris direct from London, to which she had returned from Paris (36), there is no confirmation that she is English, as is often claimed or assumed.[5] References to her 'Englishness' all derive more or less directly from her sense of others perceiving her to be so (36) – or present it as something performed rather than innate, as when she recalls resolving 'to be [...] devastatingly English' (62). This ambiguity opens a space for one of the most important strands in Rhys scholarship, which mines a Caribbean background for Sasha as the novel's 'submerged text' (Savory 1998: 117). The most striking 'clue' (117) is when the artist Serge puts on some *béguine* music from Martinique, prompting a kind of reverie: 'I am lying in a hammock looking up into the branches of a tree. The sound of the sea advances and retreats' (*GMM* 77). Yet even this is suggestive rather than declarative, pitched between memory and daydream; alongside the protagonist's frequent references to 'Anglaise stuff' (113), it opens up, rather than shuts down, the question of the narrator's background. Intriguingly, too, this most explicit Caribbean reference resists assimilation into Rhys's own biography, shifting from Dominica to the French Caribbean.

We cannot be entirely sure, then, of the passport information on 'the fiche' that so puzzles Sasha's hotel patron: we too are left with 'Name So-and-so, nationality So-and-So' (*GMM* 13). As Annette Gilson notes, whatever the signs of Sasha's background, Rhys 'has chosen to obscure them' (2004: 640). At some level it may be 'one way that Rhys negotiates difficult parts of her identity when writing for an audience that she feels is hostile to elements of her "true" self' (640). But this conflates Sasha's reticence with Rhys's, locating the cause of the aesthetic in Rhys's sense of herself rather than her sense of the writing; and Rhys does voice more explicitly Caribbean perspectives in both earlier and later work. And while a kind of intimacy is achieved through the lack of any need of introductions, Sasha makes emphatic statements of identity by negation – 'I have no pride – no pride, no name, no face, no country. I don't belong anywhere' (*GMM* 38) – and her anonymity and facelessness are scrupulously maintained. How subtly, for example, this narrative of a woman so often looked at, who so often scrutinizes herself in mirrors, withholds any reference to identifying features beyond the cosmetically or sartorially variable. The elusiveness of Sasha's identity in conventional terms is thus explicitly and pervasively drawn attention to, and appears to be less a reflection of Rhys's fear of an audience hostile to her '"true" self' than a defiant choice – and one that questions the stability of identity implicit in the idea of a 'true self' at all. The withholding of coordinates of identity is of a piece with what V. S. Naipaul identified as a hallmark of Rhys's style: her refusal to '"set" her scene' (1972: 29). It was this quality – a part of Rhys's modernist experimentation with the traditional role played by space in characterization and plot – that Ford pointed to in explaining why he 'butted in' with his scene-setting preface to *The Left Bank* (Ford 1927: 26). There is an emblematic irony in the fundamental tension between Rhys's resistance to traditional characterization in these terms, and the biographical grandeur of Ford's closing hope that 'when [...] her ashes are translated to the Panthéon [...], a grain or so of my scattered and forgotten dust may go in, too, in the folds' (27).

If we do not know her legal name, the elective name of 'Sasha' is tellingly unassimilable: multinational, and androgynous as a familiar diminutive of Alexander or Alexandra. As a Russian nickname combined with the Scandinavian name 'Jansen', also borrowed, 'Sasha Jansen' serves less as a guarantor of identity than as a hybrid transnational mask. If her names give nothing away about her identity, they also resonate with literary associations alerting us to further biographical enigmas. The name 'Sasha' is shared with Orlando's Russian love – exotic, androgynous and enigmatic – in Woolf's *Orlando: A Biography*; 'Jansen' is strikingly close to 'Jensen', the author of *Gradiva*, a novel in which an archaeologist is so taken by the bas-relief in a museum in Rome that he goes in search of the real woman on whom he imagines it must have been based, and which Freud analysed in terms of dream and delusion on the author's as well as the protagonist's part. The name Sasha means 'defender' or 'helper of mankind', and it may be that the act of choosing this mask of a name is itself an act of protest, a 'defence' against pernicious social contexts. Sasha's personal exposures and evasions are intricately intertwined with a pervasive culture of exhibition and spectatorship – in fashion, sexuality, tourism, and commerce, all under the sign of the Paris Exhibition – while her withholding of the most conventional markers of biographical identity is central to Rhys's exploration of transnational identity. Sasha is repeatedly drawn to restlessly international figures, whose 'identities' are largely the work of the stories they tell of themselves – most centrally to the 'gigolo' René, whose claim to be French-Canadian Sasha doubts (*GMM* 62–3), and who is looking to secure fake papers. Intriguingly, Sasha notes at one point: 'I tell him my name, my address, everything' (66). By contrast, it is the store manager, Mr Blank – the most nationally fixed, 'the real English type' (17), the figure who most overtly 'represent[s] Society' (25) – who most aggressively probes the 'facts' of her background.

While it might be claimed that it is in the enigmatic aspects of her identity (including the adoption of a name) that Sasha Jansen is most 'like' Jean Rhys, any attempt to decide on Sasha's heritage, or to read the novel as Rhys's autobiographical fiction on the basis of the narrator and author sharing 'vital statistics', involves an approach that is brought into question within the book itself. Albeit with diametrically opposed motivations, it bears an uncomfortable proximity to the suspicious questions of the hotel patron on Sasha's right to stay in the hotel, or the English store manager's testing of her curriculum vitae, or the look Sasha sees caught in a West African mask – the look 'when they are saying: "What's this story?" Peering at you. Who are you, anyway? [...] Are you one of us?' (*GMM* 76–7). What might seem innocuous biographical questions – what is your family name? where do you come from? – take on sinister inflections in the approach to the Second World War. If, as Helen Carr has suggested, *Good Morning, Midnight* should be recognized as one of the great anti-fascist novels of the century ([1996] 2012: 25), Rhys's subversion of the uses of life writing plays a politically engaged role here.

'No time region', or: *Mémoires d'outre-tombe*

A fundamental issue in all autobiographical life writing is that the self is both subject and object. To express the self involves objectifying that self (every autobiography is also a biography of self as other), and narratives of the past are always also documents of the present (every memoir is also a diary). *Good Morning, Midnight* pervasively literalizes this distinction between self as subject and self as object, giving literary form to Rimbaud's famous claim that 'Je est un autre' (2004: 238). In haunting her old haunts, Sasha measures her own ageing on the reactions of others, and meets the memory of herself as she once was, almost literally: 'I can see myself coming out of the Métro station at the Rond-Point every morning at half-past eight [...]' (*GMM* 15). As with the repeated mention that Sasha's hotel room with its 'two beds' overlooks 'what they call an impasse' (9, 31), the 'Rond-Point', designating both a closed circle and a radiation of paths, might nod towards Proust's emblematically circular narrative with its two 'ways' at Combray (by Swann's and by the Guermantes). At points, Sasha's narrative fractures, with two 'Sashas' in dialogue with each other. But throughout, Sasha's is a deeply enigmatic, inside-outside, disembodied narrative position – such that it is not only her background that is uncertain but her position as she narrates. A grammar of displacement and doubling is deployed throughout. Consider the following:

> I must go and buy a hat this morning, I think, and tomorrow a dress. I must get on with the transformation act. But there I sit, watching the same procession of shabby women wheeling prams, of men tightly buttoned up into black overcoats.
> (*GMM* 53)

The grammar displaces the narrator: not 'here I sit', but 'there I sit'. Sasha is watching herself watching the procession; but where is she as she watches? It is as if she were her own familiar, or as if in her 'film-mind' (147) she were performing the voiceover for the film of her own life, or as if, Scrooge-like, she were looking in on her life from outside. It can resemble a reconstruction – like a witness testimony, or dream narrative, or as Nagihan Haliloğlu (2011: 89) has illuminatingly observed, the narrative of a stand-up comedian. It suggests a sense of audience, and the transportation of oneself and an audience into a different place and time. Delia Konzett argues that this externalization allows us to read the novel as a kind of 'anti-memoir' (2003: 69) which 'abandons the project of interior reflection altogether' to show instead the ways in which 'consciousness is as much, if not altogether, constituted from without rather than within' (70), in particular by mass, commodity culture. In more psychoanalytic terms, there is also an animating tension in the way in which this narrative of self-as-other involves a distancing from the self, but also, through the levelling of time periods in the tense, a grammar for traumatic memory, as if Sasha's voice registered the melancholic compulsion to repeat, reliving rather than working through her (often traumatic) memories.

Rhys's predominant use of present tense is usually taken to be 'simultaneous narration', in which there is a synchrony between the narration and the event narrated (Haliloğlu 2011: 88). Thus we speak of 'a tidal wash between Sasha's *current* life in Paris and the time she lived in London' (and in Paris previously) (Kloepfer 1989: 80; emphasis added). Sasha herself tells us (and herself) as much: 'This is late October, 1937' (*GMM* 76). Yet what is usually seen as Sasha's here and now – Paris, October 1937 – can also be read, at least in parts, as a composition in the historic present. Sasha often narrates her former life in a present tense indistinguishable from the present tense used to narrate her return to Paris, and while phrases like 'last night' (11) rather than 'the night before', seem to confirm the use of simultaneous narration for the October 1937 time frame, this anchoring grammar is not deployed consistently. Towards the end of even the first chapter, Sasha narrates what we often assume to be her present as follows: 'At four o'clock *next* afternoon I am in a cinema on the Champs Elysées, according to programme' (15; emphasis added). The narrating Sasha travels backwards and forwards in time around a nominated 'today'. And if there is no certain mark by which we could decide whether Sasha's present tense is simultaneous or historic, it becomes possible to read the narrative as an act, or re-enactment, of memory, or even as Rhys's performance of Sasha's written memoirs. In its basic substance – the source of the narrating voice, the question of whether the narration represents a written document or not – the novel is radically indeterminate.

In one of the few commentaries Rhys offered on the writing of *Good Morning, Midnight*, she explained of the novel, and the ending in particular, that she 'wanted Sasha to enter the No time region there. "Everything is on the same plane"' (*L* 138). To take a further, tentative, step here: in occupying a 'no time region', Rhys's novel challenges the deep-seated security implicit in one of the most mundane yet profound features of autobiographical life writing: that the storyteller lives to tell the tale. Of Rhys's five novels, only *After Leaving Mr Mackenzie* is free from ambiguity over whether the protagonist survives the story. In *Quartet*, the last we are told of Marya is that she has been struck by Stephan 'with all his force', and that 'as she fell, she struck her forehead against the edge of the table, crumpled up and lay still' (Q 143). In the original version of *Voyage in the Dark*, Anna narrates – in the past tense – her own death by botched abortion (1990: 381–9). *Wide Sargasso Sea* culminates in 'Bertha' narrating, again in the past tense, the fire in which, as we know from the beginning, she is to die. Is the possibility of reading *Good Morning, Midnight* as *Mémoires d'outre-tombe* – to borrow Chateaubriand's title, and his sense of posthumousness in having 'always imagined I was writing these Memoirs in my coffin' (2014: xvii) – among the implications of the much-debated ending of the novel? Two Sashas are in conflict with each other: the 'myself who is crying' and 'the other' who 'isn't me', whose voice sarcastically indicts Sasha: 'What an amusing ten days! Positively packed with thrills. The last performance of What's-her-name And Her Boys or It Was All Due To An Old Fur Coat' (*GMM* 154). But it is not the now longed for René, but the neighbouring *commis voyageur* – so often compared to a ghost, unseen by anyone but Sasha – who enters her room:

> He doesn't say anything. Thank God, he doesn't say anything. I look straight into his eyes and despise another poor devil of a human being for the last time. For the last time. ...

Then I put my arms round him and pull him down on to the bed, saying:
'Yes – yes – yes ....'

(159)

What might that repeated 'last time' imply? That Sasha resigns to despise this 'poor devil', but simultaneously resolves, with whatever degree of irony, never to let this happen again afterwards? That Sasha is about to give herself to the *commis*, 'forswearing hatred' (Angier [1990] 1992: 382) – allowing us to read the echo of Molly Bloom's 'yes' either as tragically ironic, since it is thus that Sasha loses 'the wolf in her' which is the 'real self, better and more real than the docile dog' (382), or as a 'protracted sigh of relief, uttered when she realizes that she will finally stop living in death' (Wittman 2014: 190)? Or might it also be that Sasha is about to die, even literally, by her own hand if not that of the *commis*? As with Rhys's holding back of background, it is the openness of the novel's 'conclusion' that has the most far-reaching implications here. Simply put, it is a story in which life and death are at stake. In shaping a voice poised between life and death – a voice as 'strong as the dead', *fort[e] comme la mort*,⁶ as if giving form to Walter Benjamin's remark that the storyteller 'has borrowed his authority from death' (Benjamin [1936] 1999: 93) – Rhys gives voice to a speaker who may have no voice, and any given place and time could be the here and now of that voice. Paradoxically, it is in harbouring the possibility that what we are reading in *Good Morning, Midnight* is a ghost's story in a literal sense that the narration is both most tragically spectral and most defiantly alive.

La vie littéraire: Uses of the writing life

In her letters Rhys repeatedly stresses the subordination of the writer to writing, claiming not to 'believe in the individual Writer so much as in Writing. It uses you and throws you away when you are not useful any longer' (*L* 103). Or again: 'The writer doesn't matter at all – he is only the instrument. But .... he must not be smashed. Or *he* goes bust. Then no music if you smash the violin' (270; emphasis in the original). Rhys combines in this choice of metaphor both a superlative artistic commitment – a sense of the writer's vocation as sacred, sacrificial, involving the extinction of the self and social ties in unreserved service at the altar of art – and a worldliness. Rhys's writer inhabits a violent economic sphere – is 'instrumentalised', 'used', 'smashed'; can go 'bust', and be 'thrown away when no longer useful' – rather than any rarefied, sanctified aesthetic realm. While

Rhys does often portray writers and artists and their milieu, she rarely shows her protagonists explicitly making use of – or being used by – art. That Rhys was a writer of such uncompromising dedication while her protagonists are not presented as such is one of the most fundamental ways in which Rhys frustrates as much as she invites identification between her protagonists and herself. Sasha is unusual in that there is explicit reference to her life as a professional writer – even if as a ghostwriter. In this sense it is the novel that most directly gestures towards, and distances itself from, the *Künstlerroman*, as well as being pervasively concerned with the diverse uses of the writing life.

Forms of life writing are among the most prominent textual presences within Rhys's fictions, deftly deployed as dramatically and thematically revealing devices – something sidelined by approaching the fiction as a form of autobiographical life writing in itself. Letter writing is usually the only kind of writing her protagonists are shown to engage in, and the epistolary is often pivotal. In *Quartet*, for example, Marya Zelli attempts to write a letter requesting money from Heidler so that she might return to Paris after he had forcibly arranged for her to move to Cannes (*Q* 121); in *Voyage in the Dark*, Anna Morgan voices in a parenthetical aside: 'You make up letters that you never send or even write. "My darling Walter ..."' (*VD* 64). Letter writing in such scenes poignantly connects the act of writing with dependency, vulnerability, and disempowerment. The status of the letter writing of Rhys's female characters is to be sharply distinguished from that of her male characters, who often oppress them not least through letters – often pay-offs and brush-offs – for which the only vulnerability takes the form of a fear of blackmail: both Julia Martin (*ALM* 249) and Anna Morgan (*VD* 81) are asked to return letters from lovers for fear of compromise. *Good Morning, Midnight* is full of letters – from the first act of writing we encounter directly in the book, when Mr Blank calls for Sasha, then ignores her while writing the ill-fated letter he instructs her to deliver to the 'kise' (mispronouncing 'la caisse') (*GMM* 21-6), to Sasha's recollection of an acquaintance, Paulette, reading from 'letters written to her by a lover in the provinces' (112), to what sounds like an early agony aunt column ('answers to correspondents' [52–3]). Life writing is thus shown to be put to very different uses according to the writer's position and context.

The novel stages something of a stand-off between two very different kinds of life writing. Early on, Sasha incorporates a quotation and responds to it: '"At first I was afraid they would let gates bang on my hindquarters, and I used to be nervous of unknown people and places." Quotation from *The Autobiography of a Mare* – one of my favourite books' (*GMM* 37). Sasha's 'favourite' book is thus an autobiography of a peculiar kind: self-evidently fictional, from the perspective of an animal put to the service of humans, by a human author whose name is withheld. The book appears to be fabricated: it might allude to Anna Sewell's *Black Beauty: The Autobiography of a Horse*, as well as to Leo Tolstoy's 'Strider: The Story of a Horse' (a story which, in its questioning of 'how and why I could be called a man's property' ([1885] 2005: 86), has strong affiliations with the politics of Rhys's novel).⁷ The alignment of Sasha's sensibility with so anonymous a work is set off against a pervasive, grand biographism in the fabric of European culture. The novel is detailed in its references to statues and streets named after the great and good, and the lionization of literary figures and the literary tourism attendant on it. Sasha recalls having 'waited for a couple of hours to see Anatole France's funeral pass', but at her husband's bidding, 'because, Enno said, we mustn't let such a great literary figure disappear without paying him the tribute of a last salute' (*GMM* 15). And what does it augur exactly that Sasha finds herself in the very hotel in which Rimbaud and Verlaine – that happily fated couple – reportedly lived together (33–4)? This implicit questioning of the politics of biographical literary history culminates in the novel's most explicit reference to Sasha's own literary life, late in the book, as a ghostwriter of 'fairy stories for a very rich woman' in Antibes. It is an encounter in which the genre of biography adds a distinct note. The very rich woman of Antibes expresses reservations about Sasha's work:

> 'I'm afraid Samuel didn't like your story. [...] Well, I'm afraid he didn't like the way you write. [...] Madame Holmberg is most anxious to collaborate with me. And she's a real writer – she's just finished the third volume of her Life of Napoleon.'
>
> (139–40)

A three-volume biography of a man whose name is synonymous with military leadership, ambition, *la gloire*, memorialized in countless biographies, often depicted on horseback, is the domain of the 'real writer' who can be admired by wealthy and powerful patrons.⁸ If this domain admits women, it is in a three-way relationship among women in which, nevertheless, a man in the background is appealed to as patron and authority, and it is a woman whose name sturdily fuses 'home' and 'mountain', preserved from first-name terms by a respectable title. Might 'Madame Holmberg' allude to Madame de Staël – a writer formidable enough to be considered by her contemporaries a country unto herself, as one of the 'three great powers' struggling against Napoleon alongside England and Russia (Herold 1958: 432–3)? What is clear is that Madame Holmberg and her book represent not only a threat but also a jarring antithesis to Sasha as a writer, to her own self-narration, and to a book like *The Autobiography of a Mare* as a favourite. Whatever *Good Morning, Midnight* is, *Napoleon: Volume III* by Madame Holmberg is what it most specifically is not.

As already suggested, one of the questions the form of the novel opens up is of whether the novel represents Sasha's own written memoirs. But the refusal to offer any confirmation of Sasha's having made use of her experiences in this way is among the principal ways in which Rhys foregoes, and rejects, the satisfactions of a fulfilled *Bildung*: the *Künstlerroman* would risk turning attention away from the mechanics and repercussions of debasement and towards a transformative triumph, which would not only be compensatory but would also depend on, and in a sense justify and valorize, the suffering it makes use of. While Sasha's narration involves a profound critique of the self-indulgent confidence of a certain kind of bourgeois European life writing, her 'strained particularity' – to borrow Emily Wittman's suggestive phrase (2014: 195) – also unsettles the idea that her own narrative approach could be made use of as an alternative 'model'. To do so would be to see Sasha as an example and her narrative as a variation of the exemplary life – a form that finds its superlative expression in the life of the saint. The comparison is tutelary. The summaries in the table of contents of *The Life of Saint Teresa of Ávila* – to which Rhys attributes a quotation in 'From a Diary' in *Smile Please* (160) and from which she cites, 'from memory', in her letters (*L* 144) – evaluate many of the chapters in terms of being 'essential and profitable' or, as in Chapter 13 concerning 'certain temptations the devil sends at times': 'very useful' (Teresa of Avila [1562–5] 1957: 8). What would it mean to make use of Sasha and her voice in this way, to make an example of her, to make her 'very useful'? The dark humour in Sasha's voice, as well as the traumatic nature of her experiences, sound less like the exemplary life than like Vladimir Mayakovsky's suicide note: 'I do not recommend it to others' (quoted in Alvarez 2005: 11). We must, of course, distinguish between the experiences Sasha undergoes and her responses, her actions, her ways of thinking, feeling and narrating. Yet still, one of the questions Rhys provokes is whether it is possible for us to encounter a life narrative without seeking out the exemplary in it (which includes its negative or inverse: the cautionary) – without making use of it as a means to our own ends. In becoming exemplary, Sasha (or anyone else) would be elevated but also obscured – drained of irreducibly, intrinsic individual content, in that value would be accorded extrinsically, instrumentally, as if to a template rather than the thing itself. To read Rhys's fiction as furnishing us with a 'model' of subjectivity risks capitulating to the normative traditions we purportedly see Rhys as undermining.

After life

Rhys's work so fundamentally and subtly engages with the ways in which a 'life' might emerge – or be submerged, perceived, conceived, obscured, shaped, replaced (etcetera) – in being spoken about, written about or in any way represented, that we should be wary of thinking we know what we refer to when we speak of the person who went by the name of 'Jean Rhys' or of Jean Rhys's 'life' at all, never mind when trying to articulate the relation between the work and this entity. The stakes for these questions in Rhys's work are high: the biographical scripts we use in framing ourselves and others, the use we put life stories to, are shown to be instrumental in the social practices Rhys so acutely brings into question. As it challenges the various traditions and backgrounds Rhys brings into contact in her writing, so it speaks presciently to present preoccupations – whether concerning global migration, social anxieties over exposure and privacy in the era of online social media, or the concomitant ascendancy of what has been termed an 'age of memoir' (Miller 2007: 545) in which experiments in 'autofiction' have an increasingly prominent presence. Rhys's anatomization of the stakes of female exposure, and her critical and performative challenge to an assumption of straightforwardly autobiographical foundations in her work, resonate powerfully with the issues eloquently explored in Olivia Sudjic's *Exposure* in its critique of a still resilient tendency in responding to women's writing: 'Whether she is writing an account of a real encounter or being inspired by one to write fiction, light ends up directed not to the world she's created – or the worldly issues the text raises – so much as back at *her*' (2018: 99). Most fundamentally, in being very much about the processes through which human beings are seen and reconstituted by one another (which is also to be unseen and taken apart), Rhys's writing prefigures the dynamics of her own reception, and the uses to which her life and work might be put. It would perhaps be too easy to say that if we think we apprehend the biographical figure of Rhys in the carpet of her writings, we see only a tree walking, and that the more difficult task would be to turn on ourselves Rhys's 'inflexible rigour' in what is always, at some level, 'parler de soi'. We might well make an example of Rhys. But it would not be Rhys anymore. And what would be the use?

Notes

1 A literal translation of the original passage in Bernanos's novel (1936: 9), from which Rhys omits 'cette tendresse', might be: 'It would be necessary to speak of oneself with an inflexible rigour. And at the first effort to seize this self, where does it come from – this pity, this tenderness, this relaxation of all the fibres of the soul, this desire to cry?' In what follows, I allow some flexibility in translating 'parler de soi' as to 'speak' or 'talk', 'de' as 'of' or 'about', 'soi' as 'oneself' or 'the self', according to the context.

2 The slash in 'auto/biography' serves as shorthand for discussing autobiography and biography together, and acknowledges the ways in which autobiography and biography almost inescapably interpenetrate (see Marcus 1994: 273–4).

3 See especially Saunders 2013: 1–17.

4 I follow Smith and Watson's definition of 'life writing' as an 'overarching term used for a variety of nonfictional modes of writing that claim to engage the shaping of someone's life' (2001: 197).

5 Shari Benstock writes, for example, that 'Sasha Jansen is English, […] is recognizably – even predictably – *Anglaise*' ([1987] 1994: 438), while in her introduction to the 2000 edition of the novel, A.L. Kennedy describes Sasha as 'Englishwoman Jansen' (2000: xii).

6 An allusion to Maupassant's novel *Fort comme la mort* (1889) – the book, as it happens, that the narrator of 'The Day they Burned the Books' saves from the fire (*CSS* 149).

7 It is worth noting, too, that 'Sasha' was the name of Tolstoy's daughter and secretary. Rhys may also have had in mind Woolf's 'biography' of Elizabeth Barrett-Browning's spaniel, *Flush: A Biography*.

8 A woman writing about Napoleon also appears as a counterpoint to Rhys's protagonist in *After Leaving Mr Mackenzie*: George Horsefield 'would say, 'D'you see that girl in the cocked hat and the top-boots? She's writing a novel about Napoleon' (*ALM* 28).

5

Jean Rhys and Indonesia: A lineage and alienage

Christopher Gogwilt

Jean Rhys and Indonesia may seem an odd pairing, since there are very few direct references to Indonesia in Jean Rhys's fiction. The only place where the nation is named as such appears in the late story 'Who Knows What's Up in the Attic?' (and here it is a somewhat fleeting, spectral reference to the childhood memories of a Dutchman, Jan, who has become friends with the story's unnamed main character). Indonesian spectres nonetheless haunt Rhys's texts, even if her fiction elsewhere does not explicitly name the nation which, after all, only emerged as a nation-state with the declaration of the Republic of Indonesia in 1945, and was only officially recognized in 1949. I focus here on two significant references to Indonesia in the earlier fiction (before Indonesia became a nation-state), and a third, less obvious reference in *Wide Sargasso Sea* (whose composition coincided with the turbulent early years of the Republic). All these references may appear accidental, fleeting allusions to a cultural formation quite distant from the European and Caribbean coordinates of Jean Rhys's fiction. Alien though the earlier references certainly seem both to Rhys's characters and to her own family experience, their spectral appearance becomes all the more significant in light of her daughter's later move to Indonesia and her own interest in her daughter's family's experience of Indonesian life and politics. The direct lineage linking Jean Rhys with Indonesia through her daughter, Maryvonne Moerman, and her granddaughter, Ellen Ruth Moerman, adds another layer of complexity to what Peter Hulme has called the 'Creole family romance' (1994) informing *Wide Sargasso Sea*.[1]

The earliest reference to Indonesia is a passage quoted in *After Leaving Mr Mackenzie* from *Almayer's Folly*, Joseph Conrad's first novel, set in Borneo (present-day Kalimantan), Indonesia:

She picked up the book lying on her bed-table – *Almayer's Folly* – and had begun to read:

> The slave had no hope, and knew of no change. She knew of no other sky, no other water, no other forest, no other world, no other life. She had no wish, no hope, no love.... The absence of pain and hunger was her happiness, and when she felt unhappy, she was tired, more than usual, after the day's labour.
>
> Then she had got up and looked at herself in the glass.

(*ALM* 103)

The second reference to Indonesia comes in *Good Morning, Midnight*, referring to the 'Spécialités Javanaises' on a menu from a restaurant in Paris:

> All this time I am reading the menu over and over again. This used to be a place where you could only get hot dogs, choucroute, Vienna steak, Welsh rabbit and things like that. Now, it's more ambitious. 'Spécialités Javanaises (par personne, indivisibles): Rystafel complet (16 plats), 25.00, Rystafel petit (10 plats), 17.50, Nassi Goreng, 12.50....' The back of the menu is covered with sketches of little women and 'Send more money, send more money' is written over and over again. This amuses me. I think of all the telegraph-wires buzzing 'Send more money.' In spite of everything, the wires from Paris always buzzing 'Send more money.'

(*GMM* 38)

I'll turn, later, to consider the third possible reference in *Wide Sargasso Sea*.

These first two references to Indonesia – a landscape description and a restaurant menu, respectively – are characteristic montage pieces for Jean Rhys, if unusual in their reference to the East (rather than the West) Indies. Obscure though they may be, these spectral images reveal an Indonesian lineage underwriting European Modernism. This lineage may appear more of an estrangement than an affiliation, more alienage than lineage. The first presents a literary evocation of an Indonesian landscape through the perspective of a slave. The second describes the displacement of staple European food by exotic Indonesian items on the menu. Whether looking back to an earlier moment in colonial representations of the East Indies, or looking forward to the emerging formation of Indonesian anti-colonial nationalism, Indonesia might be seen to figure an estrangement of narrative consciousness in Jean Rhys. This might also be a way to explain the single reference to the nation-state of Indonesia in 'Who Knows What's Up in the Attic': the strangeness of the main character's identification with the friend named Jan is underscored by Jan's childhood experience growing up in Indonesia, a childhood experience the story appears to identify with without sharing. These Indonesian spectres may be all the more telling, as moments of strange narrative identification, in light of the active interest Jean Rhys took in Indonesia in the period during which her daughter's family lived there, from 1948 to 1957. This happens to be the decade in which *Wide Sargasso Sea* crystallized as a book. Considered simultaneously as both lineage and alienage, these spectres invite a reconsideration of the overall profile of Jean Rhys.

The reception of Jean Rhys continues to be shaped by various versions of the argument that her work unearths a Caribbean lineage of European literature and culture.[2] How might the Creole lines of Caribbean transmission in her fiction point a way to assessing the Indonesian lines of transmission – and vice versa? I propose that each of these first two Indonesian references offers a miniature scene of reading culture that recapitulates the ambiguity of Rhys's response to the decolonizing imperatives of Creole Modernism. So, one might ask about these East Indies coordinates a similar question to the one we find ourselves repeatedly asking about the West Indies coordinates of her fiction: is her work *remembering* or *forgetting* those lines of decolonial transmission that have produced the food we eat, the landscapes we inhabit and the texts we read?

Jean Rhys provides not only, as Caryl Phillips's recent novel about Rhys richly evokes, 'A View of the Empire at Sunset.' Her work also offers a resource for understanding the interrupted history of decolonization. As Phillips's work as a whole suggests – making his recent turn to Jean Rhys all the more interesting – any view of empire depends on the experience it seems most to exclude. Ambiguity is the hallmark of Jean Rhys's fiction. It is an ambiguity akin to what Walter Benjamin, writing about the streets of Paris and the image of the woman in Baudelaire's poetry, theorized as the ambiguity of the dialectical image:

> It is the unique provision of Baudelaire's poetry that the image of the woman and the image of death intermingle in a third: that of Paris. [...] Decisive for Baudelaire in the 'death-fraught idyll' of the city, however, is a social, a modern substrate. The modern is a principal accent of his poetry. As spleen, it fractures the ideal [...]. But precisely the modern, *la modernité*, is always citing primal history. Here, this occurs through the ambiguity peculiar to the social relations and products of this epoch. Ambiguity is the manifest imaging of dialectic, the law of dialectics at a standstill.
>
> (Benjamin 1999a: 10)

There is a close affinity between Rhys's characteristic form of montage and the citations of history that make up the form and substance of Benjamin's *Arcades Project*. One reason to attend to Jean Rhys – besides retracing the shared interest in Baudelaire, the streets of Paris and the image of the woman from the perspective of a woman writer's experience – is to unearth the fuller colonial and postcolonial coordinates of that social hieroglyph Benjamin reads in the arcades of Paris, the metropolitan capital of the nineteenth century.

The first of our two references to Indonesia (from *After Leaving Mr Mackenzie*) has already formed an important part of my reading of Jean Rhys as a writer uniquely suited to measuring the interrelation between English, Creole and Indonesian genealogies of Modernism. In *The Passage of Literature* (2011), I read this montage from Conrad's *Almayer's Folly* in *After Leaving Mr Mackenzie* as a complex instance of Rhys's rereading of English Modernism and its simultaneous dependence on and erasure of non-English cultural coordinates. As a carefully selected collage piece from Conrad's tropical landscape descriptions, the passage enacts a paradigmatic problem of cultural memory. An enigmatic montage from a book the main character's sister, Norah, picks up to read, it marks an aesthetic certainty of nonmemory. While the reader is surely invited to consider an affinity between the slave in Conrad's narrative and Norah's feeling of enslavement to the care of her sick mother, Norah cannot possibly identify with, let alone recall, the cultural experience of the Siamese slave described in the passage.

This reading positions the reference to Indonesia largely in terms of the *forgetting* of the importance of the East Indies enacted by English Modernism. The passage of literature enacts a forgetting of its own Indonesian coordinates in the repetitive formation of English Modernism (from Conrad to Rhys, via Ford Madox Ford). My argument seeks to emphasize the traces of what continues to be (repetitively) forgotten and erased. What it foregrounds, however, is a kind of negative dialectic (or dialectical impasse): in the geographical and historical reference to Indonesia there is no authentic lineage of Indonesian affiliation or identity to be recuperated. The lineage is more precisely a form of alienage – as it is, indeed quite literally and specifically, in the passage from Conrad's *Almayer's Folly* that Rhys quotes, in which the slave is described as being alienated from any sense of her own country of origin (she is a Siamese slave to Buginese settlers living in northeast Borneo): 'She knew of no other sky, no other water, no other forest, no other world, no other life.' This determinate negation of Indonesian lineage in the quotation has its counterpart in the determinate negation of Caribbean lineage evoked in Norah's sister Julia's thought (at the very beginning of the novel) of 'a dark-purple sea, the sea of a chromo or of some tropical country that she had never seen' (*ALM* 12). The East Indies reference stands in counterpoint to the forgotten South American family lineage. The unnamed East Indies reference recapitulates a logic of forgotten (or displaced) West Indies lineage, suggesting that the East Indies and West Indies may only ever name forms of cultural, historical and familial displacement.

The second, later reference to Indonesia in Rhys's fiction, from *Good Morning, Midnight*, seems to register – by contrast to the first case of *forgetting* – an instance of *remembering*. Like so much else about Sasha Jansen's experience in the novel, the memory of a restaurant specializing in Javanese food is most likely taken from Jean Rhys's own experience. In the novel, the palimpsest of memories it registers is especially interesting and important in establishing Sasha Jansen's living conditions. It is in the return to the memory of this restaurant scene that we learn about the terms of her two pounds ten a week and a room off Gray's Inn Road; and we even get a glimpse of what might be her real first name, Sophia. Once made to 'look like an olde English tavern' (*GMM* 34) and formerly run by a proprietor called 'Pecanelli' (hence she recalls her former friend calling it the 'Pig and Lily'), 'now' the place is run by a 'new proprietor – a fat, bald man with a Dutch nose' and the restaurant's specialty is 'Javanese food', although 'the English hunting-scenes' are still there and 'look very exotic' (35). Whereas the tropical setting of the Conrad passage is not specified, the Indonesian cuisine of the 'Pig and Lily' is specified repeatedly: first in English ('The specialty now is Javanese food' [35]); then in French ('Spécialités Javanaises' [38]), then in Dutch ('Rystafel'), then again in the Indonesian name for the fried rice dish 'Nassi Goreng'. The scene of this Indonesian restaurant, then, situates the English coordinates of the novel's main character within the multilingual, multicultural and cosmopolitan coordinates of the specifically Indonesian cuisine of its metropolitan French setting.

The restaurant setting of *Good Morning, Midnight* offers (at least potentially) concrete material cultural reference to an Indonesian lineage in pre-war Paris. Ambiguity attends every aspect of this image: the restaurant, a scene of exotic tastes in cuisine, attracting a cosmopolitan clientele, reproduces the global ambiguity of transnational exchange and chauvinistic nationalism, all on display at the 1937 Paris Exhibition. All of this is distilled into the ambiguous profile of the restaurant's 'new proprietor' – the 'fat, bald man with a Dutch nose' (35) – who simultaneously embodies a Dutch colonial appropriation of Javanese specialties and a foretaste of Indonesian anti-colonial national identity.

This is only to begin to read the ambiguity of Indonesian lineage and alienage in Rhys's work. Each example appears to point in a different direction. The quotation from Conrad looks back to a longer colonial prehistory of literary and cultural exchange between English and South/Southeast Asian lineages.

The restaurant menu looks forward to the post-war emergence of the new postcolonial nation of Indonesia. In both cases, the allusion to Indonesia produces only spectres, rather than clear social, ethnic or national profiles. The significance of these Indonesian allusions, indeed, may be seen to hinge on the ambiguity of social, ethnic or national profiles – as well as ambiguity in the narrative's identification with, or estrangement from, those profiles. The 'slave' in the Conrad quotation from *After Leaving Mr Mackenzie*, though never named in Rhys's montage piece, is Siamese, and so figured as coming from beyond the East Indies setting of the novel. The restaurant scene in *Good Morning, Midnight* figures only a spectral sense of Indonesian identity through the colonial (possibly mixed Indo-) Dutch figure of the proprietor with the 'Dutch nose' and through the fleeting appearance of 'five Chinese' customers who enter and then leave. To the extent that both of these examples refer to the Dutch colonial territories that would come to form the new nation-state of Indonesia after the Second World War, they characterize the East Indies as an ambiguity of ethnic, racial or national lineage: a lineage *and* alienage that stands in counterpoint to Jean Rhys's more vexed personal and familial relation to the West Indies.

This brings us to the possibility of an Indonesian lineage and alienage underwriting *Wide Sargasso Sea*, something that remains to my knowledge quite unexplored in critical responses to Rhys. Although there would appear to be no direct reference to Indonesia in *Wide Sargasso Sea*, there is a direct biographical link, a lineage that can be traced through Jean Rhys's letters to her daughter. In the years during which she began writing *Wide Sargasso Sea* in earnest, her daughter's family moved to Indonesia, living there between 1948 and 1957. Her daughter, Maryvonne, married Job Moerman, a Dutchman who was born and grew up in Indonesia (not unlike Jan in the story 'What's Up in the Attic?'). Job Moerman worked for the big Dutch shipping company KPM (Koninklijki Paketvaart-Maatschappij) that remained under Dutch ownership and management after Indonesian independence. Moerman maintained ties to childhood friends, including the prominent nationalist figure Abdul Nasution (who was targeted in, but escaped, the coup attempt of 1965 that became the pretext for mass executions, the toppling of Sukarno and the rise of Suharto as President of 'New Order' Indonesia). According to Rhys's granddaughter, Ellen Moerman, it was Nasution who advised the Moerman family to leave Indonesia in 1957.[3]

In September of 1949, Rhys wrote to her daughter: 'I read all the news from Indonesia I can find' (*L* 54); and in February of 1958 she is still reading 'all the news about Indonesia' (*L* 152). Jean Rhys's biographer, Carole Angier, writes that these were the years of her 'least containable disasters' ([1990] 1992: 440). She puts it this way to emphasize that these were 'exactly the right years' for her daughter's family to be away from her, crediting the ironic insight to Jean Rhys herself – quoting a letter to Diana Athill from 1967 – "'As for me, I had such a – Well, a trying time after the war that I was thankful that Maryvonne had her own life and wasn't involved with mine'" (*L* 440). Reading Rhys's letters to her daughter suggests an involvement with her family that is also a distance from her family – a lineage and an alienage. All those 'least containable disasters' of her life during these years unfold in counterpoint to her reading of 'all the news from Indonesia'. The lineage and alienage of this family correspondence, moreover, looks both forwards (to *Wide Sargasso Sea*) and backwards (on all her pre-war fiction). Side by side with her comments on the political situation in Indonesia are comments hinting at the protracted, slow work towards *Wide Sargasso Sea*. The correspondence with Maryvonne is also punctuated with references to Selma Vaz Dias's rediscovery of her work (in 1949) and the BBC broadcast of a version of *Good Morning, Midnight*. In 1957, she writes to Maryvonne 'I'll ask about broadcasting to Indonesia' (*L* 141).

It is perhaps not too far-fetched to describe this as Jean Rhys's Indonesian family romance – in contrast with what Peter Hulme has called 'the Creole family romance' (1994) that underwrites *Wide Sargasso Sea*. As Ellen Moerman has said (in response to a version of this essay delivered at the Paris 'Transmission Lines' conference), following the Moermans' return from Indonesia, her grandmother would repeatedly inquire about her childhood growing up in Indonesia, and she (Ellen Moerman) recalls her grandmother having numerous conversations with her father, Job Moerman, about Indonesia. The seeds of this interest seem to have been planted even before the Moerman family left for Indonesia. Consider a letter Rhys wrote to Peggy Kirkaldy about the family's impending departure for Java. The letter (dated 8 July 1948) includes a family photograph of daughter and granddaughter: 'Here's a snapshot of these only hopes of mine – but send it back for it's precious.' I am not sure if the photograph itself has survived, but the image of what makes it 'precious' for Jean Rhys is inscribed in what she writes to Kirkaldy: 'Well Maryvonne's baby is a darling – she has slanting eyes and red brown hair – I fell in love with her and pray that they'll get safely to Java. / Sun to sun in one generation. It's true there's a war over there. / Still even a war would be better than this ghastly hopelessness and treachery in Europe' (*L* 47).

'Sun to sun in one generation' — there's a striking resonance in this phrase with Christophine's articulation of the 'Creole' stereotype in *Wide Sargasso Sea*: 'She is Creole girl, and she have the sun in her' (*WSS* 95). How might the shaping of the 'Creole' family romance of *Wide Sargasso Sea* be informed not only by the West Indian Lockhart family ancestors (Hulme), but also by her Moerman family descendants? That family romance (as this letter illustrates) is directly linked to what is happening in Indonesia during the period in which Jean Rhys is shaping the Creole family romance of *Wide Sargasso Sea*.

The 'war' she refers to in that letter is the war for independence fought against the Dutch and allied forces seeking to reassert Dutch control over the colonies occupied by the Japanese during the war. The Indonesian Republic was declared in 1945, following the defeat of the Japanese, but full sovereignty was not recognized until the end of 1949 (see Appendix 1 for a chronology of events). Jean Rhys's daughter's family moved to Indonesia in the middle of this war for independence. In letters to Maryvonne, Jean Rhys expresses concern about what she reads in the news. On 7 September 1949, she writes 'I read all the news from Indonesia I can find but it's very contradictory depending a bit on the politics of the editor' (*L* 54). On 24 October of the same year, she writes 'My dear I often read news about Java that worries me – one paper says one thing one another – so send me anything – a post card even to say you're all OK' (*L* 57). On 9 November (again, the same year) she writes 'My dear your last letter disturbed me, though it was very interesting. I don't like much what I read about the situation in some newspapers – others are optimistic, it's so difficult to judge' (*L* 61). All of these letters were written between the official ceasefire (1 August) and the recognition of full sovereignty (27 December). These are the foundational moments of Indonesia's hard-fought independence.

Between 1957 (when the Moermans left Indonesia) and 1965 (when *Wide Sargasso Sea* was completed), Indonesia's experiment in revolutionary independence was severely tested. There are parallels to be found elsewhere during this period of struggle for decolonization worldwide. Third World independent nation-states faced aggressive forms of destabilization and containment (notably in the US war in Vietnam). This is the moment, too, of the short-lived West Indies Federation (1958–62) that brought independence from Britain (momentarily) to Dominica. Indonesia's revolutionary form of anti-colonial nationalism (a model for Third World independence) was spectacularly reversed in the aftermath of the aborted 'coup' of September 1965 that became a pretext for mass killings and led to the toppling of Sukarno and the establishment of the corrupt and repressive 'New Order' regime of Suharto.

Jean Rhys's writing of *Wide Sargasso Sea* parallels this turning point in the history of decolonization, when worldwide, the fate of anti-colonial nationalism in the West Indies and the East Indies hung in the balance. Considered from the perspective of Benjamin's messianic Marxist vision of history, the fate of decolonization still hangs in the balance. The full historical import of that moment has yet to be grasped, even as its significance flares up in the images we glimpse here and there in the historical record or the archive of fiction. One especially intriguing document related to the historical record of Indonesia just before the events of 1965 is a secret report written by Jean Rhys's son-in-law detailing the corruption he had witnessed as an employee of the KPM. It was very likely because of this document, according to Ellen Moerman's account, that Abdul Nasution advised Job Moerman to leave Indonesia.

Even several years after the Moermans' return, Jean Rhys is still reading about Indonesia (and presumably still asking her granddaughter and her son-in-law about their time in Indonesia). In a letter from 4 March 1962, she writes to Maryvonne about a book she has been reading called *The Net of Gold* – the translation of a German novel by Alice Ekert-Rotholz about the decline of the colonial Dutch East Indies. Contrasting the exotic romance of this novel with what her daughter has told her about Indonesia, she writes: 'It is so very unlike what you wrote me that it must be a complete fake.' She then goes on to critique the book with a turn of phrase that echoes the description of 'this cardboard house where I walk' (*L* 107) at the end of *Wide Sargasso Sea*: 'Besides it is enormously long with dozens of characters all made of cardboard – the sort of book most people like and I detest. Still, I read it because it was about Indonesia' (*L* 211).

'This cardboard house where I walk at night is not England' (*WSS* 107). *Jane Eyre* is, of course, the book that Rhys is evoking here, and the power of her reimagining of Brontë's Bertha Mason has had the effect of making Antoinette haunt the pages of that canonical novel. We read it differently now – as indeed we might read all of modern literature – to recapture the Creole profiles on which it is premised. In what sense, though, does Rhys's investment in Indonesia show how the 'not England' of that 'cardboard house' is premised, too, on an Indonesian lineage? How might the earlier references to the East Indies in Jean Rhys's fiction relate to *Wide Sargasso Sea*, and how might they be explored from the wide-angle lens of this comparative perspective in decolonization?

This brings us to one important, if buried allusion to Indonesia in *Wide Sargasso Sea*. The fictional post-Emancipation West Indian historical setting of Coulibri estate famously captures an important geopolitical shift in its reference to Mason's plan to import 'labourers – coolies he called them – from the East Indies' (*WSS* 21). The labourers or 'coolies' invoked in this important reference may not seem to constitute a reference to Indonesia at all. 'East Indies' might more likely be glossed by reference to the Indian or Chinese indentured slave labour brought to Jamaica after the Emancipation Act of 1833/4 (see, for example, Judith Raiskin's note in the Norton Critical edition [*WSS*: 21, n. 7]). Yet historically the schemes for introducing indentured labourers into the Caribbean involved a range of West Indian-bound migration routes originating in the British- and Dutch-controlled 'East Indies'. In the early years of the nineteenth century (reaching back to the earliest such schemes, before Emancipation, in 1806), contract labour systems organized in Java and the Malay Peninsula offered a model for immigration schemes throughout the nineteenth century. Although the vast majority of indentured labourers brought to the Caribbean after Emancipation were from India, with a smaller but significant proportion from China (and a much smaller proportion from Java and elsewhere), the term 'East Indies' names the migration routes through which these workers were transported.[4] And as Jung Moon-ho has noted in *Coolies and Cane*, 'Coolies were never a people or a legal category. Rather, coolies were a conglomeration of racial imaginings that emerged worldwide in the era of Emancipation, a product of the imaginers rather than the imagined' (2006: 5). In *Wide Sargasso Sea*, the spectre of these indentured slave labourers is really just that, a spectre (not unlike the shadowy slave figure in the Conrad quotation from *After Leaving Mr Mackenzie*; or the spectres crowding round the Paris restaurant in *Good Morning, Midnight*). But this spectre plays a crucial role in the novel's plot, the rumour of Mason's plan precipitating the act of burning down the Coulibri estate. The spectre of East Indies labourers or 'coolies', moreover, signals that wider geopolitical shift in the global economy of West Indian sugar production worldwide which figures as a crucial turning point (from the Atlantic to the Indian Oceans) in the mid-nineteenth-century reorganization of global trade, labour and commodity exchange. It is a turning point (from West to East) that is itself more than symbolically written into the form of *Jane Eyre*, the novel Jean Rhys is rewriting. As a number of critics have noted, the burning down of the Coulibri estate ought to be read as a palimpsest of historical events condensed and displaced into the fictional image. Peter Hulme productively asks of this palimpsest of historical moments, 'What history are we talking about?' (1994: 74). Considering the fictional image as a Benjaminian 'dream image' – what Benjamin theorized in the ambiguity of Baudelaire's poetry as the 'manifest imaging of dialectic' (Benjamin 1999a: 10) – and affirming that Jean Rhys's fiction is precisely a palimpsest of different historical moments, I suggest we add to this palimpsest the spectral image of Indonesia's political history and prehistory.

Ambiguity attends all these questions of lineage and alienage – in a literary sense, in a material cultural sense, as well as in a biographical familial sense. We have yet to read the full significance of these spectral images of Indonesia, and the lineages of decolonization they harbour, almost like citations from a history yet to be written. They are all, in a sense, like the 'Dutch nose' of the proprietor in the Paris restaurant in *Good Morning, Midnight* (which might evoke a colonial white identity, an anti-Semitic stereotype or possibly even a mixed 'Indo' lineage). These spectres condense and displace into a single profile a range of lineages offering a 'dream image' (in Benjamin's sense) of the simultaneity and synchrony of colonization and decolonization. The spectre of the 'coolies' from the 'East Indies' in *Wide Sargasso Sea*; the spectral image of the Siamese slave in the passage from a book read in *After Leaving Mr Mackenzie*; the spectral figures of the proprietor of the Paris restaurant and its fleeting Chinese visitors – all of these spectral images of Indonesia mark an important ambiguity of reference. A similar ambiguity may be found in the singular reference to Indonesia in 'Who Knows What's Up in the Attic?' If the main character's enigmatic friendship with Jan suggests a familiarity based on affinities between the Dutchman's East Indies past and Jean Rhys's West Indies past, the story is framed by another kind of strange familiarity. At the beginning of the story, the main character has been expecting the visit of a 'Mr. Singh', a travelling salesman, who reappears at the end of the story as the expected visitor who will succeed in selling her some familiar article of clothing. Between the two strangers, the story evokes a sense of home as displacement, a remembering and forgetting that implicates spectral memories of the West Indies and the East Indies, of Caribbean and Indonesian lineages, combined into a characteristically Rhysian lineage of contemporary English identity. A lineage *and* alienage might be a way to articulate the significance of this ambiguity in its historical, demographic and cultural significance.

Appendix 1. Jean Rhys and Indonesia: Chronology

	Jean Rhys's Family (Moermans)	Indonesia
1945		**Independence declared** (17 August); revolution against Dutch (1945–9)
1948	Moermans move to Indonesia	**Renville agreement** (19 January: divides Republican and Dutch territories); **Madiun affair** (18 September: communist uprising suppressed)
1949		**Official ceasefire** (1 August); **full sovereignty recognized** (27 December)
1957	Moermans leave Indonesia	**State of war and siege; Guided Democracy begins; Dutch enterprises nationalized**
1965		**'30th September Movement' 'coup'** (in response, from 1965–6 more than 1 million people killed; thousands interned in prison camps)
1966	*Wide Sargasso Sea*	**Suharto formally declared President; New Order regime begins**

Notes

1 For information on Maryvonne Moerman's family experiences in Indonesia, I'm indebted to Ellen Ruth Moerman for many conversations conducted during the conference in Paris where this paper was first delivered as a talk.

2 A partial list of critics who have shaped this argument includes Wilson Harris (1983), Peter Hulme (1994), Mary Lou Emery (1990, 2007), Veronica Gregg (1995), Sue Thomas (1999), Judith Raiskin (1991), Elaine Savory (1998) and Denise de Caires Narain (2000).

3 For information on Abdul Nasution's role in contemporary Indonesian history, see M.C. Ricklefs, *A History of Modern Indonesia* (1993: 255–82), and John Roosa, *Pretext for Mass Murder: The September 30th Movement and Suharto's Coup d'État in Indonesia* (2006: esp. 107–16).

4 See Walton Look Lai's *The Chinese in the West Indies* (1998: Chapter 1 and passim).

Part Two

Lines of flight:
Rhys's transnational legacy

6

Jean Rhys in Australian neo-Victorian and Great House imaginaries

Sue Thomas

'Works of literature take on a new life as they move into the world at large, and to understand this [...] we need to look closely at the ways the work becomes reframed in its translations and in its new cultural contexts', comments David Damrosch in elaborating the scope of the field of world literature (2003: 6, 24). Creative engagement, like adaptation across media and genre, reframes source texts and extends the cultural reach and contexts of story. Jean Rhys's late modernist *Wide Sargasso Sea* ([1966] 1999) and John Fowles's postmodern *The French Lieutenant's Woman* (1969) are routinely identified as the progenitors of neo-Victorian fiction: fiction influentially characterized as '*more than* historical fiction set in the nineteenth century', fiction 'in some respect [...] *self-consciously engaged with the act of (re)interpretation, (re)discovery and re(vision) concerning the Victorians*' (Heilmann and Llewellyn 2010: 4; emphasis in original). Especially since the mid-1980s Rhys's critical engagement with Charlotte Brontë's *Jane Eyre* in *Wide Sargasso Sea* has inspired writers of neo-Victorian fiction, and influenced adaptors of *Jane Eyre* for opera, the stage, television and cinema. The publication of a selection of Rhys's letters in 1984, edited by Francis Wyndham and Diana Melly, drew out the scope of her creative engagement with Brontë's novel and made her reflexive project of 'writing back' to an English canonical text common property for writers, fans, scholars and students. *Jane Eyre* has functioned, Cora Kaplan argues, as a 'mnemic' symbol for generations of readers, writers and artists, a text which excites a complex 'affective dynamics', a 'memorialis[ation] and renew[al]' of the 'melodramatic excess of nineteenth-century fiction' (2007: 15).

In this chapter I trace shifts in Rhys's influence on Australian writers of neo-Victorian fiction, as well as on a sound and video installation that explores the legacies of the Great House in the present-day Caribbean and its Australian diaspora. I seek to draw out nuances of the aesthetic and 'affective dynamics' at play in the way Rhys's project and innovation in *Wide Sargasso Sea* are memorialized through these artistic and literary forms. To recover the Australian reaches of *Wide Sargasso Sea*'s path to becoming world literature, I discuss, in particular, Barbara Hanrahan's *The Albatross Muff* ([1977] 1986), Amanda Lohrey's 'Jane Eyre' (1995), Jennifer Livett's *Wild Island* (2016) and Willoh S. Weiland and Halcyon Macleod's *Crawl Me Blood* (2018b) against a backdrop of a broader range of novels, stories, a libretto, a film, opera and plays.

'Re-vision, Recovery, Circulation, and Collage' have been proposed by Susan Stanford Friedman as a methodology of transnational literary inquiry (2011: 5). She limits such inquiry to critical scholarship. These methods, though, are crucial to the writerly praxis of the texts I examine. Rhys's project in *Wide Sargasso Sea* has become, like British Victorian literary and cultural works, a 'site within which the memory of empire and its surrounding discourses and strategies of representation can be replayed and played out' (Ho 2013: 5) in acts of re-vision: 'looking back, […] seeing with fresh eyes, […] entering an old text from a new critical direction' (Rich 1972: 18). In relation to the field of neo-Victorian literary studies, the authorial affiliations with Rhys, which are inscribed in the texts I discuss here, challenge dominant logics when it comes to the circulation of texts and influence: centre/home (Britain) to periphery. The affiliative poetics of *Crawl Me Blood*, staged at the Tasmanian Botanical Gardens in Hobart from 11 to 14 April 2018 and the Royal Botanical Gardens in Melbourne from 29 August to 1 September 2018, routes Rhys's influence through shared authorial Caribbean heritage. Not all Australian creative engagements with *Wide Sargasso Sea* have had a global circulation. Staged performances and installations, for instance, are venue specific. Engagement across genres has, too, arguably obscured appreciation of the depth of Rhys's influence on Australian cultural production.[1] The term Creole as a descriptor of peoples has a complicated history across different imperial formations. Some Australian writers assume, or give credence to, Rochester's anxieties that Bertha Mason Rochester/Antoinette Cosway Mason Rochester is of mixed-race heritage (*Wide Sargasso Sea* 1993; Lohrey 1995; *Wide Sargasso Sea* 1997; Malouf 2000; Livett 2016). Friedman describes collage as 'radical juxtaposition, […] a montage of differences where setting texts side by side illuminates those differences at the same time that it spotlights commonalities' (2011: 7). Collage in my archive of texts takes various forms: intersecting narrative strands, generic and stylistic juxtaposition, and counterpointing of narrative and musical tracks.

In an Australian historical context, the Victorian period is marked by Indigenous dispossession and genocide, convict transportation, settlement, federation around a White Australia policy, shifting class, gender and racializing formations, and the discourses that underpinned them. There were manifold connections between the West Indies and Australia in its colonial period (1788–1901). They include transportation of convicts from the West Indies, migration, 'movement of colonial officers, merchants and professional men between the two locations' (McMahon 2016: 50), the transfer of capital to Australia after the abolition of slavery in the West Indies, the flow of plantation management practices, and the production and dissemination of scientific knowledge of, for example, botany, tropical agriculture and tropical medicine.[2]

Hanrahan's allusions to Jean Rhys's last novel *Wide Sargasso Sea* in *The Albatross Muff* signal a parallel writerly interest in extending the narrative reach of the memory of empire. This allows the text to encompass the psychodynamics of racialized and racializing intergenerational intimacies between a white middle-class colonial girl and female servants – surrogate mother figures, who function as phallic mothers for their charge. In colonial terms Stella is a 'currency lass' ('currency' meaning Australian-born),[3] and as such English characters position her foreignness as 'convict's filth' (Hanrahan [1977] 1986: 68), 'too hot for a proper human', 'a bit of convict […] got in' (171), 'exotic' sexual precociousness (125) and 'evidence of some nigger variety of sweat' (178). Exploring the global translatability of ideas of white colonial degeneracy, Hanrahan draws on elements of Rhys's representation of the relationship between white Creole Antoinette Cosway Mason Rochester and black servant and emancipated slave Christophine Dubois in *Wide Sargasso Sea*, and turns them into a story of an uncanny 'web of love' (80) between the vulnerable Stella Edenbrough and a 'dark' emancipist (ex-convict) servant Moak, whom Stella thinks has magic powers, and whose skin was, in Stella's eyes, 'brown as a gypsy's' (13).

Rhys and Hanrahan evoke the subjectivity of the webs of desire and dread in the minds of Antoinette and Stella respectively. Hanrahan takes Rhys's authorization of intergenerational female agency and blurring of the lines of the real and the imagined to centre stage. In line with dominant nineteenth-century troping of the Romany the suggestion of Moak's heritage makes her a symbol of 'dispossession', 'homelessness' (Nord 2006: 67) and 'heterodox femininity' (14).

Like Antoinette with Christophine, Stella attributes occult powers to Moak. Hanrahan's analogue to the colonial plantation with its Great House is the sheep station and homestead owned by Stella's grazier father, who dies in a horse-riding accident.[4] Sargassum, a type of seaweed, and drift, both emblematic of the Sargasso Sea, are central motifs of the 'web of love' which develops on the voyage from Australia to England in 1855. Stella's English mother Bertha is widowed and retreats into grief and care for Stella's needier baby sister Louise Victoria on the voyage 'home' to England. As an emancipist Moak is free to return to England. Hanrahan's use of the sea as a narrative point of departure, as narrative tension, metaphor, affiliative allusion and occult unsettlement of assimilation to English domestic imperialism and English domestic realism predates what Elizabeth Ho identifies as a 'turn to the sea' in much more recent post-millenium neo-Victorian texts (2013: 175).

In 'Three Women's Texts and a Critique of Imperialism' (1985) Gayatri Chakravorty Spivak writes that one of the two axes of 'feminist individualism in the age of imperialism' is 'childbearing', 'domestic-society-through-sexual-reproduction cathected as "companionate love"'; the second is 'soul making', 'the imperialist project cathected as' social responsibility for Christian humanization (244). The historical moment of *The Albatross Muff*, the mid-1970s, is apparent in its feminist questioning of the patriarchal imperative underpinning domesticity and childbearing within marriage – and its underside pioneeringly exposed by Steven Marcus in *The Other Victorians* (1966). Hanrahan's imaginative world is a place of sexual peril for women, as is suggested by the punning and symbolic title *The Albatross Muff* and, as an example of her internationally renowned printmaking, *Run Rabbit Run* (1978). In *The Albatross Muff* the sexual perils are predatory English paedophilia, colonial fortune-hunting and grotesquely excessive, indeed vampiric, Victorian childbearing. *The Albatross Muff* culminates in a conflagration, and there are allusive and stylistic parallels to and pointed contrasts with the endings of Rhys's *Wide Sargasso Sea* and Rhys's *Voyage in the Dark*. With what is seen as an 'animal intensity' (Hanrahan [1977] 1986: 202) identified as 'low Chapel' (166) and 'mad' (205), Moak, who may be a schizophrenic double of Stella (brought on by the trauma of sexual abuse on the trip to England), damns the souls of the predatory English paterfamilias William Hall and his home, the punningly named 6 Percy Villas, to the fires of apocalypse. Like Antoinette's, Stella's future in death (she dies after childbirth) is projected in poetic richness as a return to a colonial home, but to an uncorrupted father figure rather than a childhood playmate.

Assimilation to gendered white English heteronormative middle-class propriety is the 'soul-making' plotline of the novel around both Stella and Edith (Dissy) Hall, who appears as a writer in the making. Stella's difference is marked both by the fire and by a 'rosella-red cloak' (57); English Dissy's sexual dissonance is accommodatable in a counter-family of women in Wales, to which she takes Stella's baby daughter at the end of the novel. The Dissy plotline was inspired by a cache of Hodge family materials – letters and a family history 'recorded [...] in a brown paper-covered exercise book' from the Victorian era – purchased at London's Church Street Market (Stewart 2010: 118).

Hanrahan very much admired the 'grey' of the 'worlds' of Rhys's novels (1998: 337, 339). In Rhys's fiction, grey is a metonym of her protagonists' marginality in England and France and their difficulties in assimilating to the homogenizing sameness of dominant cultural values, what Rhys terms the 'huge machine of law, order, respectability' (*CSS* 110). Hanrahan's affiliation with Rhys in *The Albatross Muff* is grounded in critical awareness of the stakes of assimilation by that machine, including its reach within metropolitan literary cultures.

In the late 1970s and the mid-1980s (when *The Albatross Muff* was first reprinted) no reviewers recognized Hanrahan's allusions to *Wide Sargasso Sea* or Rhys's inspiration of a narrative examination of gendered, classed and racialized aspects of Australian colonial history and their representability. This is partly because of a blind spot around the possibility of a Caribbean-Australian circuit of affiliation and because *Wide Sargasso Sea* and Rhys's project in it had not yet acquired mythic status. The cover blurb of the 1986 British edition of *The Albatross Muff* indeed describes the novel as 'a tender and intensely individual evocation of Victorian childhood merge[d] with a Dickensian fairy story which becomes a feverish nightmare'.

Chris Baldick suggests that a text's mythic status 'strips down the longer stories from which they may be derived, reducing them to the simplest memorable patterns. [...] The process of myth-making violates the multiplicity and interplay of meanings which the novel's narrative complexity sustains, and sets its radically foreshortened story free to attract new narrative or interpretative elaborations around it' (1987: 3). By the 1990s the circulation of both *Jane Eyre* and *Wide Sargasso Sea* was underpinned by mythic status. The reprinting of extracts from Rhys's letters about writing *Wide Sargasso Sea* under the title 'Love's Dark Face' in *Regarding Jane Eyre* (Geason 1997), a collection billed as 'Writers Respond to Charlotte Brontë's *Jane Eyre*' (cover blurb), suggests that Rhys's self-reflexivity in the letters grounds the mythic status of her project. A cluster of 1990s

Australian adaptations of *Wide Sargasso Sea* – Paul Monaghan's *Obeah Night* (physical theatre, opera and spoken text, 1993), John Duigan's *Wide Sargasso Sea* (film, 1993), and Brian Howard's *Wide Sargasso Sea* (chamber opera, 1997) – foreshorten the novel and its complex interplay of narrative voices, refracting it entirely or predominantly through the point of view of the Rochester figure.[5]

In 1995 Rhys provides for Amanda Lohrey a model for the audacious remaking of a canonical text – a remaking which poses fresh questions about labels of madness and depravity, and their imbrication with the racialization of empire. A four-page story in six subtitled parts, Lohrey's 'Jane Eyre' begins with '*The Story So Far* by Charlotte Brontë', a very short plot summary of Brontë's text, a 'public thing', 'common property' (Stoneman 1996: xi) by virtue of its cult status and, unlike *Wide Sargasso Sea*, being out of copyright. Lohrey then offers five clever postmodern plot variations, a collage of scenarios that play on the representability of 'suppressed histories of gender and sexuality, race and empire' in the Victorian period (Kaplan 2007: 3), at times to the point of parody. The last variation takes the character Jane Eyre, mothered now by Mrs Deronda from George Eliot's novel *Daniel Deronda*, to a politically volatile Sydney in the aftermath of republican revolutions in Europe in 1848. Rochester's first wife is identified in the plot summary as a 'mad mulatto' (Lohrey 1995: 76), in the first variation ('The Visionary Bride') as a 'mad and depraved Creole heiress from the West Indies' (76), and in the third variation ('Adèle') as a 'black ravaged form [...] dozing lumpenly in her chamber beneath the battlements' (78). In the second variation ('The Crisis Was Perilous but Not Without its Charm'), Rochester and a 'worldly', 'slaver[ing]' Jane have 'heartless, carnal, greedy and hot' animalistic sex. Their 'monstrous couplings' take place, at Rochester's insistence, in a bed on the 'third floor of the Hall'; 'they thrash and writhe, roaring like bulls, neighing like horses, drowning out the laughter of *her* in the attic'. Rochester here is a Bluebeard figure; 'her' the monitory figure of the abandoned, now caged sexually 'delinquent' partner; and Jane fresh sexual curiosity (77). The scenario draws on Rochester having sex with Amélie in *Wide Sargasso Sea* within Antoinette's hearing, and reframes it as initiating serial tauntings of *her*, the first wife. The first wife's laughter suggests not madness but knowingness about Jane's potential fate. The monstrous figure of the variant 'Revisionism (i)' is Jane's now alive, socially conservative mother who pushes her daughter to marry St John and procreate, offering her a deeply symbolic 'gift of a snakeskin purse' with 'sugared almonds' inside, 'nestling in the red silk lining of the purse like a cluster of eggs' (79). She dies of smallpox in India.

The story's historical moment is the 1990s campaign for Australia to become a republic. Australia's current constitutional status – it was founded in 1901 as a federal constitutional monarchy – is a throwback to the Victorian era in which the constitution was framed. The explanatory subtitle of the journal *RePublica* in which the story was published was 'from *res publica*, the public thing, that which is ours and of our own making' (Lohrey 1995: 281). In none of Lohrey's scenarios is there a marriage between Jane and Rochester or indeed a hint of companionate romantic love, and there is no realization of the grand narratives of 'childbearing' or of 'soul making'. Rochester is represented as a sexual predator in the first and second variations; he is a 'morose and provincial bore' in the third, in which Jane develops a paedophilic interest in Adèle (77). The variations, then, pointedly resist Brontë's sexualization of Rochester's power, founded as it is on the prestige of his English whiteness, civility and class position, and of course, Bertha's dowry.

Billed on the cover as 'A novel of Jane Eyre and Van Diemen's Land', Jennifer Livett's *Wild Island* (2016) combines in generic and stylistic collage historical bio-fiction about Lady Jane Franklin, the controversial wife of Arctic explorer Sir John Franklin, the Lieutenant-Governor of the convict colony Van Diemen's Land (now Tasmania) from 1837 to 1843, and a resiting of foreshortened plots of *Jane Eyre* and *Wide Sargasso Sea* with Gothic melodrama. *Wild Island* includes at the front separate lists of historical and fictional characters (vii–xi). Sir John was recalled as governor over the alleged improper influence of Lady Jane: petticoat government. Harriet Adair, one of two narrating voices, positions the text as a challenge to British authority, produced as a colonial composite from accounts by 'those of us' who witnessed 'the Franklin debâcle [*sic*] and the Rochester matter' and 'who know what really happened' (xii–xiii). Lady Jane's civilizing mission (which includes a projected botanical garden) is beset by fractious, faction-ridden masculinist politics and misogyny. Harriet, who has been the keeper/'nurse-companion' of Bertha/Antoinette (Anna for short) after the death of Grace Poole (19), comments of Jane Eyre and Edward Fairfax Rochester:

> Reader, she did not marry him, or rather, when at last she did, it was not so straightforward as she implies in her memoirs. Jane Eyre is a truthful person and her story is fascinating, but some things she could not bring herself to say. Certain episodes in her past, she admits, 'form too distressing a recollection ever to be willingly dwelt upon'.

(xii)

Livett suggests that her Jane Eyre writes the story of Rochester and Bertha we read in Brontë's novel to suppress and bury Fairfax Rochester family scandals and secrets, including a mixed-race child of Rowland Rochester and Antoinette Mason. Jane Eyre's self-censorship is juxtaposed with the reported ruthless familial censorship of Lady Jane Franklin's published diaries (Livett 2016: xiii) and the repression of women's and homosexuals' histories. 'Where better to go than towards unknown regions?' comments Harriet (57). Lohrey mentored Livett in the later stages of manuscript development under the auspices of the Australian Society of Authors' 'Mini-Mentorship' scheme (432). They both show boldness in imagining repressive Victorianism.

As narrator, Harriet compares 'intrepid' Janes, Jane Eyre and Lady Jane, adjudging that they share 'cool intelligent appraisal, the feeling of energy suppressed' and, alluding to *Jane Eyre*, that both are 'struggling free of the nets cast around them' (Livett 2016: xii, 153, 406). Readers might say the same of Harriet; also, like Jane Eyre, she has an artistic sensibility. The pun on Harriet's family name (ad-eyre) underlines the comparison, the Latin 'ad' meaning 'toward', 'up to'.

Livett's narrative of Tasmanian settlement addresses the routing of English sensibility to the island and the roots it develops there in the wake of the brutality of Indigenous dispossession and of convictism under former governor Sir George Arthur. Sensibility is the register of colonial humanization as social good in the novel (Livett 2016: 244). In talking about conceptualizing her first novel *Wild Island* (Dawkins 2016), Livett, a now retired academic, who migrated to Tasmania with her English parents as a child, points to the importance to her of Spivak's essay. This suggests that Postcolonial Studies framed her route to and through *Wide Sargasso Sea*. Livett does not gloss over the limits of Victorian sensibility on questions of class, race, gender and sexuality. She has her Grace Poole, a 'vicious old woman, by all accounts' (Livett 2016: 31), die of apoplexy to replace her with Harriet. In addition to Harriet's domestication of English sensibility and Lady Jane Franklin's pursuit of an English civilizing mission, Livett develops civic humanization narratives around the historical Charles O'Hara Booth, the commandant at Port Arthur penal station from 1833 to 1844, and the fictional repressed homosexual clergyman St John Wallace, a variant of Brontë's St John Rivers.

Tasmanian history is a frontline in Australia's current History Wars around Indigenous genocide and dispossession. Drawing on the life and diaries of Lady Jane, accounts of Sir John's governorship and documentation of the emergence of professional classes in the history of Tasmanian settlement, Livett engages with earlier bio-fiction and bio-narrative about Lady Jane, but most pointedly

Richard Flanagan's novel *Wanting* (2008). Flanagan represents his childless Lady Jane as consumed by thwarted maternal desire, played out tragically in her adoption and abandonment of the Indigenous child Mathinna. Mathinna is a very minor character in *Wild Island*. In Sitka, questing for news of her husband, Livett's Lady Jane reflects briefly on her failings with respect to her. The cover image of *Wild Island* (a woman holding a bowl of fruit) alludes to a particularly egregious troping of the question of the fitness of Julia Gillard, Australia's first female Prime Minister (2010-13), for the office: the empty fruit bowl as a symbol of her decision not to have children.

Like other authors, to establish her Janes as credible heroines of sensibility for a contemporary audience, Livett has to reinvent Bertha, largely as a cipher for more empathetic Jane figures than Brontë's. David Malouf, for example, does the same in his libretto for the neo-Victorian chamber opera *Jane Eyre* in which Mrs Rochester has a voice, sympathy being the dominant affect he explores.[6] In her reanimation of Bertha, Livett flagrantly revives the melodramatic excess of Victorian fiction and pseudoscientific twaddle about the tropics. Bertha/Anna falls into a state of 'suspended animation' after the aborted wedding, the doctor pronouncing to Adèle that her awakening 'may take one hundred years as it does in fairy stories' (Livett 2016: 51). She revives in warmer latitudes on the sea journey to Van Diemen's Land during which Rochester sickens. Rochester and Jane are taking Anna to the colony in an effort to prove that her marriage to Rochester was bigamous and thus void, her first secret marriage having been to Rowland Rochester, who like many, has 'take[n] refuge in the colonies from an awkward situation at home' (56). The story of Rowland and Anna being violently parted by the Fairfax Rochester and Mason families and Anna being violently parted by Rowland from their child is over-the-top Gothic. Once the reawakened Anna affirms that she was married to Rowland, who was alive when she married Edward, Rochester and Jane are free to marry and return to England. The fate of Anna's dowry is not a narrative issue for Livett. The conflagration in the novel is not caused by Anna.

'What Anna was made of, we had yet to discover', Harriet concedes, Livett's metacritical implication perhaps being that we would need to wait for a Creole perspective – Rhys's *Wide Sargasso Sea* – to 'discover' this (2016: 101). Harriet also posits Anna, 'madwoman, invalid, sleeping princess', as an everywoman figure: 'if Anna could escape the prison of Bertha, then anything was possible. We might each be more than we had imagined' (99). The Antoinette of *Wide Sargasso Sea* is invoked through bare mention of names: Coulibri, Coco, Pierre, Christophine. As copyright in *Wide Sargasso Sea* extends until 2049, the scope for any new narrative use of Rhys's character Antoinette is very limited. Livett's fresh backstory for her in Harriet's narrative accords Anna little granularity of character: she is impractical, likes fine clothes and is lethargic to the point of ennui – a white Creole stereotype. She is off the Van Diemen's Land narrative stage travelling with her lover Captain Quigley for much of the action of the novel, freeing Harriet from the caging of the nurse-companion role to establish herself as an ornithological illustrator and artist and romantic interest for and eventual wife of Gus Bergman, a secular Jewish surveyor, whose skin colour Harriet describes as being 'brown' (212, 278).

There are multiple scenes of reading in *Crawl Me Blood* and its site-immersive experience. Weiland and Macleod have cleverly reread and reworked motifs of *Wide Sargasso Sea*: sargassum, the Great House, the fall of the planter class, the white cockroach, fire, the threat of hurricane, the burning parrot, the loyal black employee, the beloved local pool. In *Crawl Me Blood*, set in 2018, the audience hears and imagines two apparently white Australian women, Gwen Clifton and her daughter Antoinette Clifton, experience a homecoming to the Caribbean occasioned by the death of Antoinette's grandmother, Gwen's mother Elizabeth Mary Clifton, owner of the Great House Clifton Hall. Short videoclips frame the sound installation. With the help of Afro-Caribbean gardener Charlie, Elizabeth had turned Clifton Hall, a relic of colonial days, 'rotten to the core', Gwen insists, into a tourist attraction for visitors in search of 'Old World glamour', who Gwen realizes, 'wanted to be ignorant of the blood in the ground and the bones beneath their feet'. History is 'just in us', says Gwen, remembering her flight from that history to Australia, while pregnant with Antoinette. History is the snake that moves in the shadows of the garden at Clifton Hall. For both Gwen and Antoinette in the present, the Caribbean can be a metaphorical 'jungle': 'a place of bewildering complexity or confusion', 'a scene of ruthless competition, struggle, or exploitation', according to the *OED Online* (2018). Antoinette has never been to the Caribbean before. Gwen has been away for eighteen years. There are family secrets to be negotiated and threatening winds foreboding a hurricane to be (mis)read. *Crawl Me Blood* is 'inspired by the Belizean Kriol phrase "what crawls your blood" are the secrets you sense but are not told to you', 'akin to saying "it gave me the shivers"' (Weiland and Macleod n.d.). Single mother Gwen has kept secret from Antoinette her father's identity and the complex and conflicted intertwining of deep motherly love and trauma in raising a child of rape. The written texts referred to are Elizabeth's will, which dispossesses her children, leaving the Great House instead to Antoinette, and the estate agent Cynthia's notes towards a property evaluation of Clifton Hall, requested by Gwen before she learns she has been disinherited. Cynthia has been Gwen's Tia figure in childhood.

Crawl Me Blood takes the audience through some of the subtropical and tropical parts of botanical gardens, institutions with a long colonial heritage.[7] Micro-climates, like glasshouses, have been created to allow tropical and subtropical species of plants to flourish outside the tropics. The gardens are defamiliarized, made strange by a night tour, encouraging audiences to think in fresh ways about the history in them, the secrets they and their families withhold, particularly around racial heritage, the family similarities between colonial histories and struggles for decolonization, 'the blood in the ground, the bones beneath their feet'. The site immersion also extends to Caribbean rites (the wake), and Caribbean accents and sounds, such as street sounds, insect noises, birdsong and a hurricane siren, recorded by Weiland and Macleod during a research trip to the Caribbean.

Audiences are also challenged to interpret the collage of narrative and embedded histories in the musical soundtrack by Felix Cross, which includes calypso (The Mighty Sparrow's 'Congo Man' [1964]), Yoruba chant, reggae (Lady Saw's 'Sycamore Tree' [1997]) and hip-hop/rap (Princess Nokia's 'Brujas' [2017]). The musical cultures that have emerged from the Caribbean and circum-Caribbean plantation complex and its 'interlocking workings of dispossession and resistance' are one of the creolized 'modes of survival' for people of African heritage (McKittrick 2013: 3). Calypsos are a topical comic form, albeit making serious political and cultural comment. Opening with 'Congo Man', which satirically uses the jungle stereotype of the tropics to mock both tourist culture and stereotypes of black people, establishes the humorous ambit of *Crawl Me Blood*.

The garden of Clifton Hall is a liminal space in and from which Gwen can critically distance herself from her mother's and alcoholic Uncle Anthony's values. Like many of the plantocratic elite after slave emancipation, Elizabeth has made a social fetish of Christian respectability, property ownership (though she is asset-rich and cash-poor), inheritance and European cultural tastes. 'Respectability', Deborah A. Thomas observes, 'is rooted in the system of stratification imposed by the old colonial social order. It was reproduced through the teachings of the colonial church and was associated with "whiteness," British culture, and formal authority' (2011: 143). Brian L. Moore and Michele A. Johnson have traced the genealogy of the cult of respectability in Jamaica back to the Victorian period (2004: 137–43). Gwen left the Caribbean for Australia after she was raped by Sonny

Griffiths, the son of the local policeman, in the garden and became pregnant as a result. Her mother demanded, in the interests of respectability, that she marry him. Sonny is socially white, a 'red bones' (light-skinned), associated with propriety and law. In 2018 he is the local police and fire chief. Gwen tersely introduces him to Antoinette as 'king of the jungle round here'. Gwen remembers witnessing in the orchid house Uncle Anthony's auto-erotic fetishization and use of objects (a whipping stool, a neck chain) that were part of the 'repertoires of violence' and terror exacted on enslaved people of African heritage (Thomas 2011: 115). From the garden Gwen begins to look at tourists when they ask about race relations in the wake of slave emancipation thinking about Charlie's responses to the question, 'What is it really like here? Between black and white they meant.' Gwen learns to code switch between the respectable and the coarse or vulgar. The coarse – street smarts, 'hav[ing] spunks' in the language of Christophine in *Wide Sargasso Sea* (*WSS* 69) – grounds her survival and speaking of trauma. The garden is also the place where, acting on her anger towards Elizabeth over being disinherited in favour of Antoinette and over her fetishization of respectability, she makes a bonfire of Elizabeth's personal effects, which evince Eurocentric taste. The embers of the fire reignite in potential hurricane winds, burning down Clifton Hall and causing severe burns to Antoinette.

Antoinette begins a journey of reconciliation to place and history, resolving to stay in the Caribbean in the immediate future. That redemptive move contrasts with Gwen's negativity formed under pressure of trauma. The razing of the Great House by fire, as in Caribbean literature more generally, opens fuller possibilities of a 'realignment of social and political hierarchies' (McGarrity 2008: 51). The Great House is one of a nexus of tourist sites in *Crawl Me Blood*, the others being the sexualized beach bar (a site of Gwen's rebellion against her mother when she was growing up) and the beach under threat by sargassum seaweed – here a sign of the detritus of imperial history and its legacies under globalization. Massive beachings of sargassum seaweed are indeed currently threatening tourism in the Caribbean, a dominant industry in the region. The sexually predatory Leroy Griffiths, Sonny's dark-skinned son, who works at the bar has the job of raking the seaweed out of tourists' view to the sea each day. Unbeknown to both Antoinette and Leroy, who have vapid sex, they are half-siblings.

Antoinette's healing after the fire takes her not back to the bar or beach, but to Indian River, her grandmother's favourite part of her estate, where mutual respect and platonic love between Elizabeth and Charlie developed. Princess Nokia's 'Brujas' on the music track suggests sustaining spirit presences in the landscape. The name Indian River seems to commemorate an Indigenous presence and the 'blood' of dispossession and genocide. Charlie and Antoinette wade out of the river together after a rafting mishap while strewing Elizabeth's ashes there. Charlie has helped Antoinette when she struggled in the water and she 'tak[es] up his rhythm' of swimming. The image offers a counterpoint to Gwen's and Sonny's rendering of assistance to the burnt Antoinette: Gwen sings lullabies and wraps her 'own crumpled white linen dress around her', replacing the 'fire blanket' Sonny has 'smother[ingly]' thrown over her. Gwen curls up beside Antoinette, calling her 'my baby'.

Weiland and Macleod position *Wide Sargasso Sea* as integral to a 'rich history of dialogue about race' in the Caribbean (*Crawl Me Blood* 2018a: 3). Their reading of that dialogue has been sharpened through broader inquiry and experience. They have researched *Crawl Me Blood* in the Jean Rhys Papers held at the University of Tulsa, through a creative residency with the Fresh Milk Art Platform in Barbados, and through interviews in the Caribbean around racial formations in '*race-founded & race-foundered*' cultures that are a legacy of plantation capitalism (Brathwaite 1995: 74; emphasis in the original). Weiland was 'born and raised in Belize to white Australian parents'; Macleod's 'black Jamaican' great-grandfather arrived in Australia in the late nineteenth century. Felix Cross, MBE, the composer of the musical soundtrack of *Crawl Me Blood*, 'was born in Trinidad, made his career in the UK', and migrated to Australia in his fifties. Performers Natasha Jynel and Zahra Newman migrated to Australia from Barbados and Jamaica respectively (*Crawl Me Blood* 2018a).

Rhys herself was exhilarated by the allusive layering of *Wide Sargasso Sea* after the breakthrough occasioned by her writing of 'Obeah Night', layering that cites *Jane Eyre*, Charles Baudelaire's 'Le Revenant', William Shakespeare's *Othello* and *Macbeth*, Joseph Conrad's *Almayer's Folly* and *Heart of Darkness*, Aesop's fable of the oak and the reeds, Derek Walcott's early poetry, and Francophone *doudou* mythology. Rhys has in turn inspired Australian writers Hanrahan, Lohrey, Livett, and Weiland and Macleod to actively extend and revise the representation of domestic 'intimacies' of empire intertextually and through collage and to take up the aesthetic challenges of memorying them. Hanrahan, writing before *Wide Sargasso Sea* achieved mythic status, engages with the granularity of Rhys's characterisation of Antoinette and Christophine and of her aesthetic innovation. '*Wide Sargasso Sea* has literally wound its way into other texts, subsequent rewritings of *Jane Eyre*', comments Armelle Parey (2006: 5). Lohrey and Livett's engagement with *Wide Sargasso Sea* through *Jane Eyre* predominantly drives plots, functioning in Lohrey's narrative to undermine grand narratives of empire and imperial loyalty and in Livett's to complicate them. Like *Wide Sargasso Sea*, *Crawl Me Blood* is a finely wrought and layered, compressed narrative which explores the fraught intimacies – racialized formations of sexuality, gender and class – that are the legacies of the Great House and its economic and cultural ties to imperial centres.

Acknowledgement

The Australian Research Council has supported my research on Jean Rhys through DP140103817.

Notes

1 Conceptualizing the literary narrowly, Elizabeth McMahon does not even mention Rhys as an influence on Australian cultural production in *Islands, Identity and the Literary Imagination* (2016), which very selectively addresses Caribbean and Australian literature.
2 For wide-ranging partial overviews, see McDougall 2002; and McMahon 2016: 47–85 and Appendix.
3 The term originated in distinctions made between the value of sterling and Australian currency in the early colonial period. Sterling meant British-born (Ransom 1988: 186–7).
4 The sheep station functions as an analogue of Thornfield Hall in two Australian rewritings of *Jane Eyre* influenced by Rhys, which have contemporary Australian settings: Coral Lansbury's novel *Ringarra* (1985) and Jean Bedford's short story 'Crown Me with Roses Pastiche' (1997). In each of the texts Bertha has a voice.
5 On Monaghan and Duigan, see Thomas 1997. Monaghan had played Rochester in *Woman in the Attic* (1987), an effort to combine adaptations of *Jane Eyre* and *Wide Sargasso Sea*.
6 See Thomas 2015b on Rhys's influence on Malouf's libretto for Michael Berkeley's chamber opera, performed in 2000, 2005 and 2006, and released on CD in 2002.
7 On botanical gardens and empire, see Brockway (1979) and McCracken (1997).

7

Twisted lines in Caribbean postcolonial Modernism: Jean Rhys and Edward Kamau Brathwaite

Françoise Clary

In his 1974 monograph *Contradictory Omens*, Edward Kamau Brathwaite declares that white Creoles have forfeited their claim to the spiritual life of the Caribbean. Whereas Édouard Glissant defines creolization as the object of an 'unceasing process of transformation' through which people create a collective sense of identity from multiple cultural sources (Glissant 1989: 142), Brathwaite describes creolization as the slaves' capacity to preserve the essence of their African cultural identity, in spite of the brutality of colonization, through a posture of racial identity characterized as a strategy of withdrawing, disguising and submerging the self, which results from the denigratory identities projected onto Afro-Caribbeans by colonialist racism. As such, the strain and rupture in identity reflect back in Brathwaite's insurgent Afro-Caribbean understanding of West Indian culture. More exactly, the cultural perspective on creolization is indicative of a revolutionary identity politics as Brathwaite insists on piecing together remnants of Afro-Caribbean connections. So doing, however, he underscores the reality of West Indian cultural fragmentation while mediating Afro-Caribbean experience through a language whose figural characteristics account for the interdependence of history, politics and sociology.

When viewed from the margin of otherness that displays identification, Brathwaite's pronouncement on creolization should be understood as a questioning of cultural identity in its connection to race and in the historicization of an individual's identity, or 'one's historical and historically received image of oneself' (Brathwaite 1974: 34). In other words, Brathwaite's model of creolization is best understood as a product of cultural heritage grounded in a racial identification. With the contention, 'my own idea of creolization is based on the notion of a historically affected socio-cultural identity' (25), Brathwaite brings attention to his own identity defined as that of a 'black West Indian' (38).

There is no denying that within the conjunction of multiformity and neocolonialism, white Creoles have been subjected to oscillating patterns of historical ambivalence and have consequently inherited a double perspective. But when Brathwaite depersonalizes white Creoles, he does not merely object, like Glissant, to 'what threatens Caribbeanness, the historical balkanisation of the islands' (Glissant 1989: 423). He also extends his statement about white Creoles to Jean Rhys specifically, going as far as to raise doubts about the standing of *Wide Sargasso Sea* in the Caribbean canon: 'A white Creole cannot meaningfully identify or be identified with the spiritual world of the contemporary West Indies. That spiritual world is essentially the culture of the black ex-African majority' (Brathwaite 1974: 38). What, then, is really at stake in Brathwaite's discomfort with Rhys's identity as a descendant of the white Creoles, whose agenda was supposedly one of cultural domination? It is, obviously, a matter of misrecognition of the cross-currents illustrating the need for responses to historical articulations of race and ethnicity. No doubt the cultural diversity of the Caribbean region produces a metaphor of difference to be understood as a 'sociological process' reflecting collective memory (Alexander 2014: 22).

Not only have critics deemed Brathwaite's 'judgment of the inadmissibility of *Wide Sargasso Sea* into the Caribbean Canon unsettling', but they have blamed him for acting 'as an aggressor' while positioning himself as the inheritor of a traumatic history of Afro-Caribbean victims (Metz 2015: 99). Interestingly, Brathwaite's strategic claim that Afro-Caribbeans are the victims of the incompleteness of history concerning past traumas is illustrative of Cathy Caruth's trauma theory, since Caruth glorifies the person who listens to (or writes about) the traumatized, making it seem as though the listener to trauma is playing the heroic role, willingly becoming traumatized (Caruth 1996: 36). According to Metz, Brathwaite discards Western criticism on *Wide Sargasso Sea* for failing to 'historicize the text' and thus entertaining a postcolonialist mentality. In fact, by clearly connecting race to culture, Brathwaite applies his personal identification with Afro-Caribbeans, described as victimized by white Creoles, to his reading of *Wide Sargasso Sea*. At the core of Brathwaite's opposition to Peter Hulme's critique and claim to be indifferent to the colour of the writer, one can find a violent debate published in *Wasafiri* (1994–6). At stake is Brathwaite's concern with ethnological identity and attention to the subalternity of the voice.

Brathwaite's ambivalence towards Rhys does present a prejudiced vision of creolization in terms of perceptual and cultural self-understanding. In his discourse – the historical and cultural specificity of which lies in the splitting between the black West Indian and the white Creole identities – Brathwaite makes his argument apparent that Rhys's white background and her alienation from the essence of West Indian culture are connected:

> White Creoles in the English and French West Indies have separated themselves by too wide a gulf and have contributed too little culturally, as a group, to give credence to the notion that they can, given the present structure, meaningfully identify or be identified, with the spiritual world on this side of the Sargasso Sea.
> (Brathwaite 1974: 38)

This statement recapitulates other notes of insurgency present throughout Brathwaite's writings. He does not want the articulation of West Indian culture, now politically independent from British culture, to be confused by attempts to identify its essence with 'the work of a white Creole expatriate' (39), a phrase which suggests that, for Brathwaite, Rhys is accidentally, rather than genuinely, a West Indian, whereas a Creole person can be either white or black, colonizer or colonized. By disrupting the equivalence between culture and identity, Brathwaite changes the terms of our recognition of West Indian identity, turning instead to the articulation of the notions of dislocation and doubleness. A differential discourse of affiliation addresses the questions of cultural métissage and positional mutability. Whatever may be Brathwaite's controversial viewpoint, it is intimately bound up with the shifting paradigms of history focusing on the idea that 'trauma is not locatable in the simple violent or original event of an individual's past, but rather in the way that its very unassimilated nature – the way it was precisely not known in the first instance – returns to haunt the survivor later on' (Caruth 1996: 3).

In *Wide Sargasso Sea*, Rhys describes the main protagonist's relation to her racial identity in such a way as to show that race is constructed primarily by a racist society, and then by the individual's reaction to that society. Thus, in the first part of *Wide Sargasso Sea*, Antoinette – through whose voice the story of her childhood is first told – explains: 'They say when trouble comes close ranks, and so the white people did. But we were not in their ranks' (*WSS* 9). Then, revealing the fragmented aspect of her memories of the Coulibri Estate, she confides: 'I never looked at any strange negro. They hated us. They called us white cockroaches. [...] One day a little girl followed me singing, "Go away white cockroach, go away, go away'" (13). Rhys was born a white Creole of European descent, which placed her at an identitarian distance both from Afro-Caribbeans and from the English, because of her West Indianness. Her fate was that 'of a woman, belonging to a group which no longer has a place' (Olaussen 1993: 66).

Significantly, the creative ambivalence of West Indian consciousness is developed in Caribbean poetics of loss. It functions both in Rhys's fiction (implicitly concerned with the disastrous relationship between England and her colonies) and in Brathwaite's poetry (centred on the story of the annihilation of selves that accompanied colonialism). Considering that T.S. Eliot's idea of 'Modernism' (characterized by the fragmentation and diversity of contemporary culture) draws on the same strategies as Brathwaite's – including an awareness of the impossibility of modernity's humanist ideal – the best approach to Rhys's and Brathwaite's staging the complex poetics of identity in the Caribbean context is to examine how these two writers deal with the structure of memory in their relationship to history. This implies contemplating the possibility of interdependence and resistance.

This chapter follows the twisted lines of literary filiation and the subsequent intertextuality between Rhys and Brathwaite, to rethink the dichotomy of forgetting and remembering as well as the dialectic of creolized consciousness or *antillanité* as articulated by Glissant (1981: 222). In fact, the entangled relations between life and memory, between history and story-writing, make up a nearly perfect symbol for the way the two West Indian writers have preserved their cultural heritage through readapting it to changed conditions. This chapter proposes therefore to examine the intertextual connections between Rhys, Brathwaite and T.S. Eliot drawing from Glissant's 'poetics of relation' (Glissant 1997: 179).

Glissant's 'poetics of relation'

There are two predominant representations of Caribbean identity: one – Rhys's – which is connected to the history of British colonization of the West Indies and deals with the question of identity with an explicitly gendered experience of self-alienation; and one – Brathwaite's – which deploys a recuperative archaeological procedure of excavating the fragmented terrain of Caribbean history. Both adopt an approach to history that helps to portray a world that is the countercultural reality of colonial culture as it celebrates a diasporic version of Caribbean philosophical reality.

Rhys's uses of black history have been examined by Veronica Gregg. Arguing that history can be a site where different narratives collide, Gregg criticizes the weight of British culture imposed on West Indians, such as the poems of William Wordsworth: 'I was tired of reciting poems in praise of daffodils [...] I don't much wish to be English' (Gregg 1995: 10). Gregg is determined to analyse the question of identity in Rhys's novel through literary investigations of race, gender and colonialism. She acknowledges that history itself can be a site where different narratives collide, notably through the rewriting of discourses on the West Indies and of European canonical texts. Yet, whereas Rhys's treatment of the issues of cultural alienation has been studied by several critics, such as Sandra Drake who turns her attention to the growing social tension in *Wide Sargasso Sea* (Drake 1990), and while the uniqueness of Brathwaite's theory of creolization relying on an understanding of self and community has been examined (Savory 1996: 23–44), the trajectories of cultural exchange between Brathwaite and Rhys have not been probed in fruitful ways. I propose therefore to consider the structure of memory in Brathwaite and how that structure can be applied to Rhys as evidence that they write from a stance which implies a similar relationship to history, where to take up Glissant's theory, forgetfulness begets memory. Glissant's use of the notions of 'conversion' and 'diversion' as critical concepts testifies to his concern with a theory of the incompleteness of history, and of memory emerging from forgetfulness premised on the idea of African cultural survivals, which brings us back to Caruth's argument that authors respond to historical traumas (Caruth 1996).

For Brathwaite, 'the word becomes a pebble stone or bomb that demands a politics of life, not death' (Brathwaite 1984: 35). In the postcolonial discourse of identity, what is enacted is the splitting of the subject through a questioning of the frame of representation. Thus, the familiar space of the 'Other' in the process of identification develops a graphic specificity in Rhys's *Wide Sargasso Sea*, more particularly when words become weapons. This invites the reader to see what is invisible, an invisibility linked to the articulation of an iconic language. For instance, the association of the image of the 'white cockroach' (*WSS* 61) with the theme of Caribbeanness makes the reader suspect Antoinette's awareness of her in-between identity.

There is a 'modernist' ambivalence in the struggle for identity at the heart of Rhys's *Wide Sargasso Sea*, just as there is one in Brathwaite's overview of poetry's social function. In Rhys's fiction writing and Brathwaite's poetical work, the return to issues of shared voice, in relation to dominant discourses of gender, race, ethnicity and nationality, are indeed quite close to the different models for social organization that modernist writers developed while confronting their anxieties with cosmopolitan versions of community (Berman 2001). The use Rhys and Brathwaite make of a variety of genres to capture the experiences of the subaltern plays an important part in their quest for an identity which resists representation. Theirs is a search for a voice, haunted by some sense of loss. *Wide Sargasso Sea* dramatizes the loss of identity experienced by Antoinette as she desperately struggles to fit into both the Caribbean culture and the English culture.

Subalternity and the strategies of selfhood

When examining *Wide Sargasso Sea*, the emphasis should be put on the ways in which the meanings of 'place' and 'origin' – the crucial coordinates of cultural identity – are constantly disturbed in the experience of flight, departure, displacement, loss and marginalization. This raises the question of subalternity, if indeed 'the subaltern is one on whose domination citizenship and the state are founded' (Beverley 2001: 47). To illustrate this point, one can look at the two systems of domination evoked by Rhys: the colonial and the patriarchal. The reversal of emphasis which focuses the reader's attention on the marginalized Creole underscores the idea of subalternity in a society whose structure and history are predicated on the inferiorization of a category of people. Antoinette Cosway is illustrative of this struggle against forgetting. She has deep feelings for the landscapes of her childhood and for the place where she grew up: 'I love it more than anywhere in the world. As if it were a person' (*WSS* 53). As she travels from one geographical location to another, from the West Indies to Europe, Antoinette is constantly questioning her place in the world. Her story is one of displacement and loss, and also of the subalternity of a West Indian woman whose voice does not count, an issue famously taken up by Gayatri Chakravorty Spivak (1988).

Antoinette's story is that of a white Creole caught in a process of marginalization/exclusion confronting spousal abuse. From different angles of vision (gender, family, class, religion), Rhys provides insightful explorations of these issues. When imprisoned by Rochester, she can take no action on her own behalf. She lacks a family as she lacks a home and religion to provide a valued sense of self. Besides, as Antoinette's husband becomes increasingly distanced from his wife and the West Indies, he comes to hate his wife and the place she lives in, adopting a type of behaviour which matches the authoritative ethnocentricism and sexism of white patriarchy, behaving like the old slave owners when he renames his wife 'Bertha' and keeps her prisoner.

To this extent, Rhys's story of the unvoiced, disempowered Creole, and Brathwaite's theory of creolization as a poetics of ambivalence follow a logic similar to Eliot's poetic method of complementarity and consensus. This parallel is grounded on Eliot's poetics that collocates a variety of cultural resources and perspectives to eventually reach a sense of cultural wholeness (Eliot 1964: 6). It is worth emphasizing here that there is no overlapping of the notions of 'creolization' and 'cosmopolitanism' in either *Wide Sargasso Sea* or Brathwaite's poems, but the enactment of Eliot's Modernism, that is to say, 'an ever-increasing series of points of view, which struggle towards an emergent unity and continue to struggle past that unity' (Levenson 1983: 192). This provisional unity is identified by Eliot as a collocating method, which Brathwaite finds attractive because it recognizes not just the reality of cultural fragmentation but also the aspiration to cultural unity (Brathwaite 1984: 11). Indeed, it values West Indian experience as representative of the modern condition. Just as Rhys leads the reader to the heart of exclusion and prejudice, Brathwaite's poetics implicitly shows that the introduction of subordinated cultures entails an association of the subaltern with lateral creolization, a phrase to be understood as a transformation of culture, language and identity in response to the historical context of colonialism and neocolonialism. This is what happens in *Barabajan Poems*, where the poet's name, 'Kamau', is presented through a litany of split syllables, as a descent into the self.

Symbolic language, or the power to reinvent reality

In an approach to *Wide Sargasso Sea* as a political construct, the disempowered Creole Bertha/Antoinette is the very symbol of 'otherness', whether seen from the perspective drawn by Sandra Gilbert and Susan Gubar's picture of the untamed female ([1979] 2000: 43), or from Sandra Drake's evocation of what English colonizers did to black slaves by changing their African names or giving them surnames (1990: 98). Antoinette is called names '*Marionette, Antoinette,*

Marionetta, Antoinetta' (*WSS* 92; italics in the original). More than anything else, it is important to examine how a West Indian Creole from *Wide Sargasso Sea* may fit into Gilbert and Gubar's presentation of women's necessary struggle against the stereotyped images of either 'the angel' or 'the monster' used in Victorian literature to categorize female characters. In fact, Rhys's dramatization of Antoinette's revolt against her husband's contemptuous and tyrannical behaviour draws on the clichés applied to rebellious, unkempt women, and by extension to 'mad' women, as when Rochester exclaims: 'She laughed at that. A crazy laugh' (89).

Part two, told largely in the voice of Mr Rochester, except in the sequences when he reports his wife's rebellious attitude, is illustrative of the 'fantasies in which maddened doubles functioned as asocial surrogates for docile selves' (Gilbert and Gubar 1979: xi). As a matter of fact, Antoinette loses her name, but also her identity, when her husband starts calling her Bertha: 'Bertha is not my name. You are trying to make me into someone else, calling me by another name. [...] I hate it now like I hate you and before I die I will show you how much I hate you' (*WSS* 88–9). This postcolonial novel can thus also be read as a feminist text in which Rhys points out the social and psychological reasons why Antoinette/Bertha is said to be 'mad': She can be locked up. Her life is in the hands of her husband, a metropolitan white man. She desperately tries to find her place within the boundaries of constructed racial and gender identities, but fails to do so.

And yet by being offered access to 'symbolic' language, a language in which inner experiences, feelings and thoughts are expressed as if they were sensory experiences, the Caribbean subject from the margins is given the ability to reinvent reality. By making use notably of techniques akin to magic realism, such as the black legend of the African flying to freedom, Antoinette dreams she owns the secret knowledge that will enable her to escape from Thornfield Hall, England, away to freedom: 'The wind caught my hair and it streamed out like wings. It might bear me up, I thought, if I jumped to those hard stones' (*WSS* 112).

This use of symbolic language also enables the writer to create nuances of sound and feeling in a merger of the visual, oral and auditory, as can be observed in Rhys's imaginary landscapes, for example when Rochester is about to tear Antoinette away from her native place:

> Here's a cloudy day to help you. No brazen sun.
> No sun ... No sun. The weather's changed.
>
> (*WSS* 100)

Such symbolic language is equally present in Brathwaite's dream stories. In *The Arrivants*, for instance, the poet suggests that through the intercession of the god that translates the messages of the gods into human language, the Caribbeans' language will be reclaimed:

> So on this ground,
> write;
> within the sound
> of this white limestone *vévé*
>
> (Brathwaite 1973: 265)

In this context, questions about strategies of selfhood press directly on West Indian society in whose exilic imagination the concept of space articulates oblivion and memory. In *Wide Sargasso Sea*, Antoinette is confronted with a distorted image of herself or at times with no image of herself at all. She is in many ways almost unseen, concealed from others and even from herself. What is recovered – by her use of symbolic language, or of understatements drawn from African magic realism – is the ability to remember and to create a new reality, notably through the eruption of the unconscious into the conscious.

The logical conception of Antoinette's discourse is to imagine the past as a succession of moments of disempowerment. When the heroine specifies 'we have no looking glass in the dormitory' (*WSS* 32), she realizes she is trapped in a socially restrictive culture. Besides, the convent appears to be a place of erasure: there is no representative of the larger society, no one from the outside world to look at Antoinette and constitute her as a social person. Brathwaite's poetics also illustrates such strategies. For instance, *The Zea Mexican Diary* (1993) subverts usual ways of thinking. Brathwaite tries to rebuild his world, to piece it whole with personal memories. The more he endeavours to create a sense of peace, the more his sense of isolation increases:

> I came to reach far
> out far out in space and into the very wound & darkness of
> our/selves out there/far out/deep down in/side ...
> out there ... And it seemed as if I might win ...
> *was winning* ... if only I cd find the strength ...
>
> (Brathwaite 1993: 43; emphasis in the original)

We can observe a similar dynamic at work in *Wide Sargasso Sea*. In much the same way as Brathwaite gives voice to his pain descending into the darkness of the Caribbean psyche, searching for light and celebrating the purgatorial experience of black people – the dispossessed – Rhys compensates for the lack of happiness in the convent she has been sent to by proceeding to an enactment of the ritual of pain that is very close to the one used by Brathwaite. The use of imaginative power serves as a liberating device in the work of each writer. While Brathwaite plays with broken words, Rhys plays with the metaphorical overlapping of brightness and darkness. Thus, Antoinette's decription of the days she spent in the convent is openly creative in the interplay of light and darkness:

> But what about happiness, I thought at first, is there no happiness? [...] Everything was brightness, or dark. The walls, the blazing colours of the flowers in the garden, the nuns' habits were bright, but their veils, the Crucifix hanging from their waists, the shadow of the trees, were black. That was how it was, light and dark, sun and shadow, Heaven and Hell.
>
> (*WSS* 34)

Brathwaite has his own political approach to distortion as an act of power when he writes that '[it] was in language that the slave was perhaps most successfully imprisoned by his master, and it was in his (mis) use of it that he perhaps most effectively rebelled' (Brathwaite 1971: 237). Using metaphors is a way of recovering the language of myths to help us make sense of a senseless world. In Caribbean poetic output, oblivion is thus on the surface only, generating memory in fact, a remark which applies to Rhys's novel too. The relationship between history and poetry brings with it a sense of cultural identity because, as Brathwaite claims, in *History of the Voice* (1984) insight is at the core of Caribbean philosophy. The language of myth struggles against forgetting, while colonial contact disrupts Indigenous culture.

While in *Wide Sargasso Sea* the fragmentation of Antoinette's perceptual and practical unity is paralleled by a ceaseless unnaming and renaming, in Caribbean poetical discourse, crucially twisted by race and the history of colonial contact, a representational idea predominates: 'the Sea is History'. It is correlatively central to Caribbean self-reflective identity. In the same way that Brathwaite declares that 'unity is submarine' (1975: 10), Derek Walcott describes the ocean as a metonymic history of the Caribbean:

> Where are your monuments, your battles, your martyrs? Where is your tribal memory? Sirs, In that grey vault. The sea. The sea Has locked them up. The sea is history.
>
> (Walcott 1986: 364)

Under the oblivion of the oceanic grave lies cultural identity, as is also underscored in Glissant's 'The Open Boat': 'the abyss is a tautology: the entire ocean, the entire sea gently collapsing in the end into the pleasures of sand make one vast beginning, but a beginning whose time is marked by these balls and chains gone green' (1997: 6).

Wide Sargasso Sea is assuredly a complex and multilayered space but it articulates the same reversal of paradigm, from oblivion to memory. Indeed, in the convent, despite the lack of reflective image and the threat of erasure, Antoinette maintains a sort of tense identity. Ultimately, when the heroine is displaced to England, her incarceration in the attic of Thornfield Hall, deprives her of any self-image. As an abrupt end is put both to her seeing and her being seen, she is condemned to oblivion. But oblivion generates memory through a distorsion of the usual paradigm, a distorsion which becomes an act of power, according to Brathwaite. Eventually, in her living tomb, Antoinette endeavours to recall her appearance and reclaim the perceptive part of her reflective identity even though in the nightmare of history.

What is recovered through symbolic language is to be seen as a move to transformation. This manner of suggesting ideas instead of making the meaning of sentences explicit accounts for Rhys being ahead of her time in her willingness to deal with race. An example of this use of symbolic language is given when Rochester about to leave for England expresses his contempt for the dispossessed West Indians: 'They can be recognized. [...] The way they walk and talk and scream or try to kill (themselves or you) if you laugh back at them. Yes, they've got to be watched. For the time comes when they try to kill, then disappear. But others are waiting to take their places, it's a long, long line' (*WSS* 103).

It comes as no surprise that the reversal of the paradigm concerning the concepts of memory and oblivion is a pivotal element in the transmission lines whose criss-crossing process reflects what Glissant analyses as the sociological process of transformation through which people create a collective sense of identity (1981: 225). It is from the overlapping of these two concepts that the symbolic pattern of oblivion breeding memory emerges in Caribbean verse, uniting the imagery of forgetfulness, the incompleteness of history and rememory as myth-making.

It is not surprising that Brathwaite and Rhys should share a common heritage and make strategic truth claims to expose the constructedness of Creole identity, using a language appropriate for a literature in which 'everything takes on a collective value' (Deleuze and Guattari 1975: 57). Indeed, Rhys's and Brathwaite's writings fit within a literature that allows the writer to reach another consciousness and is 'positively charged with the role and function of collective, and even revolutionary enunciation' (57). As a matter of fact, both Rhys and Brathwaite conquer new modes of expression in which the literary is the ground on which the revolutionary can develop. Thus, in *Wide Sargasso Sea* Rhys's choice of imagery linking hate with racial difference is not accidental, while in *Barbajan Poems* Brathwaite creates a violent irruption into the present world giving face to new oppressors: Imperialists in a Global world.

Just as the literary gives voice to the revolutionary – Deleuze and Guattari assert that in such instances 'the literary machine [...] becomes the relay for a revolutionary machine-to-come' (Deleuze and Guattari 1975: 57) – the relationship between history and poetry transforms Brathwaite's text into a theatre. Subverting ways of thinking and language itself, discarding lines of demarcation between prose and poetry, merging reality and illusion, Brathwaite gives the unvoiced new modes of transmitting memory. The move from oblivion to memory can, notably, be observed in *DreamStories* in which the inverted process of forgetting giving way to remembering is made meaningful by the interplay of three images: the canefield, the slaveship and the New World plantations. Similary, be it in the poems 'Charcoal' by Wilson Harris, 'Epigraph' by Dennis Scott, 'Harbour' by Brathwaite or 'A Far Cry from Africa' by Derek Walcott, it is precisely the reversal of the usual Memory/Oblivion paradigm, replaced by a new Oblivion/Memory paradigm, with the sense of an incompleteness of history attached to oblivion that catalyzes the efforts of postcolonial poets, generation after generation, to urge the reader to go beyond the dichotomy of remembering and forgetting.

Thus, in his early works, *The Arrivants*, *Mother Poem* and *X/Self*, Brathwaite penetrates oblivion to get to the unnamed and bring into being an awareness of the hidden meanings of the historical past. In *The Arrivants* we read:

> The Word becomes again a god and walks among us; look, here are his rags, here is his crutch and his satchel of dreams, here is his hoe and his implements/on this ground on this broken ground.
>
> (Brathwaite 1973: 266)

The underlying idea is that under forgetting is memory and that through a move backwards to one's cultural past (here the image of Legba the god of road is made clear), Caribbean language will be reclaimed. The same dynamic can be observed in the last part of *Wide Sargasso Sea* when Antoinette, now a prisoner in England, goes beyond oblivion to reach memories of the past. Using smells to create nuances and feelings, Rhys conquers new territories while discarding conventional lines of demarcation between reality and illusion, memory and myth: 'The scent that came from the dress was very faint at first, then it grew stronger. The smell of vetiver and frangipani, of cinnamon and dust and lime trees when they are flowering. The smell of the sun and the smell of the rain' (*WSS* 109).

Both Walcott's 'The Sea is History' and Glissant's 'The Open Boat' underscore the watery origins of the people of Africa relocated to the Caribbean. Both Walcott and Glissant reverse the process of 'remembering' and 'forgetting' as they reconstruct the reality of a historical past by moving beyond oblivion, historical negation or absence. So doing, they discard the straight lines of transmission for a circular order that offers a reinterpretation of the historical past through a new paradigm: 'forgetting and remembering'.

Alienating hybridity and the incompleteness of historical representation

When it comes to apprehending the paralyzing conviction that one has no identity, no roots, no cultural home, the sense of loss and alienation is easily associated with madness as one is faced with the challenge of remaking the world for oneself. And yet if the question of cultural wholeness is raised, one should not fail to see the implications of the trajectories of cultural exchange, first from the centre to the peripheries, then from the peripheries to the centre. The poet explores the power of words eventually to reproduce a 'circular nomadism' (Glissant 1997: 29). Glissant's notions of a creolized Caribbean culture and a *poétique de la relation* – to be understood as a cross-cultural poetics – articulate a discursive practice that reflects the tensions of colonial encounter in the equivocations of the antagonistic overlapping of disjunctures and linearity. Within this conjunction, Glissant's definition of creolization can address the questions of cultural métissage, including plural perspectives.

A differential discourse can indeed address the questions of creolization and cultural métissage. In the context of Brathwaite's ongoing research into 'creolization', a term used by the poet to articulate the notions of dislocation and oppositional identities, the reason for the emergence of an alienating hybridity is that the Caribbean experience, which Caribbean poets offer to share with readers in Europe and North America, presents in an extreme form the dilemma of modern society, in that the tensions between the old

Eurocentric world and the new West Indian one may prove to be a test for a schismatic vision of society. Paul Ricœur's concept of the 'Other' may be useful here (Ricœur 1984: 36): the past is what is missing and recreated by 'the force of re-enactment and of distancing', which highlights the sense of temporal distance and otherness in transforming historical blankness into the historical knowledge of different cultures.

James Clifford underscores the importance of travelling cultures (Clifford 1988: 98–100), but one must remain aware of the way Caribbean poets, in the search for an adequate poetic language, gather fragments of experience to create a cross-cultural sense of individual and collective wholeness. This can be observed in Rhys's poem 'Obeah Night' with graphic descriptions of 'the sea strewn with wrecks', 'the stains of tears covering the marks of blood' and 'the slave-owner's gravestone' (Burnett 1986: 147). The same is to be observed in Brathwaite's 'Horse Weebles', and its description of the 'plantation shop at pie corner', with its 'fifteen pigeons in a coop, razzle-neck fool-hens, a rhode island cocklin, yam, pumpkin, okro, sweet potato, green pea bus' (Burnett 1986: 255). Walcott's 'A Far Cry from Africa' would be another example, with the picture of the tormented soul of a man torn between two cultures:

> I who am poisoned with the blood of both,
> Where shall I turn, divided to the vein?
> I who have cursed
> The drunken officer of British rule, how choose
> Between this Africa and the English tongue I love?
> Betray them both, or give back what they give?
> How can I face such slaughter and be cool?
> How can I turn from Africa and live?
>
> (Walcott 1986: 18)

If one considers the complexities of racial prejudice and interaction that have been instrumental in shaping present-day Caribbean society, it is clear that Rhys's, Brathwaite's and Walcott's poems illustrate the 'creolization' of a European literary tradition through the portrayal of a uniquely Caribbean landscape, society or experience. For instance, in Rhys's 'Obeah Night' the use of metaphors representing night as 'Lord's dark face' and turning Love into a 'cruel' and 'mocking' entity (Burnett 1986: 147), evokes the spells obeah practitioners could cast, using witchcraft against their victims, to change them into zombies, or living dead. The specificity of the perspective chosen by Rhys is its borrowing from 'traveling culture' (Clifford 1988: 98).

One notes how Brathwaite reworks a master principle in Eliot's Modernism – poetry's relationship to speech and poetry's social function – in a constructivist approach to tradition, since he builds from a different fragment, choosing to chronicle the experience of African Caribbeans' alienation and dispossesion, conquering new modes of expression through the use of Afro-Caribbean vernacular, broken words and fragmented syllables as in *The Zea Mexican Diary*. Meanwhile, a continuum can be observed in the language chosen by Brathwaite as it borrows from the oral tradition typified by the vernacular of the English-speaking Caribbean that shows strong African influence in its syntax and intonation. 'Horse Weebles' is thus mainly in standard English, but Brathwaite also makes partial use of one of the vernaculars of the Caribbean, accessible to non-speakers with the occasional help of a glossary:

Uh bet-
'cha feelin less
poorly a'ready !
i int know, pearlie,
man, any-way, de body int dead.
no man, you even lookin more hearty !
(Burnett [1986] 1993: 256; emphasis in the original)

The creative juxtaposition of various tones of voice is a Caribbean literary device of great subtlety. So doing, Brathwaite's choice of the expression 'nation language' as an alternative to the term 'dialect' illustrates which point of the language continuum he uses to develop his own insurgent Afro-Caribbean folk tradition. In fact, while Brathwaite adopts Eliot's Modernism, sharing his view of poetry's social function, he also creolizes it through a cross-cultural process inseparable from violent histories of displacement; transplantation; and economic, political and cultural interactions, creating New World poetics that draw upon several diaspora cultures, that is to say, the experience of simultaneously participating in a transnational and Indigenous cultural community, as illustrated by the use of Barbadian vernacular in 'Horse Weebles'.

Fragmentation, dislocation and alienation are all common themes in Rhys's and Brathwaite's writings that reflect the high degree of severance experienced by colonized people, and the rootlessness associated with creolization generating some sort of alienating hybridity. It seems important to explore how Rhys's rejection of neocolonialism and Brathwaite's reliance on travelling cultures can convey the complexity of uniting Caribbean writers in a modernist cosmopolitan tradition. But it involves risks, namely the risk of reinscribing too easily alienating hybridity within the cultural hierarchy of colonial and neocolonial experiences in the New World.

Mixing prose or poetry with history, both Rhys and Brathwaite disclose an alternative history of the Carribean and bring a mythic dimension to postcolonial fiction and poetry as a way of giving a voice to disempowered people. Because they provide new ways of illuminating areas of darkness in the diasporic world, Rhys and Brathwaite create a new world in which they fight against historical incompleteness by re-enacting the historical past in the present. Men make their own history, but they do not make it just as they please, they do not make it under circumstances chosen by themselves but from the past. In *Wide Sargasso Sea*, Rhys's rewriting of the story of *Jane Eyre* from the point of view of the 'other' woman, can be easily apprehended as an illustration of Drake's analysis of Antoinette's loss of identity that points out how one form of despair arises when one no longer knows one's place in society, and when one's aspirations become meaningless (Drake 1990: 99).

Glissant extends the idea of creolization to a 'new global level' in developing his 'poetics of relation' (Dash 1995: 179), a cross-cultural poetics fit to refer to the ambition of examining the relationships between Rhys, Brathwaite and Eliot. In this examination, the trajectories of cultural exchange are a collocation of the interactions between these writers to express a series of points of view making up a modernist poetics. The combined perspectives introduced with the creolization of history in the Anglophone Caribbean by Rhys and Brathwaite give a face to a new cultural type of modernity, interwoven with Western modernity and reaching a provisional unity Eliot identifies as 'the theory of points of view' (Eliot 1964: 192). Both Brathwaite and Rhys develop a challenging discourse in so far as the text (whether poetry or fiction) maps the contours of a culture torn between the submission to a dominant country and the simultaneous articulation of its creolized double identity, implicitly acknowledging the intrinsic intricacies of Caribbean history and sociology.

An alternative vision of transmission lines?

Brathwaite's poetics is meaningful in its representing the complexity of the experience of colonization in the Caribbean. Particularly significant is the transmission line of polyvocality used by Caribbean poets, and notably

Brathwaite. The pattern of transmission is continuous with the one adopted by Rhys as she gives voice to the marginalized. When this type of transmission is examined from the perspective of the unceasing process of transformation defined by Édouard Glissant, it is the creation of a New World poetics that one bears in mind, recognizing the possibility of interdependence and resistance.

Fiction reveals its ability to remake the world and transform or transfigure reality (Ricœur 1991: 467). In *Discours sur le colonialisme* ([1950] 1955; *Discourse on Colonialism* 2000), Aimé Césaire argues that true poetry is subversive to the extent that it arises from out of the depths of oneself and that it establishes itself as a counter-communication. Be it prose or poetry, Rhys's and Brathwaite's transmission of the historical past is submitted to the twists of a transformation of reality and counter-communication. Indeed, Rhys and Brathwaite present an alternative vision of the world that challenges the codification of accepted history. By inventively repatterning historical facts, Rhys and Brathwaite recreate a historical reality likely to transmit a personal and cultural perspective that incorporates their personal and cultural visions. As such, history is constantly rectified and transformed by a process of counter-communication to combat the incompleteness of historical representation and fulfil their desire of rectifying history and enlarging reality by opposing the subalternity of the voice.

8

Dressing and addressing the self: Jean Rhys, Jamaica Kincaid and the cultural politics of self-fashioning

Denise deCaires Narain

The politics of clothing have always had a strong symbolic function in the Caribbean. Ever since Columbus's arrival in the New World, clothing has been instrumental to the production and (re)definition of race, color, class, and ethnicity.
—Fumagalli, Ledent and Del Valle Alcalá (2013: 3-4)

Good clothes, new clothes, this year's clothes will cover up my flaws, straighten me out, measure me up to the approving eye.
—Young (2005: 66)

About clothes, it's awful. Everything makes you want pretty clothes like hell. [...] 'All right, I'll do anything for good clothes. Anything – anything for clothes.'
—Anna in *Voyage in the Dark* (22)

They were special, everything about them said so, even their clothes; their clothes rustled, swished, soothed. The world was theirs, not mine; everything told me so.
—Kincaid (1991b: 35)

Clothing matters in the Caribbean: as objects of desire; as symbols of power or powerlessness; and as crucial markers of status for colonizer and colonized, as Fumagalli, Ledent and Del Valle Alcalá make clear. Clothing has also functioned to index women's status; she must be well dressed to measure up favourably to the male gaze. Iris Young succinctly conveys the complex, gendered circuits of desire that are mediated through clothing, 'well-trained to meet the gaze that evaluates us for our finery, for how well we show him off, we then are condemned as superficial, duplicitous, because we attend to and sometimes learn to love the glamorous arts' (2005: 69). Jean Rhys's protagonists often enact this dynamic, appearing oppressed and obsessed in equal measure by 'pretty clothes', as indicated in Anna's impassioned declamation in *Voyage in the Dark*, cited above. In my fourth epigraph, Jamaica Kincaid approaches clothing from a different perspective to foreground the 'softer, almost not there' power of the canonical literature of her colonial education, in which even the protagonists' clothing is saturated with the cultural authority of its wearers, consolidating her exclusion and making her 'really feel like nothing' (1991b: 34). In this chapter, I argue that Rhys and Kincaid share an interest in clothing that is intricately and intimately connected to an embodied sense of self, manifested in their distinctive engagements with self-fashioning. In their respective oeuvres, 'the psychic life of clothing is woven into the very flesh of existence', as Julia Emberley argues in her discussion of clothing in contemporary women's fiction (2007: 466).

Jean Rhys's fascination with the accoutrements of femininity, clothes, make-up and hair, is evident across her entire oeuvre, as Joannou notes: 'As an essential condition of subjectivity dress articulates the body and in "articulating the body, it simultaneously articulates the psyche"' (Kaja Silverman cited in Joannou 2015: 123).[1] All Rhys's protagonists understand the value of clothing in establishing status and value; in *Voyage in the Dark*, Maudie recalls a man saying, '"It's funny, [...] have you ever thought that a girl's clothes cost more than the girl inside them?"' (*VD* 40). In this overdetermined context, the right outfit takes on talismanic significance: if only the right outfit can be acquired, all will be well, at least momentarily. This is the logic prompting Anna's exclamation, 'All right, I'll do anything for good clothes', and Sasha's conviction that had she been wearing the coveted black dress, she'd 'never have stammered or been stupid' in response to her employer in *Good Morning, Midnight* (25).

Jamaica Kincaid's engagement with dressing is not as precisely anchored in detailed references to women's fashion as Rhys's, but clothes have a similarly powerful, definitive function in her work, signalling the status and significance, or *in*significance, of the wearer. Kincaid's interest is more obviously geopolitically oriented, fuelled by anger about the history of conquest, enslavement and colonization that began with Columbus's arrival in 1492 and continues into the present in the region's dependence on service industries, such as tourism. So engrained is this history of exploitation and servitude that it is presented in many of her texts as an article of clothing, or second skin: Lucy describes the precariousness of her position as a newly arrived au pair in New York, as having 'around my shoulders the mantel of a servant' (Kincaid 1991a: 95); Xuela understands that her teacher has internalized 'self-loathing' to such an extent that 'she wore despair like an article of clothing, like a mantle, or a staff on which she leaned' (Kincaid 1996: 15). Sharrad's comments in relation to *The Autobiography of My Mother*, can easily be extended across Kincaid's oeuvre: 'References to cloth and clothing therefore permeate the text, as both metaphors and specific material references' (2004: 57).

Both writers, then, identify dress and the paraphernalia of femininity as important targets in their critique of patriarchal, postcolonial structures that doom women to flounder, unless they acquiesce to ladylike decorum and dependency on men. Where Rhys's critique tends towards ambivalence and melancholy, Kincaid's register is that of lament, energized by anger. Across their work, the restricted parameters within which a 'woman' is expected to make a life and a living, and indeed, author a sense of self, is bleak and perilous. In response to this challenge, they persistently thematize self-making in their texts in protagonists who display a marked uncertainty about their identities and place in the world: Antoinette's oft-quoted plaint, 'I often wonder who I am and where is my country and where do I belong and why was I ever born at all' (*WSS* 61), or Sasha's declaration, 'I have no pride – no pride, no name, no face, no country. I don't belong anywhere' (*GMM* 38). No sooner has Lucy written her name and first sentence in her pristine notebook, 'Lucy Josephine Potter' (Kincaid 1991a: 163) than it is erased by her tears; *The Autobiography of My Mother* ends with Xuela's poignant assertion: 'This account is an account of the person who was never allowed to be and an account of the person I did not allow myself to become' (Kincaid 1996: 228).

The fictional engagement with self-making that is characteristic of both Rhys and Kincaid is informed by a similarly compulsive inscription of the autobiographical in their oeuvres, so that the narrative trajectories of their texts frequently echo their own lived experiences. So similar to her own bohemian life in Paris and London are Rhys's protagonists that the phrase 'the Rhys woman' used to be applied to author and fictional counterparts alike. The protagonists in Kincaid's texts likewise echo details of her Antiguan childhood, migration to America and family life, stated attitudes to colonial history and, often, her own family names. While both writers are aware that, for women writers, 'the autobiographical' risks being read reductively as 'confessional', they offer similarly contradictory responses to the label, variously refusing *and* embracing it. In an interview with Mary Cantwell, Rhys rejects the suggestion that her work is thinly disguised autobiography, only to add 'the feelings are all mine' (Cantwell 1990: 24). In the Foreword to *Smile Please: An Unfinished Autobiography*, Diana Athill notes Rhys's worry that 'much of her life had already been "used up" in the novels' (Athill 1979: 6). So persistently does Kincaid mine her life experiences in her work that she blurs 'the lines between autobiography, fiction, non-fiction and memoir' (Nasta 2009: 64). Asked frequently in interviews about the autobiographical in her work, Kincaid is as likely to say all of it is autobiographical as she is to insist that it is *not* about her.

To my mind, the persistent inscription of recognizably autobiographical material in Rhys's and Kincaid's writing implies that self-making is a laborious and ongoing struggle in both 'life' and 'text'. There is no 'self' waiting in the wings to be 'expressed' or 'given voice' to textually, but rather, through repeated acts of self-fashioning, refracted fragments of self become momentarily recognizable, to both reader *and* writer. Clothing, in this context, makes visible the performativity of self-making so that these tentative, performative acts of self-making become serial dress-rehearsals, in a manner of speaking. As such, they chime with Judith Butler's arguments about the precariousness of self-making:

> There remains that history from which I broke, and that breakage installs me here and now. At the same time, nothing determines me in advance – I am not formed once and definitively, but continuously or repeatedly. I am still being formed as I form myself in the here and now. And my own self-formative activity – what some would call 'self-fashioning' – becomes part of that ongoing formative process.
>
> (2015: 60)

The repetitious labour of self-making is amplified for Rhys and Kincaid who seek to break from colonial history to author themselves *as authors*. We might read this in the weary, repetitive circularity of Rhys's protagonists' or the bleak *un*becoming that so many of Kincaid's texts arrive at. But it can also be tracked in their respective engagement with *Jane Eyre* and the tussle for literary selfhood it implies. Rhys's canonization as a postcolonial writer is emphatically tethered to *Wide Sargasso Sea* and the reworking of Brontë's 'Bertha' that it offers, while Jamaica Kincaid has spoken repeatedly in interviews of her lasting appreciation of *Jane Eyre*. Rhys 'rescues' Bertha from Rochester's casual, racist misogyny ('What a pigmy intellect she had and what giant propensities!'; Brontë [1847] 1985: 334) and imbues her passion with intelligence. The fiery red dress that prompts her to set fire to the house, also prompts her to wonder, '"Does it make me look intemperate and unchaste?" I said. That man told me so' (*WSS* 110), directly addressing Rochester's accusations in *Jane Eyre*. Annie John daydreams of living alone in Belgium like Charlotte Brontë had and, after a period of illness, she returns to school dressed in a too-long skirt, a too-big hat, walks with 'purposely timid' steps and had 'acquired a strange accent' (Kincaid 1985: 128–9) in an attempt to establish a writerly persona that might approximate the ladylike decorum of a figure like Jane Eyre, or Charlotte herself. If we take *Jane Eyre* as representative of the cultural authority associated with nineteenth-century fiction (populated by people whose 'clothes rustled, swished, soothed'), then the complicated legacies of literary self-making for the postcolonial writer are clear: only a certain kind of respectable, white woman, housed and dressed appropriately decorously, can aspire to the sensibility required for literary selfhood.

Rhys and Kincaid attend to women's appearance and attire in order to expose and question the power of the male gaze. In Rhys, surveillance is most memorably figured in the enormous steel machine that appears in *Good Morning, Midnight*, with its stiffly mascaraed eyes at the ends of its long arms (*GMM* 156). In Kincaid, it is often a black woman whose gaze puts 'whiteness' under scrutiny as when Mariah's benign blondness is exposed in *Lucy* (1991a: 27) or when the narrator in *A Small Place* focuses on 'an incrediby unattractive, fat, pastrylike-fleshed' tourist (1988: 13). But when writing of Caribbean people, Kincaid eschews descriptors so that 'brown' or 'black' become normative. Her frequent use of the phrase 'people who look like me'[2] (instead of 'black people' for instance) emphasizes racist regimes of looking while refusing its vocabulary. In discussing texts at the intersection of the fictional and autobiographical, my aim in what follows is to foreground the complicated ways that clothing, appearance and being looked at matter to both writers.

Snapshots of a dress

Smile Please: An Unfinished Autobiography opens with a brief account of Rhys having her portrait taken on her sixth birthday. She remembers the photographer who 'had a yellow black face and pimples on his chin' and that despite her mother's admonition to 'stay still', her hand shoots up, 'of its own accord', unsettling the portrait (*SP* 19). Rhys then recalls looking at the framed photograph in the family home in Roseau some three years later, 'I remembered the dress she was wearing, so much prettier than anything I had now, but the curls, the dimples surely belonged to someone else. The eyes were a stranger's eyes' (19–20). While her nine-year-old self is baffled by the image of her younger self, the white birthday dress, so different from the 'ugly brown holland dress' (20) she wears as she gazes at the photograph, remains clear in her memory. So clear that though she never looks at the photograph again, 'Over and over [she] would remember that magic dress' (21). The girl wearing the dress, however, is unrecognizable and Rhys presents this moment of her nine-year-old self looking at her six-year-old self as a kind of epiphany in which she realizes for the first time that she is no longer the person the photographer captured and that selfhood is a shifting, unstable concept. The dress retains its material specificity and appears to momentarily, magically, anchor the girl wearing it to a particular time and place, while perhaps also transferring some of its beauty to her.

Rhys seems clear that it is not the photograph prompting the memory of the dress; later, she recalls wearing the new dress while watching her siblings start (and abruptly truncate) a birthday performance of Red Riding Hood. Described as her 'first clear connected memory' (*SP* 23), the dress again performs an anchoring function. Photographs frequently function in autobiographical works as a way of fixing memory in verifiable 'truth',[3] but Rhys does not begin with a description of the photograph (*Smile Please* does not include any photographs of Rhys as a child) but with the act of the photograph *being taken* under her mother's and the photographer's direction. When the photograph is described in the following paragraph, it is filtered through the layered lenses of recall of the 89-year-old Rhys remembering her nine-year-old self, looking at the portrait of her six-year-old self. Rather than anchoring the autobiographical text in a relatively straightforward image of the author, we are offered a layered account of a snapshot that keeps shifting focus. A sense of loss prevails: of the beauty associated with curls and dimples and of the wild beauty of the hills of Bona Vista where the photograph was taken. Unable to recapture the beauty in the portrait, or to adapt her ugly brown convent school uniform, Rhys describes taking a 'perverse pleasure' in being as untidy as possible and becoming 'one of the untidiest girls in the convent' (*SP* 20). From the outset, then, Rhys establishes the importance of appearance, and of regimes of looking, to her sense of self as a girl, while also suggesting the centrality of dress as a kind of stylized self-staging, as well as an important, visual aide memoire.

In other places in *Smile Please*, anxiety about appropriate apparel is compounded by a persistent worry about not being pretty enough to attract a marriage proposal: 'In those days a girl was supposed to marry, it was your mission in life, you were a failure if you didn't' (*SP* 51). Black Dominicans, by contrast, are presented as free to dress as their fancy takes them, whether that is girding their skirts up high as their cook at Bona Vista does or stitching paper into the hems of dresses for Sunday Mass to make 'the desired frou-frou noise' (51). She presents carnival as an event in which the freedom she associates with being black is heightened dramatically by the flamboyant use of costume and dance. In mocking contrast, Rhys describes her family, limited by decorum to looking through the slats in the jalousies (so *they* cannot be seen), 'the life surged up to us sitting stiff and well behaved, looking on' (52). While she is desperate to join in, 'I would give anything, anything to be able to dance like that', she also notes, 'my feelings were mixed, because I was very afraid of the masks' (52).

Rhys's own experiences of dressing-up as a child are not in the extravagantly public register of carnival but for modest dramatic performances at home and, occasionally, for a fancy dress ball. For one such event, organized by Mr Hesketh,[4] Rhys, then in her early teens, was eventually persuaded out of her choices of Zouave (too complex for her aunt's sewing skills) or gipsy (she was told she was too fair) and costumed instead as 'yachting', 'but dressed to go to the dance I stared at myself in the glass with rising happiness and excitement, for I was transformed' (*SP* 90). Returning home after a night of dancing, Rhys describes another epiphanic moment of looking in the mirror: 'I knew that that night had changed me. I was a different girl, I told myself that I would be just as happy the next day, now I would always be happy' (91). The 'yachting' dress effects a transformative change, akin to that of the 'magic' of the white birthday dress, while resonating with precarious promises of happiness that so many dresses in Rhys have so frequently signalled.

Jamaica Kincaid's 'Biography of a Dress' also focuses on a 'birthday dress' made especially for her by her mother to celebrate her second birthday and she, too, has her portrait taken wearing her (yellow) birthday dress. In *Smile Please*, we are not told where the photograph is taken; perhaps, befitting her family's status, the photographer came to Rhys's home. Kincaid, however, provides details of her photographer, Mr Walker, that indicate how far removed he is from her own social milieu: the house in which he has his studio is 'mysterious' (1992: 98) because it has four rooms and a verandah, unlike her own small, one-room house; he is unlike men she knows because he compliments her on her dress and ribbons. Both photographers are described as being of mixed ethnicity and have pimply skin: in Rhys, he 'had a yellow black face and pimples on his chin' (*SP* 19); in Kincaid, 'he touched his hair often, smoothing down, caressing the forcibly straightened hair' (1992: 99). Once he has taken the photograph, Kincaid notes that he walks to the mirror and squeezes a pimple on his chin that emits a curl of pus 'imitating, almost, the decoration on the birthday cake that awaited me at home' (100). The detailed resemblance between the two photographers is uncanny and probably coincidental, but it suggests a degree of racially inflected unease in both narrators about the respective roles of the photographers in capturing their girlhood selves on camera.

Clearly, Rhys's focus on her younger self, however changeable, is expected in an autobiography, however reluctantly and belatedly produced. Kincaid, writing at a relatively early moment in her career, approaches the autobiographical tangentially via the unexpected focus of the biographer on her dress rather than herself. The story, published in *Grand Street* in 1992, included a slightly blurry copy of the photograph in question, the child looking wide eyed and slightly nonplussed. The 'biography' of the dress is presented prior to the moment of being photographed and includes descriptions of purchasing the bright yellow fabric (poplin, from Avignon) and of the mother's labours in cutting, sewing and embroidering the dress. She has her ears pierced by a woman from Dominica and is then given gold hoop earrings from British Guiana '(it was called that then, it is not called that now)' and a silver bracelet for each arm '(and that place too was called one thing then, something else now) and a pair of new shoes from Bata' (1992: 98).

Layer upon layer, Kincaid details the provenance of each item with which the mother dresses her daughter, indicating their colonial origins matter-of-factly before reflecting directly on the mother's aspirations for her daughter to look as 'English' as possible in the portrait. Kincaid notes that her mother embroidered elaborate decorations on the dress, including flowers and birds seen only in picture books, not 'in real life' (1992: 96). The dress itself is inspired by one seen in an advertisement for expensive soap in an almanac, featuring a flaxen-haired, blue-eyed girl in a pastoral setting. Kincaid muses that this image 'created in my mother the desire to have a daughter who looked like that or perhaps created the desire in my mother to try and make the daughter she already had look like that' (97). It is significant that *before* describing the image that inspired her mother, Kincaid asserts that: 'My skin was not the color of cream in the process of spoiling, my hair was not the texture of silk and color of flax, my eyes did not gleam like blue jewels in a crown' (96). This affirmation of what she is *not* is a syntactical construction Kincaid frequently uses to consolidate her wider arguments about the structural constraints on self-making for people who look like her. In 'Biography of a Dress', Kincaid's step-by-step account of how she is dressed by her mother is accompanied by the narrating daughter's rhetorical act of *un*dressing in which she lays bare the ideological implications of a colonial history that lies heavily on her child self, set-up so carefully in the photograph.

In *Smile Please*, it is the loss of the dimpled, curly haired younger self, and the prettiness and innocence associated with her, that both nine-year-old and 89-year-old Rhys lament. In 'Biography of a Dress', Kincaid's excavation of the photograph is more forensic, the dress so saturated in history that it appears to determine the subjectivity of the child wearing it. In both, the photograph prompts reflections on what time passing might mean and how that might be represented. Rhys presents the memory of herself at nine years old looking at the photograph of her six-year-old self as a decisive, foundational moment in the portrait of the writer-to-be: 'It was the first time I was aware of time, change and the longing for the past' (*SP* 20). She is also pleased that her photograph is 'by itself, not lost among the other photographs in the room' (19), so that it confirms her singular importance. By contrast to this zooming in to the child's eyes, a familiar visual shortcut to indicate access to interiority, Kincaid pans out widely to draw out the insignificance of her child-self to the wider world. Though Kincaid indicates the care and love with which she is dressed, the shadow of her mother's desire for a flaxen-haired daughter troubles the portrait. The two-year-old girl cannot approximate this ideal, however beautifully she is attired. In offering a biography of the *dress*, Kincaid seems to imply that the girl herself does not qualify as an appropriate subject for biography; the negative terms in which the adult narrator remarks on its significance to anyone, including herself, is similarly equivocal: 'My second birthday was not a major event in anyone's life, certainly not my own (it was not my first and it was not my last, I am now forty-three years old)' (1992: 97).

'Biography of a Dress' is punctuated frequently by reminders that what happened 'then' is being narrated 'now', in self-consciously articulated reflections on the passage of time and how that shapes the perspective of the 43-year-old author. As in *Smile Please*, memory is anchored momentarily in a specific dress but the epiphany in Kincaid is associated more strongly with pain. For example, when she remembers the pain that having her ears pierced for the gold hoops causes, Kincaid describes it as her 'first and only real act of self-invention', a moment of sudden self-awareness that causes a separation between the one experiencing and the one observing the pain, the latter being 'the one of the two I most rely on' (1992: 98). This resonates with Rhys's realization that she is no longer the girl she was, but in Kincaid there is no 'longing for the past' because the past is linked to wider histories of suffering and loss in the Caribbean and to the collective denial of selfhood.

Dressing *up* and dressing *as*

I want to shift direction here to attend to a story by Rhys that mediates the autobiographical through the fictional in rather different ways. 'Let Them Call it Jazz' is unique in Rhys's oeuvre in being narrated in a stylized Creole by Selina Davis, a 'mixed-race' woman whose father is 'white', mother is 'fair coloured' (*CSS* 155) and grandmother is 'quite dark and what we call "country-cookie"' (156). Formerly a seamstress, Selina is out of work and struggling to pay her rent. Following a chance encounter in a café, she is offered accommodation by Mr Sims, who installs her in one of his shabby properties where she is kept in a limbo-like state with the promise of a job. While she waits, Selina thinks, remembers, sleeps, drinks a lot and eats a little, a pattern that recalls many of Rhys's protagonists.

But Selina also dances and sings when she has been drinking, sometimes indoors but also outdoors in the garden or street, without her stockings and shoes. The neighbours object to her 'obscene' dancing and 'abominable language' (*CSS* 161), positioning themselves as upholders of English respectable legality in the face of the racialized disorder and difference that Selina represents. Enraged by the smug hostility of their taunts – 'At least the other tarts that crook installed here were *white* girls' – Selina's 'arm moves of itself. I pick up a stone and bam! Through the window' (159). One is reminded of the hand that shoots up 'of its own accord' as the photographer takes the shot in *Smile Please*, and of the similarly involuntary, disruptive potential of the body that it implies. When taken to court, Selina tries to regulate her voice and body language into acceptably 'decent' form but speaks loudly and gesticulates, so that she knows she won't be believed. She is not believed and is incarcerated in Holloway prison where she spends time in hospital, having lost her appetite for food, and life. It is only on hearing the Holloway song sung by a woman in the punishment cells that she revives. The song stays with her after her release but when she hums it at a party, a man takes note of it, jazzes it up and sells it, giving her £5.00 by way of acknowledgement, with which she buys herself 'a dusky pink dress' (167).

What interests me about the story in relation to questions of dressing and self-making is that while Selina's experiences closely echo those of Rhys herself, she chooses to narrate them in a voice that is much less easily or obviously read as autobiographical than that of her other protagonists; she gives her reader the slip, as it were. Carole Angier documents that Rhys spent five days in Holloway in 1949 after being charged several times with being drunk and disorderly and then with assault. She spent time in the psychiatric ward, where 'the doctors pronounced her sane. She was put on probation for two years and allowed home' (Angier 1985: 80). Given that Rhys wrote from the experiences of her own life, it is particularly intriguing that she refracts an experience as significant as her own imprisonment in the way she does in 'Let Them Call it Jazz.' We have some indication of Rhys's thoughts on 'Let Them Call it Jazz' from her letters to Francis Wyndham: 'The other day I wrote a short story as a holiday. It's called "*They thought it was jazz*" and is not typed. A bit of a crazy story. For fun' (*L* 184). In another letter, she writes the story 'is about Holloway Prison – So, all things considered, must not be taken too seriously' (*L* 186). She also sent it to her daughter to type up, rather than the woman she usually asked, to avoid providing the villagers in Cheriton with any more ammunition for labelling her 'crazy' (*L* 263), a recurring theme in her letters. Helen Carr notes that 'in the 1920s and 1930s Rhys's books were frequently described as "sordid"' (2003: 98); so, quite reasonably, Rhys may not have wanted to court further gossip or infamy by suggesting any alignment between her own experiences and Selina's.

Leaving aside Rhys's avowed opinions on the story in her letters, which in any case, are as layered a textual form as any other, what are we to make of Rhys's decision to mediate her own experiences of incarceration for drunk and disorderly behaviour through a mixed-race, Creole-speaking protagonist like Selina? It is not that Selina is completely at odds with Rhys's other white protagonists; like them, she is in similarly perilous financial circumstances that prompt her into dependency on men and into states of anxiety, inebriation and aimless wandering. As with Sasha, Anna, Julia, Marya and Antoinette, clothing features prominently in indexing Selina's affective state. In the opening paragraph of 'Let Them Call it Jazz' Selina's 'best dress' falls to the floor when her landlady maliciously kicks her suitcase. When she dresses in it, having determined to leave Mr Sims, the memory of it being kicked causes her to cry unstoppably (*CSS* 151). With the money the man gives her for the 'Holloway

Song' she whistles for him, she buys a 'dusty pink dress' (167). 'Let Them Call it Jazz' is bookmarked at its opening and closing with Rhys's characteristically symbolic use of dresses.

But Selina is also *unlike* Rhys's other protagonists in intriguing ways. Unlike the uncertain provenance of these, Selina's mixed-race, Caribbean ancestry is clearly stated. Rhys's white protagonists often seem ill-equipped to undertake regularly paid employment, while Selina takes pride in her sewing skills and, after being released from Holloway, finds work as a seamstress. Rhys's protagonists are often associated with a mode of speech that is hesitant, repetitious and circular and the distinction between what is internalized and externalized is not always clear. While they may occasionally use French or English patois, the vernacular register is not as obviously or consistently West Indian as it is in 'Let Them Call it Jazz'. It is striking, too, that while the protagonists of Rhys's novels are always threatening to cause a scene and occasionally do so (Julia slaps Mr McKenzie's face lightly with her glove; Anna stubs her cigarette out on Walter's hand), it is done in a more furtive register than Selina's dancing, cursing performance that ends with her pelting a stone hard enough to break her neighbour's window and be charged with causing criminal damage.

'Let Them Call it Jazz' includes sexual encounters that involve the exchange of money and, as in her novels, these scenes are presented without much fanfare or graphic detail. In light of this, Selina's removal of her shoes and stockings to sing and dance outside, signals a bold flouting of respectable norms and a more visibly performative assertion of selfhood than is characteristic of Rhys's other fiction. There is, then, something strikingly carnivalesque in Selina's display of difference and refusal to conform to acceptable standards of behaviour in public. There are similarly carnivalesque moments throughout 'Let Them Call it Jazz', notably in the description of the policewoman who comes to arrest her:

> She wear sandals and thick stockings and I never see a foot so big or so bad. It look like it want to mash up the whole world. Then she come in after the foot, and her face not so pretty either.
>
> (CSS 160)

The vernacular register and humour here is managed deftly by Rhys to allow Selina to signal a degree of picong agency, despite being roughly handled by the police:

> Then I ask her what I must wear. She say she suppose I had some clothes on yesterday. Or not? 'What's it matter, wear anything,' she says. But I find clean underclothes and stockings and my shoes with high heels and I comb my hair.

I start to file my nails, because I think they too long for magistrate's court but she get angry. 'Are you coming quietly or aren't you?' she says.

(160)

In this act of dressing, Selina takes meticulous care to present herself as respectably as she can for her appearance in the magistrate's court, as if it might help cancel out the earlier scene of her undressing, as well as the 'dressing down' of her neighbours that accompanied it. While Selina, like Rhys's other protagonists, understands the importance of dressing in establishing selfhood, the agentic humour with which she narrates these scenes implies a less constrained attitude to clothing.

From the accounts we have from various sources, including Rhys's letters and autobiography, we know that there are many aspects of Selina's experiences, beyond being incarcerated for being drunk and disorderly, that resonate with Rhys's. Rhys loved calypso, remembered and sang them, and even wrote a few; it was her strong Dominican accent that short-circuited her acting career; she had a fairly bohemian lifestyle – one that might even be described in Caribbean parlance as 'slack'; she had a flamboyant and quirky sense of style and was acutely aware of fashion; her letters are punctuated by a wicked sense of humour, as albeit more sparingly, are the novels with their 'gloomy-eyed', unhappy protagonists. Rather than reading 'Let Them Call it Jazz' as the odd one out, the one text where Rhys masquerades as a *brown* Creole, I suggest we read it as a text that magnifies the deep imprint of Dominican culture on Rhys and, in so doing, we might also recognize the layered ways in which her lived experiences of Dominica are mediated textually. Such a reading might allow more promiscuous readings of Rhys's work and a shift away from the routine alignment of her with the tragic, alienated white Creole.

Putting myself together

By way of gathering this discussion of dressing and self-making towards a close, I turn to Jamaica Kincaid's 'Putting Myself Together', published in 1995. Where 'Biography of a Dress' catalogues the mother's aspirational dressing of her daughter, 'Putting Myself Together' describes scenarios of dressing (and undressing) in which she self-consciously plays with clothing and self-fashioning in New York in the 1970s when she was then a woman in her twenties. Despite her make-shift living arrangements (a mattress salvaged from the street, very little money, no 'real food'; 1995), Kincaid establishes a lengthy, 'elaborate dressing ritual' in which she carefully selects from her array of second-hand 'stylish clothes from a long-ago time' before deciding 'what combination of people, inconceivably older and more prosperous than I was, I wished to impersonate that day'. These musings on dress are ostensibly prompted by Halloween, when she makes a costume for her ten-year-old daughter. One of the items repurposed for the costume is a black, corded velvet hat with a tassel that reminds Kincaid of herself wearing it:

> I was not afraid in those days. I used to tell perfect strangers how they should behave in public – that is, if I saw them misbehaving in public. My hat was firmly strapped in place. I was invulnerable. And if, for my interference, they threatened to kill me, I would inform them that killing me was not a proper response. None of them killed me; they only threatened to do so.
>
> (1995)

The image conjured here of the author, herself a relative stranger (having lived in New York for ten years), performing as a prim and proper enforcer of appropriate public behaviour provides a wonderfully comic counterpoint to the drunk and disorderly performance of Jean Rhys/Selina. The 'prim and proper' is a mode of self-presentation that Kincaid often deploys in mischievous or contrary ways. Here, the prim narrative voice allows less strictly 'proper' behaviour to pass by quietly in the narration: taking drugs, having casual sex, parading around in her apartment naked, taking coffee enemas, arriving at a party naked except for a skirt made from string and plastic bananas (and a theatrically discarded fur coat) in the style of Josephine Baker. If dressing-up in second-hand clothes is an opportunity for impersonation, then the primly matter-of-fact narrative voice so characteristic of her writing, appears to provide a way of controlling, managing and authorizing those impersonations.

But the authoritative tenor and definitive register of Kincaid's narrations are frequently punctured by moments when that control 'gives way'. So, although 'Putting Myself Together' conveys the verve with which she changes her name, announces she's a writer and dresses the part, it also indicates the attendant risks to the self that does the performing. When her corded velvet hat blows off her newly cropped, dyed-blonde hair and lands in the gutter, her distraught response is presented as prompting an epiphany of sorts. She recognizes the hat as 'impractical for a modern woman, suitable only as a costume' (Kincaid 1995).

The event of losing her hat 'blows her cover', as it were, and forces her to see her embodied self as she is seen. In another passage, she is told that she shouldn't be surprised that *Mademoiselle* didn't hire her because 'they never hired black girls', to which she muses:

> But how was I to know that I was a black girl? I never pass myself in a corridor and say, I am a black girl. I never see myself coming toward me as I come round a bend and say, There is that black girl coming toward me. How was I really to know such a thing?
>
> (Kincaid 1995)

Kincaid's surprise is not faux-naïve; it is a refusal to see herself as she is seen as well as a denial of racist regimes of looking; she is not denying autobiographical 'facts' but the presumptive meanings and significance of those 'facts'. This resonates with Kincaid's phrase 'people who look like me' and alerts us to the performativity that any/all autobiographical acts involve. For both Jean Rhys and Jamaica Kincaid, self-making is a painful, playful and laborious process of recovery and discovery, of expression and invention. In their deliberated engagements with dressing, undressing, dressing-up and impersonation, they provide wonderfully itinerant possibilities for Caribbean selfhood. And, I would argue, they prompt us as critics to refuse an idea of 'the autobiographical' that endlessly, unquestioningly, trails the binary legacies of colonial history that dictate what we should expect from a 'black' or a 'white' writer.

What, I wonder, would Jean Rhys and Jamaica Kincaid have made of each other if they had met? Imagine the small talk: they could mock the professed civility of English culture; they might agree that being poor and thin at least had the advantage of making them look good in clothes; perhaps they'd reminisce about going blonde? Would Jamaica be surprised at Jean's strong West Indian accent but hushed volume? Would Jean wonder what had happened to Jamaica's Antiguan timbre? Would Jean be wearing the fur coat she ruefully shortened so that it might remain fashionable (*L* 67)? Would Jamaica be wearing 'the garment that had been her own life', unravelling and trailing on the ground (Kincaid 2013: 164)? In gathering their concerns with self-fashioning and dress together here, I hope to have generated a meeting and conversation of sorts between them. The autobiographical in Rhys and Kincaid is seldom uncomplicated by a sense that they are trying out selves quite strategically, playfully and seriously. As critics, we need the flexibility to respond to that.

Notes

1. References to clothing are ubiquitous in Rhys's work but see her short stories 'Illusion' and 'Mannequin' for particularly evocative consideration of dresses and dressing. See also Joannou 2012: 463–89.
2. See for one example among many, *My Garden (Book)* (Kincaid 2000: 114).
3. See Rose 1986.
4. Hesketh Bell was a well-known colonial administrator in Dominica.

9

'Competing conversations': Voice and identity in Caryl Phillips's *A View of the Empire at Sunset*

Kathie Birat

In his fiction and his semi-fictional works, Caryl Phillips has explored the interwoven lives of characters, both real and imaginary, caught in the web of spatial and temporal relations created by slavery and its aftermath. The lifelines he draws between characters inhabiting widely diverse areas and epochs are often textual, relying occasionally on the use of historical texts as templates for reinventing the language of a time and place, a strategy he used with particular success in *Cambridge* (1991) and *Crossing the River* ([1993] 1994). Rather than attempting to capture voices directly through dialogue or first-person narration, he often filters them through the language of an unidentified narrator who moves in and out of the characters' thoughts, making it possible to focus both on the character and the context surrounding his words and acts.

Phillips's most recent novel, *A View of the Empire at Sunset* (2018a), suggests the pertinence of re-examining his narrative strategy against the background of his former works in order to understand how the narration of the real or imagined experience of a public figure brings into focus the complex relations linking a person to her historical and cultural context. In *A View of the Empire at Sunset* one can perceive, behind what seems a fluid narration by an extradiegetic narrator blending an external voice with an internal perception, the heterogeneous elements that enter into its composition. Perhaps more so than any of his other novels, it brings together multiple sources in an original way. The novel is based on the life of Jean Rhys, whose novel *Wide Sargasso Sea* ([1966] 1999) was itself a reinvention or reimagining of *Jane Eyre*, viewed from the perspective of Rochester's wife Bertha. Rhys was the author of novels and short stories published before the appearance of *Wide Sargasso Sea*. She also wrote an autobiography, *Smile Please*, which was published in its not entirely completed form the year of Rhys's death in 1979. As her biographer Diana Athill explains in the introduction to Rhys's autobiography, the writing of an autobiography was problematic for Rhys to the extent that 'much of her life had already been "used up" in the novels' (Athill 1979: 6). In his fictional reworking of Rhys's life, Phillips was recreating the life of someone who had put her own life directly and indirectly into words in a number of different ways. This situation is unparalleled in Phillips's fiction (although his recreation of John Newton's ship's log and correspondence in the third section of *Crossing the River* was based on Newton's writing) and represents a particular challenge, both in terms of composition and reception. The closest parallel in the author's work can be found in *Dancing in the Dark* (2005), a novel in which he gave a fictional representation of the life of the Caribbean-born entertainer Bert Williams. The significant difference lies in the fact that Williams left few written traces of his life, leaving ample room for Phillips's imagination in his fictional recreation. Although Williams was a performer whose art relied on his body and facial expressions rather than words, *Dancing in the Dark* offers interesting clues to Phillips's approach to public figures. His interest in Bert Williams stemmed partly from the disappearance of the performer from public consciousness after his death, producing an invisibility that Phillips saw as having cultural and racial implications that reached far beyond an individual destiny. A similar curiosity concerning the connection between a person's public performance and the cultural and historical forces perceptible in the background seems to explain Phillips's narrative approach to the life of Jean Rhys.

In looking at Phillips's representation of the life of Jean Rhys, one cannot help raising questions relating to genre and to the relationship between fiction and non-fiction, biography and autobiography. The subject of generic definitions has been discussed in connection with many of Phillips's works, as has the porous boundary between fiction and non-fiction. In a recent essay on biography in Phillips's writing, Louise Yelin stated that 'Phillips' biographical writing, like his novels, erodes distinctions between "fiction" and "fact"' (2017: 105). In her discussion of *Foreigners*, Daria Tunca likewise considers that 'a blurring of boundaries between the realms of fiction and non-fiction as well as a combination of different genres under the same cover are some of the writer's most conspicuous trademarks' (2017: 160).[1] These explorations of generic hybridity aim to clarify the functioning of Phillips's texts through a more precise understanding of the ways in which they work with and against the expectations related to generic boundaries. *A View of the Empire at Sunset* evokes similar questions concerning the novel's relation to the generic others that haunt it – particularly biography and autobiography. As in studies devoted to *Dancing in the Dark*, it is not the need to determine a label for the work that is at issue, but rather the ways in which discussions surrounding the functioning of both fictional and non-fictional genres such as the novel, the biography and the autobiography can illuminate unnoticed dimensions of a text.[2] In the case of *A View of the Empire at Sunset*, the tools for analysis made available through narratology enable us to examine the role of the heterodiegetic narrator in ways that take into account the novel's proximity to biography and autobiography, thus making it possible to perceive how Phillips suggests the impact and presence of these genres without actually crossing the boundary separating fiction from non-fiction. Beyond this generic question, an examination of Phillips's narrative strategies, by its focus on an intertextual relation between Rhys and Phillips, can offer fresh insights into Rhys's fiction. Through his fictionalizing of Rhys's life, Phillips is remapping his own experience of the discourses which Sue Thomas evokes as those with which Rhys was engaged: 'empire, gender, sex, race, class, and desire' (1999: 2). As Sylvie Maurel has convincingly demonstrated in her study of Rhys from a feminist perspective, it is often through a close examination of the author's narrative strategies, her use of voice and focalization, that one can perceive her view of women as speaking subjects (1998). From this point of view, Phillips's narrative strategies in his representation of Rhys can be seen as offering an interesting counterpoint to her own methods as described by Maurel. To the 'anxiety of influence' which Maurel mentions in Rhys's relation to Charlotte Brontë (1998: 138) it adds a potentially similar anxiety on the part of Phillips and suggests the fruitfulness of an examination of her fiction in the light of his narrativization of her life.

An approach to *A View of the Empire at Sunset* through the perspective of narratology can enable us to explore the apparent fluidity of the text and to pay attention to the effects produced by the narrator's proximity to, or distance from, the consciousness of the central character, in this case a fictional representation of Jean Rhys. From this point of view, Dorrit Cohn's terminology, developed in *Transparent Minds*, for defining the relation between the discourse of the narrator and the consciousness of the character can prove to be particularly useful. Cohn sees 'three types of presentation of consciousness […] in the context of third-person narration'. The first, which she calls 'psycho-narration', is 'the narrator's discourse about a character's consciousness'. The second, 'quoted monologue', she defines as 'a character's mental discourse', while 'narrated monologue' is 'a character's mental discourse in the guise of the narrator's discourse' (1978: 14). One of the advantages of the distinctions made by Cohn is the possibility of separating seeing and feeling from saying, and thus avoiding any possible confusion in the use of the word 'voice'.[3] While in the broadest sense of the term, the voices of both Jean Rhys and a heterodiegetic narrator can be heard in Phillips's novel, it is precisely the distinction between the physical attributes of the represented voices, the use of language by the character and the narrator, and the borderline between perception, thought and speech that makes it possible to grasp the specific nature of the author's treatment of his subject.

A View of the Empire at Sunset is written in the form of 'psycho-narration' with the narrator at times moving towards quoted or narrated monologue. This modulation of the distance between the discourse of the narrator and that of the character is a characteristic of the techniques for 'rendering consciousness in a figural context' described by Cohn (1978: 111).[4] Phillips's choice of psycho-narration allowed him to explore and reflect the consciousness of his subject without seeming to adopt her language or limit his perspective to her point of view. Given the fact that Rhys was herself a writer, it was a way to approach a representation of her consciousness from a perspective that would place it in a different light, making it possible to suggest an alternative narrative of her life. This choice needs to be seen against the background of the two genres that hover at the edges of the novel: biography and autobiography. In an article on the relation between historical fiction and biography, Cohn examines the ways in which the difference between biography and fiction reveals 'our pervasive experience of mind-reading in third person novels' as the very essence of fiction (1989: 7). It is the relation to biography, to the questions raised by the telling of the life story of a person, seen from the outside, from the point of view of events, that suggests to Cohn the pertinence of the comparison and highlights the specificity of fictional narrative as an exploration of consciousness by a third-person narrator. While Phillips is not writing a biography, the reality of his subject and the implied relation to the biographical genre suggest a meaningful tension between the novel and biography. This tension contributes to the force of the narrative voice by suggesting not only an external perspective but potentially a split within the character, perceptible in the gap between narrative voice and figural consciousness. Yet, on the other hand, the proximity of the narrative voice to the consciousness of the character, what Cohn calls 'consonance', points toward autobiography and its I-narrator. It is the overlapping of the expectations related to the three genres evoked – fiction, biography and autobiography – that allows Phillips to develop his particular perspective on Jean Rhys.

The novel begins at the moment when Gwen and her second husband, Leslie, are contemplating a trip to the Caribbean, to the island of Dominica, where Gwen was born and raised until she left for England at the age of sixteen. In ten sections bearing titles that present an abbreviated narrative of Rhys's life up to the point of her return to England, the novel tackles the moment of preparation for the trip home, then shifts back to Gwen's childhood and follows her life until it once again reaches what had been the starting point, seen now as the moment of the character's return to England from the Caribbean. The decision to situate the novel in a frame determined by Gwen's return to Dominica places her relation to the notion of home and of the Caribbean at the centre of the novel. The effect of a memoir is produced by the choice of vignettes presented in brief chapters focusing on a particular moment rather than a chronological series of events, thus emphasizing emotion rather than facts. This makes it possible for the narrator to adopt a perspective seemingly determined by the emotional impact of the things that happen, an angle that eludes certain aspects of Rhys's life which, from a biographical point of view, would seem crucial. Rhys's writing is not referred to until Chapter 45, when her future husband 'come[s] across her writing in a fairly obscure literary journal' (*View* 235).

The voice of the extradiegetic narrator serves as the concrete, practical medium in which the thoughts and perceptions of Gwen, as a character, are presented in the indirect manner in which events themselves are described, giving the narration a fluidity that hides the borderline between the words of the narrator and those of the character. This produces the 'dovetailing between the inner and outer realms of fictional reality' referred to by Cohn (1978: 49). The proximity between the narrator and the character is further increased by a series of devices – frequent shifts to the present tense, the use of deictics and first names. The first sentence of the novel – 'The bleak afternoon had been made all the more dispiriting by having to overhear Leslie on the telephone busying himself with his attempts to make arrangements for their potential sea voyage' (*View* 3) – demonstrates the blending of distance and proximity created by the placing of Leslie's name in a sentence which involves a description given by an extradiegetic narrator. Yet, on the other hand, the 'speculative or explanatory commentary' (Cohn 1978: 31) that Cohn associates with psycho-narration is abundantly present throughout the novel. The narrator's presence in Gwen's reaction to her lover Lancey's description of his failed marriage is a clear example of this:

> As Lancey poured himself another brandy, *she knew* that the man seated before her had shared this anecdote with her in order to help her better understand that wariness and discretion would inform their friendship. [...] *She knew* that Mabel would approve of this development, but it was then that Lancey posed his question about her previous experience with men, and *believing* that it was unlikely that a man such as this would have any desire to take on the responsibility of a novice, *she said nothing* and *resolved* to let the evening follow its course.
>
> (*View* 137; emphases added)

While this passage appears to be a presentation by the narrator of Gwen's thoughts, the seemingly unidirectional observation of the character's reactions branches into a speculation by Gwen on the nature of Lancey's thoughts. The interaction that in a conventional novel might take the form of dialogue in this case shifts to the interior of the character's mind, where it generates a mirror image of the narrator's function as a commentator on the behaviour of others. The pervasive use of this technique produces several effects. Most importantly, it blurs the borderline between the narrator's revelation of Gwen's perceptions and her attempts to construct a coherent narrative of her own experience. In her first encounter with Lancey, Gwen's vision of 'the chamber which contained a bed' (*View* 132) places the moment within her perception. This leads the reader to experience Lancey's telling of the story of his love affair – 'As though answering a question, he informed her that he had never married' – as being narrated from her perspective, although it is not a quoted or narrated monologue:

> Apparently, when the lady finally rejected his proposal, Miss Hambro feigned surprise that he was even interested in girls. He laughed heartily at the absurdity of such an error, but she wondered why he was even telling her this tale. In the wake of his disastrous proposal he admitted to having momentarily fallen into a sorrowful state, but his family had encouraged him to regain his mettle. According to his mother, the silly Hambro child was confused, having just lost her own mother, but if the poor foolish child didn't want her son.
>
> (132–3)

It is difficult to know whether the word 'apparently' is part of Gwen's thoughts or the discourse of the narrator. The reference to her 'wondering' makes it clear that the narrator is describing Gwen's thoughts, but the allusion to his 'disastrous proposal' could reflect either Gwen's thoughts or Lancey's words. The reference to his mother's remarks on 'the silly Hambro child' introduces a third source of narration through words repeated by her son. The blurring of narrative boundaries in this passage creates a parallel clouding of the distinction between the characters involved. This in turn makes the questions evoked – disastrous love, mothers and daughters, mothers and sons – stand out in sharp relief without the need for any explicit commentary by the extradiegetic narrator. The characters, without being aware of it, speak for each other. In this instance, the use of a single narrative voice to produce what appears to be a univocal narrative of Rhys's life reveals the fractured perspective involved in Rhys's confrontation with English society. It produces an effect similar to the one suggested by Sylvie Maurel in her analysis of Rhys's use of an autodiegetic narrator in *Good Morning Midnight*. Maurel shows how what might initially appear to be 'a highly homogeneous text with one single addresser in command' (1998: 104–5), 'often forks into two voices, one censoring the other' (106), producing an 'anonymous self in which other voices ceaselessly reverberate' (108).

This process, which appears in many passages in the novel, can be seen as another version of the 'many-tongued chorus' to which Phillips referred in *Crossing the River* ([1993] 1994: 237). Rather than being reflected through a plurality of voices emerging from different times and places, the chorus is situated within the consciousness of a character.[5] This approach permits Phillips to place Rhys's social and cultural position as a white Creole from the Caribbean at the centre of the story through a discreet use of a narrative technique which 'dialogizes' her voice, in the sense referred to by Bakhtin, and makes audible the voices of others in their encounter with hers.[6] At the same time it makes her voice complex in ways that reflect Phillips's understanding of the manner in which Rhys's '"race," "ethnicity," and cultural identifications' were 'interpellated in many everyday contexts' both during her childhood in Dominica, as Sue Thomas demonstrates, and in her European experience (1999: 33). Through a modulation of direct quotation, quoted monologue and narrated monologue as well as psycho-narration, Gwen's encounter with the language of others becomes a mirror of her situation. In a passage in which Gwen is thinking about the way her friend Mabel calls her 'a strange bird', the expression appears first as a comment by the narrator – 'Ethel occasionally called her a strange bird' (*View* 123) – then as a direct quotation of Mabel's words – 'You're a strange bird, Gwennie' (123) – and finally as a metaphor Gwen applies to herself and extends in her own thoughts: 'Eventually she began to think of herself as not only a strange bird but a bird with a broken wing' (124).

Phillips's presentation of Rhys's story through the words of an extradiegetic narrator, beyond permitting the creation of a chorus of voices within that of the narrator, allows him to produce nuances in the choice of language which reflect social, cultural and geographical specificities without thematizing them explicitly. The language spoken in islands of the English-speaking Caribbean has been represented in a variety of ways in fiction, making it possible to perceive the intimate connection between language and individual as well as collective consciousness.[7] Phillips's technique captures language on the threshold between inner consciousness and the outer world, revealing its impact in a way that illuminates the social context. The evocation of the language of the black people of Dominica is a clear example of this strategy. When Gwen's father accompanies her to Bridgetown before her departure for England, the narrator describes the 'local vernacular' of the 'elderly Negro' as 'impossible for her to penetrate' (*View* 64). One of the few direct representations of the speech of blacks in Dominica is found in a passage in which Josephine, the cook, gives Gwen a lesson in hiding her feelings, advising her to 'make [her] eyes dead like so' (29). Her direct advice to Gwen, based on her own experience as a black woman who needs to be able to read the minds of others in order to survive, stands in vivid contrast to the words of Gwen's mother concerning the death of Queen Victoria: '"For heaven's sake," continued her mother, "the Empress has died. Show some respect"' (30). Her mother's remarks reveal the absurdity of a world in which personal behaviour is governed by a distant and abstract relation.[8] The irony is encapsulated by the word 'respect', which hides a confusion in the mother's mind between her attitude towards the Empress and her expectations concerning her children. The mother's words also reflect the vacuity of the colonial world, which in the novel is evoked by the narrator as an anonymous and undefined space through which people move without acquiring a language which would allow them to make sense of their experience. Gwen's mother attends a party hosted by the Colonial Administrator 'before moving on to his new posting in the African territory of Uganda' (47). She hears her father berating 'the new settlers from the colonies of Ceylan and Malaya' who,

> claimed that having successfully tamed nature in their faraway corners of the empire, they intended now to take advantage of the construction of the island's new interior road and buy up accessible acreage in order to 'try out' the West Indies.
>
> (41)

Beyond specific references to the 'colonies', as in the headmistress's remarks to Aunt Clarice (81), the expression of people's attitudes is reinforced by the indirection of the narration itself. Many different places are evoked in a novel describing a world in which colonialism, war and economic conditions provoked numerous displacements. However, like Mr Fresh's reference to the fact that he comes from Canada and that he feels 'trapped' in Britain (161), they are treated as labels attached to characters and do not contribute to the emergence of an alternative perspective. The absence of any dialogue in the short chapter involving Gwen's encounter with Lancey's mother is a synecdoche for the woman's refusal to engage verbally with someone who comes from a place which does not exist in the language she speaks. In the following chapter, the use of direct quotation highlights Lancey's incapacity to understand what a different language – in this case French – expresses. The use of direct quotation allows the narrator to convey the ease with which Lancey expresses his lack of interest in anything that lies outside his limited world: "'Remind me. Do people speak French on your island?'" (166).

If the narrator's discourse serves to represent the ways in which the language of others is perceived by Gwen, it also conveys her reactions through a modulation of outer description and inner consciousness that captures the specificity of her dilemma. Phillips makes little use of narrated monologue (also known as free indirect discourse), preferring psycho-narration in order to maintain a certain ambiguity in the relation between the narrator's words and the thoughts and perceptions of his character. This means that Rhys as a character produces no distinctive language of her own to counter the biased discourse of others. In her discussion of narrated monologue, Cohn emphasizes the way in which this form of narration offers a highly poetic way of exploring the consciousness of a character:

> By leaving the relationship between words and thoughts latent, the narrated monologue casts a peculiarly penumbral light on the figural consciousness, suspending it on the threshold of verbalization in a manner that cannot be achieved by direct quotation.
>
> (1978: 103)

Looking at Hermann Broch's use of narrated monologue in *The Death of Virgil*, she highlights the particular effect produced by the use of this technique to imagine a poetic consciousness:

> But whereas a conjunction of poetic description and monologue is not itself unusual in novels that adopt the *vision avec*, it is rarely so effective and convincing: here the perceiving mind belongs to a creative poet, who would naturally (professionally) transmute the reality he perceives into poetic language – at the very moment when he perceives it.
>
> (Cohn 1978: 125–6)

Phillips chooses not to try to imitate or suggest the emergence of Rhys's poetic language, preferring to present her perceptions in a language belonging to someone else. This is the most significant dimension of his narrative choices in the novel and one that could easily be misunderstood.[9] In her introduction to Rhys's novel *Voyage in the Dark*, a novel that presents many resemblances to Phillips's representation of Rhys's life in England, Carole Angier describes the language of the novel as 'close to poetry': 'With all rational explanation cut, with the past as real as the present, *Voyage in the Dark* is close to poetry. And the main bearer of its meaning is a poetic one: imagery' (2000: x). In *A View of the Empire at Sunset*, the extradiegetic narrator gives both 'rational explanation' and perceived images through the use of psycho-narration. What the narrative voice does not do is suggest the emergence of the poetic language that would give life to images in Rhys's writing, something it could have done through a more intensive use of narrated monologue. Phillips's choice can be partially understood as a way of problematizing Rhys's complex relation to her Caribbean home and its role in her creative development as well as to the English context in which she felt unwelcome and uncomfortable. The inner life to which the narrator provides access through Gwen's perceptions has no language of its own, for the use of narrated monologue would distort the unstable equilibrium between the character and the social context of England, and suggest that she had found words for dealing with it. The gap between perception and language helps to convey the fragmentation that characterizes Gwen's life. Phillips uses two techniques to emphasize the impact of this absence of Gwen's artistic voice.[10] On the one hand, he suggests the existence of black voices capable of expressing a vibrant and immediate reaction to experience, something Gwen seems to envy. On the other hand, he describes Gwen's voice from the outside in a way that transforms it into an element of her estrangement from both others and herself.

In the chapter entitled 'Francine', the narrator describes Gwen's relationship with the daughter of the black man who does yard work for her family. Francine clearly takes the lead in their games and offers Gwen a range of experience and expression that she does not find in her own family:

> Everything with Francine was an adventure, and although she occasionally felt obliged to throw up an objection to her friend's suggestions based on either the weather or the sheer impracticality of the plan, she would invariably have nothing to offer in its place, and so she inevitably capitulated to Francine's schemes.
> (*View* 24)

Francine offers a freedom of expression that contrasts with the rigidity of Gwen's family:

> She sang songs with Francine, the words of which she seldom fully understood, and her friend taught her how to dance with a freedom below her waist that she intuitively understood to be unseemly.
>
> (*View* 24)[11]

In the same way, the black cook Josephine's words in her brief exchange with Gwen represent a strong and direct use of language as an expression of her relation to society. Gwen finds no comparable form of expression in her own family, whose desires are muffled by the conventions of social interaction. Josephine's reaction to the eruption of Mount Pelée in Martinique presents a disturbing but direct expression of emotion which stands in vivid contrast to her father's hesitation concerning the candlesticks he has brought back from the island as a gift for his wife. Although the narrator explains that 'the tiresome cook has intimidated her before' (*View* 38), Josephine's reactions rely on an immediacy of expression that both attracts and repels Gwen. The cook's way of speaking thus offers an inverted image of her father's inarticulateness as well as a mirror image of her own rebelliousness. This is made clear in her later conversation with Mother Mount Calvary, who accuses her of 'trying deliberately to sound like a Negress' (50).

The presentation in Rhys's own fiction of black voices and the culture that they convey as images of an authenticity unavailable to the white characters becomes a metaphor for the women's dilemma. Phillips has grasped the evocative power of a motif used by Rhys herself before the emergence of an awareness of the use to which effects of orality could be put in Afro-Caribbean literature. It signals the importance of the link between voice and identity, the necessity of finding a voice, and at the same time shows that a particular voice, the black Caribbean one, is incompatible with Gwen's hybrid identity as a white Creole.[12] This effect of estrangement is reinforced by the numerous descriptions of Gwen's voice as perceived from the outside, leaving her in a position in which she is isolated from the black Caribbean identity that fascinates her but in which she is also excluded as a foreigner by those in England who do not understand her Caribbean accent. In describing her Aunt Clarice's reaction to the arrival of her niece in England the narrator refers to 'the strange guttural tongue' (*View* 86). When Gwen begins to be involved in theatre productions, the narrator describes her attempts to speak correctly:

In the evenings she would sit alone and push and pull her mouth into the shapes that she had been instructed in at school, and try to speak in a manner which she knew would please her frustrated teachers ('It's pronounced *frawth*, my dear'), but she always felt cripplingly self-conscious and inevitably discontinued the practice.

(100–1)[13]

She is given a chance to join the chorus of a professional musical show, as this 'would offer her the opportunity to display her dramatic skills, but without her having to complicate matters with speech' (*View* 101). Gwen is described as interiorizing people's reaction to her voice to such an extent that it modifies her way of speaking: 'English people seemed to dislike her voice and so she had long accustomed herself to speaking in a whisper, but this meant that her words were often lost in the welter of noise generated by competing conversations' (200). Like Gwen's reactions to black voices, these allusions to the incomprehensibility or the inaudibility of her voice make it possible to disturb the hierarchy of voices through the use of the narrative voice to describe hers. A pattern of fracture and dislocation can be perceived within a narrative discourse that seems to produce fluidity and coherence. Gwen's perceptions do not cohere into patterns reflecting an emerging artistic awareness but remain unmoored. Many of the people that Gwen is described as observing suggest visual images reflecting her own dilemma, but the possible connection remains implicit. The dialogues involving the people with whom Gwen interacts leave her excluded by the misunderstandings that they reveal. Her own voice, perceived from the outside as if it were an adjunct to her physical appearance, remains disconnected from her search for an authentic means of expression. Rather than reinforcing the authority and control of the narrator, this strategy tends to question the authority of all voices, an effect that is reinforced by the use of psycho-narration to describe Gwen's thoughts without clearly using her words. Far from being a passing effect, this tendency to blur the boundary between the narrator's voice and that of the characters is a distinguishing characteristic of the novel. It creates zones of indeterminacy in which the notion of a controlling culture, associated with a dominant omniscient narrator, or a rebellious character, defined by an emerging artistic voice, are neutralized and questioned.

Phillips often relies on an intricate relation between fiction and non-fiction in order to explore the diasporic experience across a wide range of historical and geographical contexts. *A View of the Empire at Sunset* approaches this subject through an interweaving of voices – real, imagined and authorial – that interrogates not only the voices themselves but the way in which they have been represented in fictional and non-fictional texts. His approach may appear to be oblique and ambiguous, as he is often concerned with the way in which people's words and thoughts are influenced by forms of discourse, both oral and written, of which they are not explicitly aware. This use of intertextuality has produced the occasionally naïve voice of Emily Cartwright in *Cambridge* as well as the shockingly detached perspective of James Hamilton as expressed in his ship's log in *Crossing the River* (third section of the novel).

In his fictional portrayal of Jean Rhys, what might appear as an unwillingness to engage directly with the writer and her artistic voice is actually a way of representing the misunderstandings that characterize her perception of herself and more generally people's view of the Caribbean identity in all its complexity. Far from creating an objective distance between Rhys and the narrating voice, it subverts the expectations related to heterodiegetic narrators in both biography and fiction, problematizing the life, both 'inner' and 'outer', of the author in ways that are similar to techniques used by Rhys herself in the creation of her feminine protagonists. Phillips uses psycho-narration in a way that reveals a historical awareness of the role played by narrators in fiction. In her discussion of the development of psycho-narration, Cohn points out that 'with the growing interest in the problems of individual psychology, the audible narrator disappears from the fictional world [...] because a fully developed figural consciousness siphons away the emotional and intellectual energy formerly lodged in the expansive narrator' (1978: 25). Phillips does not try to reinstate the 'audible narrator' to which Cohn refers. His narrative choice suggests rather a different way of approaching the polyphony that characterizes much of his fiction through a narrator who, rather than speaking for the characters, exposes the fractures that make it difficult for them to find their own voices.[14]

Notes

1   The role of Phillips's formal explorations has been recognized by numerous critics. See, for example, Gunning 2012; Ledent 2012; Powell 2012.
2   Yelin takes issue with attempts to define *Dancing in the Dark*: '*Dancing in the Dark* is not a biography. Nor is it a fictionalized biography. To characterize it as a fictional biography [...] flattens the tension that stems, in Woolf's terms, from the incompatibility of the truth of fact and the truth of fiction' (2017: 110).

3   Recent studies of the notion of voice, such as Mladen Dolar's *A Voice and Nothing More* (2006), starting from the emergence of the term in psychoanalysis, have drawn attention to the necessity of avoiding a confusion between the voice as a physical phenomenon and its use as a synonym for personality or opinions, either in an individual or a collective sense. This distinction is especially important in the field of postcolonial studies, where the role of orality, but also the preoccupation with questions of identity, occasionally produces a confusion in the use of the term.

4   'Finally, the narrated monologue is by no means the only method used for rendering consciousness in a figural context: we have already seen that the consonant type of psycho-narration and the unsignaled quoted monologue often supplement, and sometimes supplant, the narrated monologue form' (Cohn 1978: 111).

5   This seems like a simple observation, but it suggests the pertinence of a re-examination of the polyphonic approach found in much postcolonial fiction as well as the validity of casting a backward glance on the aesthetic choices made by Phillips in his novels. For Phillips, as for many novelists, the use of multiple voices may have been in part a reaction to or against the assumptions underlying the use of narrative voices in realist and modernist novels. A remark by Henry James quoted by Cohn in her discussion of narrated monologue gives an idea of what might have disturbed novelists like Phillips in James's attitude: '"A beautiful infatuation this, always, I think, the intensity of the creative effort to get into the skin of the creature, the act of personal possession of one being by another at its completest"' (quoted in Cohn 1978: 115).

6   Bakhtin uses the word 'dialogism' to describe the way in which the meaning of words in actual utterances is affected by the context in which they are used, creating a tension within the word itself which he calls 'the internal dialogism of the word' (1981: 279): 'The word is born in a dialogue as a living rejoinder within it; the word is shaped in dialogic interaction with an alien word that is already in the object. A word forms a concept of its own object in a dialogic way' (279).

7   Sam Selvon's recreation of the English spoken by immigrants from the Caribbean in *The Lonely Londoners* ([1956] 2006) is one of the best-known examples. Robert Antoni gave a fictional representation of speech from Trinidad in *Divina Trace* (1992). Other novelists such as Earl Lovelace, George Lamming and David Dabydeen have integrated varying degrees of creolized speech into their fiction.

8   This absurdity was represented in a very different way by George Lamming in his novel *In the Castle of My Skin* ([1953] 1987) in a scene involving the celebration of Empire Day at school. The children's puzzlement at the way in which the king's head could be reproduced on pennies reflects the absurdity of their relation to the distant monarch (44–6).

9   In her article 'There is always the other side, always', Bénédicte Ledent refers to a remark made by Phillips himself concerning his representation of Rhys and the

absence of reference to her writing, saying 'there is nothing dramatic about the act of writing' (2019: 64). While this is true and the point well made, the decision not to present Rhys's language and art as a response to the dilemmas she faced is more complex than would appear through Phillips's statement. It is also a way of interrogating the nature of the relation between an artist's life and his work, making this relation all the more visible by its absence. Seen in the feminist perspective explored by Maurel, it also constitutes a way of problematizing the emergence of Rhys as a speaking subject in ways that can be compared with Maurel's examination of the different narrative techniques used by Rhys in her fiction to represent 'a crisis within the speaking subject' (1998: 126).

10 While Sylvie Maurel demonstrates how the voice of the autodiegetic narrator of *Good Morning, Midnight* 'forks into two voices' (1998: 106), Phillips's approach shows how the voice of an extradiegetic narrator can also reveal fragmentation.

11 The importance of blacks as the source of forms of expression that stand in contrast to those characterizing the world of whites reflects themes of the same type found in Rhys's fiction. In *Voyage in the Dark* Anna's aunt Hester reproaches her with imitating the speech of 'that dreadful girl Francine': '"I tried to teach you to talk like a lady and behave like a lady and not like a nigger and of course I couldn't do it. Impossible to get you away from the servants. That awful sing-song voice you had. Exactly like a nigger you talked – and still do"' (*VD* 56). In *Wide Sargasso Sea*, Christophine plays a similar role for Antoinette. Her remarks about Antoinette's mother are among the first heard in the novel – 'because she pretty like pretty self' – and Antoinette's mother says in speaking to her husband of the blacks, 'They are more alive than you are' (*WSS* 9, 19).

12 The complexity of Rhys's relation to black voices has been particularly well explored by Sue Thomas in *The Worlding of Jean Rhys*, who describes her use of the voice of Christophine in *Wide Sargasso Sea* as 'a nurturant corporeal presence and memory, a construction with modernist primitive resonances' (1999: 162). In her discussion of black voices in Chapter 5 'The Equivoice of Caribbean Patois and Song' she nonetheless asserts the complexity of these relations seen against the Caribbean background and announces that her argument 'goes back through historicized "social, intellectual and linguistic practices" [quoted from Irigaray *This Sex* 221] to "unravel" [Irigaray] the labyrinthine turnings (Irigaray, *This Sex* 221) of Rhys's representations of African Dominican difference' (96). Sylvie Maurel perceives the voice of Francine as represented in *Voyage in the Dark* as 'a hyperperformative speech act bridging the splits between signifier and signified, sign and referent' (1998: 86), a vision which resembles that suggested by Phillips's presentation of black voices.

13 It is interesting to note the way in which Phillips transformed the reference made by Rhys in *Smile Please* to the pronunciation of 'froth'. In Rhys's text, the conflict

over the pronunciation of the word involves a girl named Honour, who refuses to pronounce the word in the way that Mr Heath, the elocution master, does (*SP* 103). Phillips may have made this change in the interest of a clearer perception of Rhys's voice, particularly in its physical dimension, as something that separates her from others in England. A triangulation of the perception of voice by the reference to another person might have blunted the effect.

14   In Bakhtin's discussions of language in the novel, the musical image of polyphony refers to the languages that characterize 'socially significant world views' (1981: 290) and that the novelist orchestrates: 'When heteroglossia enters the novel it becomes subject to an artistic reworking. The social and historical voices populating language [...] are organized in the novel into a structured stylistic system that expresses the differentiated socio-ideological position of the author amid the heteroglossia of his epoch' (300).

10

'A journey into the familiar underworld': Revisiting Jean Rhys in Caryl Phillips's *A View of the Empire at Sunset*

Catherine Lanone

History dealt me a hand which is the only hand I've ever had to play with. […] So I am interested in people who have had to navigate, the hands they were dealt with, particularly this colonial hand.

—Caryl Phillips[1]

Caryl Phillips's 2018 novel *A View of the Empire at Sunset* explores the colonial hand dealt to Jean Rhys, a writer who shared 'modernist styles and themes' but did 'not quite fit' (Emery 2003: xi). Though Phillips's work mostly explores transnational diasporic black identity (Kral 2017: 77), Phillips was drawn to Rhys, a white Creole who moved from the 'periphery'[2] (the Caribbean island of Dominica, where she grew up) to London and Paris. For Bénédicte Ledent, her 'identity conundrum' may actually match 'the predicament of the second generation of Caribbean writers in England,'[3] 'regardless of the generational, racial and gender differences between them' (2019: 62). Ledent traces the influence of Rhys on Phillips's fiction, from early figures of lonely, alienated women, to his black Heathcliff engaging 'directly with the work of Jean Rhys, intertextually and meta-textually, via the Brontëan connection' (62), pointing to an 'affinity' between the two writers that paves the way for *A View of the Empire at Sunset*. Phillips's 2018 novel engages with bio-fiction, as 'a journey into a familiar underworld' (*View* 177) that revisits Rhys's life while opting for a differential narrative mode; this allows Phillips to address questions of race and gender, of belonging and unbelonging, through the prism of Rhys's only journey back to Dominica.

Modernist bio-fiction: From Rhys to Gwen

Susan Stanford Friedman notices that many twenty-first-century artists tend to engage with Modernism, recycling it to pass it on and challenge it at the same time. She argues that returning to the past is a way of rethinking it, turning it over 'as a precondition for imagining the future' (Stanford Friedman 2018: 6). *A View of the Empire at Sunset* recycles material from Rhys's fragmented autobiography, *Smile Please*, and echoes her transposition of her life in novels such as *Voyage in the Dark* and *After Leaving Mr Mackenzie*. Therefore, writing a novel about Jean Rhys's life raises interesting questions of genre. Marie-Luise Kohlke identifies three kinds of bio-fiction: celebrity bio-fiction, the bio-fiction of the marginal subject, and appropriated bio-fiction (2013: 4). Jean Rhys slips between such categories; are we to consider her as a marginal subject – an estranged wanderer trapped in second-class hotels, whose voice must be retrieved – or are we to consider her as a canonical writer, since *Wide Sargasso Sea* has had a lasting influence on critical theory – from Sandra Gilbert and Susan Gubar's *The Madwoman in the Attic* or Gayatri Chakravorty Spivak's subaltern onward? And what space is there for bio-fiction, when Rhys herself is famous for slippages between life and fiction? Indeed, her fiction tends to be read as 'quasi-autobiography' (Johnson 2006: 563). Besides, Rhys resisted tampering with her life's story and masculine versions of herself; for Sylvie Maurel, *Quartet* is a subversive meta-text (1998: 26) writing back to Ford Madox Ford's version of their affair. Rhys even resented David Plante's attempt to order her memories when she dictated *Smile Please*, an autobiography which strangely echoes the novels, like a kind of 'auto-ghostwriting' (Johnson 2006: 563). Writing bio-fiction, in the case of Rhys, is thus a daring proposition. This compels Caryl Phillips to slip between and betwixt genres, attempting a new kind of genre, a new kind of bio-fiction, for which perhaps no category exists as yet, the bio-fiction of the marginal, canonical, self-writing author.

Surprisingly, given the available textual palimpsest, Phillips describes Rhys in his interview with Als as 'somebody who is extremely adept at hiding their emotions, *extremely* adept, and her emotions are very bruised, and very primary, so in order to find that person, you're doing more excavation than perhaps you realize you have to do' (Als and Phillips 2018). To search for the hidden side of Rhys, Phillips peels back her gift as a writer.[4] For instance, Leslie, her husband, is presented as her editor, but his one significant gesture consists in planning the trip back to the Caribbean. Similarly, the novel does not include the core epiphany of *Smile Please*, the 'red, blue, green and yellow' quill pens (*SP* 103) found in a stationer's shop, which bring back colours into the dull grey of England – 'Rhys's personal palette' (Savory 1998: 16) that mingles poetics and the politics of colour, encoding Rhys's way out of hegemonic discourse.

This does not mean that Phillips fails to acknowledge the unique quality of her writing. The novel opens with the protagonist 'standing in deep shadow in their lacklustre Bloomsbury living room' (*View* 4). Location manifests the way in which Rhys was unfairly eclipsed by a canonical Bloomsbury figure – Virginia Woolf. Phillips suggests that Rhys was relegated to the fringes of literary London, not because she was less talented but because she was devoid of Woolf's connections, of her status and 'cultural capital', to use Bourdieu's term (2006: 257).

Yet for Phillips, writing is a performance, 'an act of self-reinvention' (Als and Phillips 2018). Distancing Rhys the writer (he calls her 'that Williams Girl' [*View* 46], Gwendolen, Gwen or Gwennie, never Jean Rhys), Phillips withdraws certain iconic episodes, like those involving Ford Madox Ford (thankfully so, given how much has been written about the affair already).[5] Whereas one might have expected the novel to deal with the period when Rhys vanished from the charts and worked on *Wide Sargasso Sea*, Phillips loops back instead to her childhood, and ends with the journey to the Caribbean, signposting Dominica as origin, destination and destiny. Rather than Rhys the writer, *A View of the Empire at Sunset* seeks to explore Gwen's 'complex positionality as a colonial Caribbean British subject' (Johnson and Moran 2015: 2).

Indeed, Phillips explains that he went to Paris and London to retrace Rhys's steps, but it was only when he travelled to Dominica that the novel fell into place: 'Unless you looked at her through the prism of Dominica, you couldn't see her. That's when it began to cohere into some kind of a shape' (Als and Phillips 2018). That 'shape', with its episodic series of 'sixty-five vignettes' or 'narrative islands' (Ledent 2019: 65), recalls the structure of *Smile Please*, while including 'misleading yet very Phillipsian headings as "Going Home" and "Home," almost antinomic indicators in view of Gwen's vagrant existence' (65). The novel opens in London, when Leslie, who has just received a legacy, suggests that they should go to Dominica and the eponymous sunset first appears in Gwen's interior monologue. The paronomasia 'show'/'share' is tinged with irony and longing, as Gwen hopes that the discovery of the Caribbean may allow her to connect with her husband at last:

I will show you the rivers and the mountains, and come evening, as the New World day convulses towards dusk, I will share with you a spectacular elevated view of the empire at sunset. Perhaps, my husband, if I show you the West Indies, then you will finally come to understand that I am not of your world.

(*View* 15)

The convulsive dusk connotes a poignant last chance; at the same time, the ironic twist on the tourist cliché, the 'spectacular elevated view of the empire at sunset', fulfils a metatextual function. Taking a view of the empire at sunset reminds us that the novel resonates with the troubled 1930s and with Britain today, convulsively poised on the brink of Brexit and shunning Europe.

The next section is called 'Home', but the projected journey does not take place yet; instead we switch back to Gwen's childhood, plunging into the early sensory experience of a 'home' where she never quite belongs either. Phillips probes into this othering of the colonial subject through a series of vignettes that offer mirror images of displacement, like the kind Irish nun, who is dying in a cold dilapidated house, or Francine, a young black servant who is dismissed by Gwen's mother. As the tension between mother and daughter grows, Gwen is evicted from the island and sent to England. In 'Performance', Phillips engages with her life as a chorus girl (which is not surprising if we think of *Dancing in the Dark;* for Kerry-Jane Wallart, Phillips 'plays with theatrical conventions and remains at heart a playwright and amateur director' [2016: 174]). Costume is part of Gwen's performance as a chorus girl and as a woman (she longs for new clothes for the trip to Dominica in the opening scene of the novel); this recalls how, in Rhys's work, dresses connote fashion (see Chapter 8 in this volume for a closer study of Rhys and fashion), financial means and problematic social status but also role-playing, disguise and dissimulation, seduction and vulnerability. Besides, feminine identity is a performance that Gwen cannot quite get the hang of either. In 'The Island Simply Doesn't Exist' (*View* 93), Harry, her lover, tries to find Dominica on the map, but it is divided into French and Spanish halves, and 'on the second map, it appeared that her island simply didn't exist' (99). The phrase mocks Eurocentrism and the colonial construction of empire: split identity, alienation and erasure are marked by the lacunae of imperial cartography. This also turns England into a non-place, where there is no I/land (in Hilton Als's interview, Phillips explains that the cruellest thing that can happen to a person is to be in a place where people fail to recognize *who* you are, leading to 'a coruscation of the soul, of the spirit' [Als and Phillips 2018]). After the 'Continental Drift' in Paris, and the visit to her daughter in Holland ('Two Journeys'), the journey that was foreshadowed in the opening section finally takes place ('All at Sea'). The novel ends with the departure from Dominica, 'A Now Empty World', a moment which is both ontological and metatextual.

Shadowing *Smile Please*, Phillips's novel thus plays on déjà-vu to create a kind of 'rhizomatic' connection with Rhys's own texts (Deleuze 1987: 3–25).[6] But Jean Rhys's signature style is terse, ironic and blooms into sudden rhythmical images. Caryl Phillips avoids mimicry. The novel opens in medias res:

> The bleak afternoon had been made all the more dispiriting by having to overhear Leslie on the telephone busying himself with his attempts to make arrangements for their potential sea voyage. Finally, her husband sat down heavily in the armchair and began to annoy her by continually seeking reassurance that the recent misunderstanding between them was now resolved.
>
> (*View* 3)

Leslie is named, but not Gwen, yet he is referred to as 'her husband', who annoys 'her'. The rift built by pronouns is widened by stiff verbs such as 'inform', suggesting Leslie's stilted inability to reach out to her at the very moment when he is trying to: 'He informed her that he had some inkling of how much it might mean to her to reacquaint herself with her island. Was a West Indian sea voyage something that she might consider?' (7). Phillips's take on the breach in communication does not aim for modernist style but for a rendering of what John Su calls the affect of empire that freezes fluidity (Su 2015: 184). Even kindness is a mode of interpellation to which the colonial subject cannot respond.

Interpellation: Race and the empire at sunset

For Judith Butler, 'interpellation' – a concept she borrows from French Marxist philosopher Louis Althusser – is a speech act which hails the subject into a subservient position (1993: 121). In *A View of the Empire at Sunset*, such 'interpellation' begins in childhood, when for instance, Mother Mount Calvary tells Gwen, who is about to be sent to England against her will, that people in England find all West Indian women 'aggravating, droning on at length about the virtues of their climate and the lushness of their vegetation' (*View* 51). She also mocks her accent: '"I'm sorry Mother Mount Calvary." She heard the nun mimic her voice. "Tell me, are you trying deliberately to sound like a Negress?"' (50).

Her aunt Clarice uses a similar racist insult, accusing her of wearing her hair 'like a golliwog' (*View* 86). In *Smile Please*, the golliwog is the black doll that Rhys wants as a small child, just as she wakes up in the morning praying to be black. Phillips appropriates and displaces the image of the black doll.[7] Both Mother Mount Calvary and Aunt Clarice differ from their counterparts in *Smile Please*, to define the plight of 'the immigrant girl' (*View* 82) as colonial, even though her skin is white. In Britain, she sees 'daylight falling and coming to rest in long blue and red streaks on the stone pavement' (79), a variation on the sunset motif and a parody of the British flag. Because of her in-betweenness, she is mocked by the other girls at school. They call her a monkey, turning her nostalgia into an insult, a nickname ('Dear West Indies'; 77): "'We don't understand what you are saying." "Do you speak English?"' (79). Her accent mars her career as a chorus girl.

Just as there is no English motherland, there is no proper mother in the West Indies. In the following excerpt, the shift from 'mother' to 'woman' connotes the sense of estrangement between the frustrated mother and the defiant child:

> When she glanced up again, her mother was angrily stripping the pink hat from her head, and the woman now declared that she would wait until her husband had returned from his duties at the hospital in order that she might urgently inform him of how appallingly his daughter had behaved.
>
> (*View* 48)

The use of 'inform' is here laced with betrayal; 'urgently' is less a temporal marker than a warning that the husband is to be summoned, and forced to choose between his wife and his daughter, prompting him to pass the sentence of exile: 'the thought of leaving the island was impossible for her to grasp. And for England?' (50).

The mother is presented as an active agent of the empire, obsessed with social performance. For instance, she organizes a formal tea party in honour of the death of Queen Victoria, but Gwen shuns the semi-official ritual. She hides into a mango tree, observing the paradigmatic view at sunset, her metonymic family microcosm celebrating the empire (her mother steering conversation, the flitting shadows of ladies taking tea, her isolated father drinking whiskey elsewhere), and the surrounding landscape and soundscape:[8]

> Dusk fell at the same time each evening, and did so swiftly, as though an expert finger and thumb were snuffing out a candle. Thereafter, a theatre of noise established itself as the air was filled with a discordant fracas of cicadas and frogs. She listened attentively, while, to both sides of her, bats began to swoop and whistle around the mango tree.
>
> (*View* 31)

The mango tree, with its surrounding natural and social 'theatre of noises', is a place of *dissensus*, in Rancière's sense of the word (an antonym for *consensus*, it accommodates the silenced noises of the imperial theatre of knowledge and power, underscoring its violence as a forceful 'distribution of the sensible' [Rancière 2004: 7]). The mango tree encapsulates for Phillips the attachment to the West Indies. As he puts it, 'she did not know what an oak tree was. She knew what a mango tree was' (Als and Phillips 2018). Here Phillips redeploys the mango tree that appears in 'The Day They Burned the Books', connoting the lush fertility of Dominica, with the lovely red and yellow hues of its tasty fruit,[9] the colours of sunset. While the mother's rule is firmly posited as colonial mimicry,[10] Gwen seeks to root herself on the island, with ambiguous results: while mocking her, calling her a monkey and partly siding with the mother they resent, the black servants praise her hybrid inability to fit in: 'It look to me like Miss Gwendolen catch somewhere between coloured and white' (*View* 32).

The view from the tree is significantly interpolated between two moments that sever Gwen's bond with Francine, her black friend.[11] As opposed to the fake mourning of the passing of the Empress Victoria, the separation from Francine and from her own father are instances of symbolic violence and of a loss that cannot be articulated. At first, the friendship with Francine allows racial boundaries to become more fluid and to free the body; Gwen sings and dances with Francine, with a 'freedom below her waist' that contradicts the mother's insistence on decorum, a freedom that her performance as a chorus girl will not bring back:

> One week they might allow themselves by crawling around the empty marketplace on all fours playing 'zoo'; the following week Francine might suggest a sandy spot by the bayfront that would be perfect for them to once again play castaway and native, with Francine always assuming the role of the tragically helpless castaway.
>
> (*View* 24)

The game allows a brief Bakhtinian carnivalesque inversion, subverting the rhetoric of colonial conquest with its ironic echo of *Robinson Crusoe*. As the girls experiment with colonial boundaries, they return with dusty clothes. Cleanliness and dirt are part of colonial discourse. As Anne McClintock puts it, 'Victorian cleaning rituals were peddled globally as the God-given sign of Britain's evolutionary superiority and soap was invested with magic, fetish power' (1995: 207). When Mother Mount Calvary blames Gwen's accent, 'commodity racism' and the judgement passed by the community on the friendship with Francine reappear: 'I hope you understand that a bad reputation can't be washed away with soap and water' (*View* 50). Though the relationship has been severed, for female figures of authority, Gwen remains tainted by racial intercourse. Phillips expands on the scenario presented in *Smile Please*, where Rhys wonders why Francine vanished and their friendship came to a sudden end, concluding that perhaps the girl never truly liked her. In Phillips's version, the mother bides her time, offering them drinks, before her sudden strike: 'Sunlight slanted through the jalousies and cast an oddly striped pattern across the floor, and she listened as her mother stepped out into the yard' (*View* 26). The steps and the stripes compose an alliterative prison, while the 'slanted sunlight' and the 'jalousies' connote the mother's spite and oblique violence. With a 'sugar-coated voice' (26), a tone that her daughter and Francine have never heard but one that Francine's father is 'attuned to' (26) and quick to detect, the mother prevents Francine from ever seeing Gwen, restoring racial barriers and severing friendship with one sharp blow.

The blow is dealt when Francine brings a puppy on a leash, a mongrel which delights Gwen – whereas for her mother, presumably, it stands for mixed identity and going native. Throughout the novel, the dog becomes a motif, hovering on the edge of vision, as a kind of lost double. When Gwen greets her father on his return from Martinique, a hungry dog walks 'jauntily beside them with the devil-may-care air of a nomad' (*View* 36). When she longs to plead with her father not to be sent to England, they sit in silence listening 'to the sound of a solitary dog barking' (52). It is significant that the term 'mongrel' (156) should come to Lancey's mind to define her, suggesting that though there is a modicum of rebellion against his mother, he still relies, unawares, upon hegemonic discourse and social and racial prejudices. In the end, when she visits her father's grave for the first time, she sees 'a mongrel bounding excitedly through the tombstones with a carefree glee illuminating its yellow eyes' (320). As E.M. Forster once put it, we are all mongrels.[12] The way in which Gwen notices stray dogs shows her kinship with the land, and reveals, simultaneously, the judgement which is passed on her connection with Dominica and the way in which people reject her as hybrid and (un)belonging.

Because the free, hungry dog is associated with both Gwen's father and Francine, it is significant that a stone should be cast, as at a stray animal, to signal the closure of the connection. Phillips revisits the split between Tia and Antoinette which takes place in Rhys's *Wide Sargasso Sea*, but he makes the white girl, not the black one, cast the stone. In the opening paragraph of 'The

Day Trip' (*View* 33), Gwen lets in the 'young girl from across the street' and leaves the covered veranda, a significant liminal space in Creole material culture. The girl is unnamed, and the colour unmentioned at first. The reader is left to wonder whether this is Francine; if so, the use of pronouns and indeterminate terms constructs the characteristic inner distance which reveals that Gwen is no longer able to identify, or rather identify with, her friend. With its prescribed movements, hopscotch is a far cry from the former games loosening body and mind. The black girl suddenly gives up and calls Gwen a 'white cockroach' (33). The inverted commas recall the intertextual link with *Wide Sargasso Sea*, and signal the force of interpellation which challenges embodiment, recasting the mongrel's hybridity as white abjection. Gwen casts a stone which misses and is scolded by the angry cook, Josephine. From then on, she fails to come close to the black figures she occasionally glimpses on the edge of her vision, in the streets of London; similarly, in one of the boarding houses, she hears a black performer practice but fails to see or meet her. Literally struck off by social invisibility, Venus, the black performer, is both the other and a double of the hybrid Gwen.[13]

Revising historiography

Interestingly enough, the moment when Gwen is called a 'white cockroach' and is forced to enter the crippling categories of colonial epistemology, is fused by Phillips with the eruption of Mount Pelée. Gwen wishes to tell her father about the insult but is silenced by his grim return from Martinique. Phillips plays on two images, the island's green skin that has been peeled back and the molten brass candelabra retrieved by the father from the ruins of a church – 'small gnarled', disfigured 'candlesticks' (*View* 36). We may think here of the powder compact that for Molly Pulda functions as an iconic image in *Smile Please* – unable to flaunt the beautiful one given by her lover, Rhys uses the old compact she is ashamed of, a token of her inability to fit in, of her shabby objectified self, the victim of mirrors and of the gendered imperial gaze: 'Most of the gilt had worn off and the black underneath showed' (*SP* 93). In *A View of the Empire at Sunset*, the twisted candelabra may perform a similar part and be considered as an iconic image of colonial disfiguration. The sudden blast of heat is in part an objective correlative for the split between Gwen and Francine, induced by the mother's sugary voice. Phillips juxtaposes the insult and the eruption, placing the conflict between Gwen and Francine in a wider colonial perspective. Lizabeth Paravisini-Gebert finds it surprising that Rhys should not have mentioned the eruption in *Smile Please* or in her novels, and that a brief short story, 'Heat', should be 'the only text in which Rhys addresses an event that was unquestionably the most momentous and devastating event of her childhood' (Paravisini-Gebert 2007: 13). For Paravisini-Gebert, 'Heat' is a case of 'traumatic amnesia, paradoxically narrated from the site of history' (19), an 'emotional defence against pain and mourning' (19) as the child sleeps through the catastrophe while the parents attempt to foster a memory of the event (the mother draws the child to the window to see the cloud, the father hangs the candlesticks on the wall).

Phillips's text further pares down the account; instead of depicting the shroud of ash covering Roseau, he imagines the father's return in terms of a gendered split – the mother does not come to wait for him (she is asleep and will not care for the candelabra) so that Gwen becomes the recipient of the twisted form. For all of the father's horror, the response of the rescue party is inadequate. The men are slightly drunk, and 'chatter excitedly' (*View* 34). The white response seems hardly more relevant than the black interpretation of God's wrath unleashed against the Paris of the Antilles and its loose women. Badiou defines an event as the irreversible split between a before and an after, and it is definitely such a fault line that the father so clearly feels: 'Can you believe that thirty thousand people were stifled by just one deadly cloud?' (36). While drawing father and daughter together, the scene is an oblique comment on colonial failure. If Phillips chooses to include the eruption in the novel, opting for the aftermath rather than direct dramatization, it may be because he wishes his readers to engage with the historical context. For although the eruption was unavoidable and the damage that could be done by a pyroclastic surge was unknown at the time, Mount Pelée's eruption still stands as a case of misplaced authority and colonial blindness. Because elections were due to take place, scientists were commissioned to proclaim that there was no impending danger. The Governor of Martinique, Louis Mouttet, ignored the volcano's increasing signs of activity and even went to stay in St Pierre, sitting just 7 kilometres from Mount Pelée. Newspapers published reports of safety, encouraging ships and people not to leave. Mouttet and his wife perished when the eruption swallowed the largest city in Martinique in the early hours of 8th May. In Phillips's novel, Gwen's father is appalled by what he has seen, by his own helplessness when walking among the 'smouldering heap of black ruins', and by 'the ghastly stench of rotting flesh' (*View* 35). Burial was out of the question in the sickening stench, and the 'black ruins' designate the erasure of the city, but also the number of black casualties far out-ranking the number of dead among the whites. With his inadequate bout of catastrophe tourism, the doctor brings back a souvenir that can be of no use: 'spent a whole day scrambling about in mud, but to what purpose?' (36). Reintroducing and repurposing the scene which was missing in *Smile Please*, Phillips expresses the trauma of history through a shape that cannot and should not make sense, like the twisted candelabra.

Gendered relationships: Father and lovers

The evocation of the aftermath of the eruption has gendered overtones. Phillips grants his Gwen a much closer relationship to her father than is the case in *Smile Please*. But Gwen's father, a doctor and a European migrant, is also weak. By surmising that the candelabra was brought back for her rather than for her mother's sake, the girl seeks confirmation of her relationship to her father, but the sign foreshadows the melting down of the connection.

The crushed connection is also signified by the coral brooch damaged by the father's last hug. The coral is a colonial trope, a marine animal that looks like vegetation, a hybrid like Gwen. In *Smile Please*, the brooch was actually given by the father. In Phillips's novel, the drunken father is unable to face this departure, though he was equally unable to resist his wife's will. The hug comes at the end of the journey taken by father and daughter, as he accompanies her to the ship bound for England; they watch pelicans dive as if united by an invisible thread, a symbol of the bond between them. The crushed brooch signifies a rupture of that bond. This breach is tentatively mended at the end, when the adult Gwen visits her father's tomb in Dominica and carefully cleans the epitaph with her handkerchief, 'so that new life was affectionately rubbed into each word' (*View* 321). The letters and the handkerchief replace or soothe absent tears.

Like the candelabra, the image of the green skin of the land peeled back by the eruption, to reveal ashy layers beneath, may be metatextual. Phillips's novel strips Rhys of the green layers of her writer's persona. *A View of the Empire at Sunset* is a dialogue with whatever or whoever lies beneath, not Rhys the flamboyant, terse writer but 'She', Gwennie or Gwendolyn, a misfit who is much less articulate when faced with lonely hotel rooms, who is often struck dumb by her position on the margins of society, not simply a jilted woman but also a woman who has to contend with imperfect husbands. Trapped in the part of the colonial other, Gwen is unable to relate to Leslie. The novel gives interesting glimpses of the other side: Leslie's, dismayed by his inability to provide his wife with what she might want and by her cantankerous addiction to drink, and Lancey's, who attempts to introduce Gwen to his world, yet proves unable to rise up to the challenge and remains daunted by his social peers.[14] At the end of the novel, Lancey makes a comeback in a dream (an ironic version of the burning dream of *Wide Sargasso Sea*) as a white-haired old man who gives Gwen pearls (*View* 303), a fantasy of compensation which also suggests that he too was the victim of social constraints and prejudices, or to use Jacqueline Rose's expression, of the 'straitjacket of symbolic forms' (1986: 157). 'There is always the other side, always', as Rhys puts it in *Wide Sargasso Sea* (81).

The dream suggests a 'decolonial epistemic shift' or de-linking (Mignolo 2007: 453) from the 'colonial matrix of power' (455) and its construction of romance. Phillips opts for elliptic moments to convey turning points rather than a more explicit stream of consciousness. In a short chapter entitled 'Christmas', Gwen is overwhelmed by the wound of Lancey's absence and by her sense of shame ('It was shameful. That was it, shame' [*View* 175]) before she begins to 'swim back to the world' (175). The cry of Mabel, her friend from the chorus line, 'You should have let me know' (175) leaves the reader to construe the scene as an abortion or a suicide attempt. In a chapter ironically entitled 'Knight in shining armour', Jean Lenglet, the husband who has abandoned her, suddenly reappears to criticize the dingy hotel room (the thin partition makes sex in the next room quite graphic). Again, the woman is silenced and shamed: 'And what is the child witnessing?' (224). Yielding, letting her daughter go for her own sake, she switches off the light: 'She snakes out a hand and turns off the bedside lamp, plunging the room into a semi-darkness that can never fully close to blackness because of the luminous moonlight' (224). The natural light brings in 'blackness', a term which connects the abduction of the child with the separation from Francine. It is also a metaphor for the conscious attempt to switch off the brain, while the subconscious grief still palely illuminates the mind. The odd verb 'snakes' suggests that the emotion is one of betrayal, while the man's return leads further away from all possible respite or Eden. The loss of a child is a familiar theme in Phillips's work.[15] Here, there is a parallel between the daughter's sense of loss, which cannot be articulated, and the father's implied sadness, when he accompanies his daughter to Barbados but fails to go all the way to England, or even to prevent her departure: 'His daughter was gone. His dear Gwendolen was on her way to England' (66).

The prism of Dominica

If there is a deep affinity between Jean Rhys and Caryl Phillips, it is perhaps best seen in the final section of the novel, when the deferred trip finally takes place. Yet once separation has occurred, it is impossible to turn back: 'there is no return', as Caryl Phillips puts it in *Crossing the River* ([1993] 1994: 2). The impossible return is at the heart of *Smile Please*. One of the goals of the journey is Geneva, the estate where, as a child, Rhys found solace with her Great Aunt Jane. The latter did not mind her bad sewing and gave her a cardboard dollhouse, a metonymic image of a home; yet the connection was severed by a family feud which the child could not understand. However, attempting to revisit Geneva only brings further loss. In Rhys's autobiography, alienation is instanced by the fact that the path is blocked (she needs a guide) and that everything has been erased:

> The only time I went back to Dominica, long afterwards, I was told I must have a guide to visit Geneva.
> I thought, 'A guide to Geneva for *me*? How ridiculous!' However there was a guide, we went quickly by car and he seemed to know exactly where to take me. Where the house had been was an empty space, the Geneva house was burnt down two, or was it three, times. I stared at it trying to remember the house, the garden, the honeysuckle and the jasmine and the tall fern trees.
> But there was nothing, nothing. Nothing to look at. Nothing to say. Even the mounting stone had gone.
>
> (*SP* 37–8)

While the polysyndeton seeks to conjure up the flowers, the scene is the opposite of a Proustian mode of recovery; the sensory appeal fails, even the stone is gone, so that there is no cornerstone on which to rebuild the Proustian edifice of memory. Like a mournful tune, the anaphoric repetition of 'nothing' strikes a blank. Geneva is a miniature Troy, a place that has been burnt down, a memory site stripped of its palimpsest. The only function of the guide is to deny access to the past, to prevent any return, any bodily connection to the long-lost land:

> When we got to the river I bent down and sipped from it. I was very thirsty and perhaps had some vague, superstitious idea that if I drank the water I'd come back. The guide caught my arm and said, 'Don't drink that. It's very dirty now. You'd be ill if you drank it.'
>
> (*SP* 38)

The river is the stream of life that might allow communion with the place, or a kind of Lethe: 'if I drank the water I'd come back'. There is no crossing to the other side of time, beyond oblivion: 'No, it wasn't as I remembered it' (38). Rhys wonders if the 365 streams of the island are polluted, a figure that brings to mind the days of the year rather than geography, suggesting both Heraclitean flux (you can never step in the same river twice), ecological 'present-day degradation' 'from modern development' (Kalaidjian 2020: 152) and colonial displacement: the migrant is alienated from the home that has vanished, from the land, and nostalgia (or longing to drink the motherland's water) is poisonous.

The inability to return home, the sense of perpetual displacement, are at the heart of Caryl Phillips's work. His characters are migrants torn from their origins, desperately trying to '[sink] hopeful roots into difficult soil' ([1993] 1994: 1) and haunted by the sense that 'there is no return' (2). His version of the return to Dominica focuses not only on the migrant's inability ever to return home but on the inability to share the complex experience of the past. Failing to communicate fascinates him. Whereas Gwen longs in the first section to open up her husband's eyes and share the island with him, the final section is a comedy of errors. Two islands are ironically contrasted, 'Leslie's England', the pastoral landscape of cows and sheep familiar to him, which they catch sight of in a shroud of mist as they depart, and the beautiful Dominica whose woods and streams Gwen gazes at as the boat is leaving in the end.

Leslie's love of pastoral landscapes does not bode well. Besides, whereas in *Smile Please* Rhys describes her niece or a Caribbean servant, the journey seems packed with Eurocentric figures, like the snob on the voyage out who praises Hitler (reminding the reader that the thirties, politically speaking, were also a crepuscular time), the couple with whom they stay in Roseau (with the wife looming large over her diminutive husband, who plays the piano but not German composers), or the Napiers, neocolonial white hosts who send their chauffeur – the wife is a social pusher while the husband displays his First World War medals. Whereas Leslie is at ease with such people, he cannot bear giving money to Owen's illegitimate children, though for Gwen meeting them was a key part of her visit. He also takes snapshots of Dominica. The path to Geneva seems both refreshing and the underworld of shades ('Entering a shaded region was like being doused by a waterfall' [*View* 306]), then there is a blank, like a fade to white, and the text switches to Gwen's annoyance as Leslie is taking pictures of the 'damn fine view' (307). Floriane Reviron-Piégay discusses the role of photographs in *Smile Please* (the title itself and the opening description refer to a photograph being taken of Rhys as a child, and photographs are actually included in the book) and warns us that we

> cannot but remember Susan Sontag's warning that 'there is something predatory in the act of taking a picture' ([*On Photography* (1971):] 14), and the use of these pictures is reminiscent of Plante's avowal in his memoir that he sometimes felt as if he were stealing her manuscripts and letters from her, dispossessing her of her identity as a writer.
>
> (Reviron-Piégay 2018: 6)

Phillips's text explores this inherent ambivalence of photographs. Leslie's clichés clash with Gwen's sense of absence, voiced by the brief description at the end of the chapter and the simple question, which echoes *Wide Sargasso Sea*, 'Why don't they like us?' (*View* 307). Here Phillips replaces Rhys's elegiac rhythm with a study of dual alienation, from the place and from her husband. Leslie takes pictures like a tourist or a voyeur, not realizing that the luscious place is the tomb of the past. Gwen herself fails to connect: ultimately, when a black man recognizes her as she wipes her father's tomb, she refuses to speak to him, only wishing to give him a few coins to tip him off.

Phillips's novel offers us new lines of transmission, reading Rhys with sympathy rather than empathy. Phillips sees as a major flaw the fact that Carole Angier did not deem it necessary to travel to Dominica to write her landmark biography; for him, there can be no understanding of Rhys's life and works without Dominica (Als and Phillips 2018). *A View of the Empire at Sunset* thus seeks to redress the map of her life by adopting a decolonial perspective, considering not Rhys the writer but Gwendolen the migrant, an unfixed diasporic subject in transit: 'The thing that she was most fearful of was this very problematic word in the English language, which is "home", where is home and can you ever return home' (Phillips 2018b; my transcription). By positioning the book as a prequel to the long gestation of *Wide Sargasso Sea,* its publication and aftermath, Phillips distances himself from the postcolonial debate that surrounds it. Indeed, while Rhys writes back to *Jane Eyre,* Spivak has argued that she fails to encompass Christophine's alternative epistemology, while Veronica Gregg claims that Christophine plays the stereotypical part of the good black servant, and that she is silenced by Rhys's 'racialist usurpation of the voices, acts and identities of "black people"' (Gregg 1995: 25). Following writers such as Derek Walcott and Olive Senior, who have claimed kinship with Rhys as a Caribbean writer, Phillips simply urges us to see Rhys 'through the prism of Dominica' (Als and Phillips 2018) and to feel, as Sue Thomas puts it, the importance of her Caribbean childhood since: 'paradoxically, her lifelong sense of homelessness begins there' (Thomas 1999: 32). At the same time, the portrait of Gwen sketched by Phillips is no eulogy and draws attention to the margins of the gaze. The final trip is the matrix of *Wide Sargasso Sea* – the novel which, diegetically, was still to be written[16] – but also of Phillips's novel, which we have just read. At the beginning of the last section, Gwen gets up early in Roseau to watch 'the sun rising over her now empty world' (*View* 299). Now, in the end, at dusk, she leaves this 'empty world' where the traces of the family estate have been erased and her father is buried. Like the hummingbird,[17] 'in a beating hurry to drink the last drops of nectar before dark', she watches not the empire but the island, with its mountain range, 'suffused' with unrequited love for the place, 'the kind of love that it is impossible to explain to another person' (324). Phillips leaves her as she leaves a piece of her heart behind, and becomes part of what Gilroy calls 'the Black Atlantic' (1993), the transitional space and time of migrants, regardless of the colour of their skin. Those who remain on land (the reader included) may watch the ship move along the launch, 'where it would eventually slip out of sight and tumble down into a landless, watery world' (323).

Notes

1 Caryl Phillips in Conversation with Hilton Als (2018). The interview is later referred to as Als and Phillips 2018.
2 The terms 'centre' and 'periphery' are used by Phillips in his conversation with Hilton Als.
3 They are perceived neither as canonical English writers nor as fully Caribbean writers.
4 To quote *Smile Please*: 'I must write. If I stop writing my life will have been an abject failure. It is that already to other people' (163).
5 Phillips also refuses to sensationalize her addiction to alcohol. The reader sees her drink, hide or throw her bottles, but this is toned down compared to Angier's biography.
6 Deleuze and Guattari use the image of the multiple root or rhizome to oppose arborescent, binary knowledge and offer instead a non-hierarchical model with multiple entries, heterogeneous connections and asignifying ruptures, a map rather than a tracing. While many episodes in the novel draw upon *Smile Please* or Rhys's novels, Phillips also novelizes her life by adding scenes of his own, such as the carriage and pub scene, in order to convey her vulnerability: 'What you are really

trying to get right is the psychological temperature, the psychological barometer of that person' (Ledent, Phillips and Tunca 2019: 3).

7   Phillips shows Aunt Clarice's instinctive dislike of her niece, yet they only differ in degree, both performing a part for a lover who simply uses them. Clarice reminisces about being infatuated with a certain Nicholas and the girls at school calling her 'knicker-less'. Her lover's response shows sexual arousal, a lack of empathy and a wish to shame all at once: 'What do you think the girls would call you if they could see you now?' (*View* 90).

8   There is a sensory dimension to the landscape, but Phillips is also wary of exotic descriptions that might 'orientalise' Dominica, and he seeks to avoid the Romantic 'landscape function' of the wilderness, 'the imbrication of nature and culture' that Carine Mardorossian reads in *Wide Sargasso Sea*, in the light of Michel Foucault (Mardorossian 2015: 112).

9   Savory points to Rhys's 'vocabulary of tropical trees' in her Caribbean stories (Savory 2015: 98). In 'The Day They Burned the Books', the outside tree contrasts with the books enshrining English culture within the house, and more specifically with Wordsworth's archetypal poem about daffodils, a flower which the two children have never seen. Rhys recasts colonial mimicry and exclusion, as the boy, Ed, rejects the poem, foreshadowing Kincaid's or Spivak's reading of the daffodils as the cornerstone of imperial culture. In *Crossing the River*, Travis offers daffodils to Joyce, and they lay a bunch on her mother's tomb. Travis does not know the flowers' name and only responds to colour. Rejecting imperial discourse, *Crossing the River* appropriates the daffodils and redeploys the motif. In *A View of the Empire at Sunset*, the mango tree echoes the debate between cultural imperialism and indigenous vegetation. By climbing the tree, the girl adopts a position that is both marginalized and radical.

10 The scene is furthered by Gwen's refusal to go to Bell's party, whereas she is happy to do so in *Smile Please*.

11 As noted above, the 'Home' section is built less as the recollection of a golden age than as a series of splits which initiate the pattern of traumatic fissure: the death of the sympathetic nun (sister Mary, a migrant from Ireland); the break from Francine; the father's return after the eruption of Mount Pelée; the intrusion of 'civilization' (electricity) and of 'Mr Howard', a married man who belittles her as a colonial sensual object; the colonial library with the obnoxious female writer; the departure for England. Mr Howard merely caresses her arm, while Rhys's version of Howard was more graphic. But Phillips captures the sense of abjection, as Gwen retreats to her mother's room and stares at her photograph. The impact of sexual molestation and the intersection between happiness, unhappiness (or the choice of unhappiness as a way of resisting the social construction of happiness) determines for Ardoin the fragmented form of Rhys's short stories: 'marked as a bad girl, she

no longer has to worry about any of the normal things – finding a husband, having children, hoping for a good future at all' (Ardoin 2013: 233).

12 In the 1930s and 1940s, in his BBC broadcasts, Forster, another writer interrogating the empire from the inside at a time when it was already falling apart, upheld culture and challenged Nazism, as well as any celebration of British national identity. In his 1939 essay 'Racial Exercise', Forster opposes the 'ridiculous doctrine of Racial Purity' and concludes that 'Europe is mongrel forever, and so is America' (Forster [1939] 1951: 30).

13 Cathie Jayakumar connects the image with the Hottentot Venus. See Cathie Jayakumar, '"I have no faith in the civilizing power of the English": Poetics of Sensibility and the Emergence of the Diasporic Self in Caryl Phillips's *A View of the Empire at Sunset*', paper delivered at the 'After Empire?' Conference, Leeds University, on 14 December 2018, unpublished.

14 As E.M. Forster puts it in 'Notes on the English Character' (1936), he does not have a cold heart, but an undeveloped one, warped by English education and prejudices.

15 We may think of Martha's lifelong pain after losing her daughter in *Crossing the River*, or of Joyce who has to give her baby up for adoption. Phillips works on childhood, rupture and cross-connections. For family disruption in Phillips's work, see Ledent and O'Callaghan (2017) for a reading of Phillips's *The Lost Child* (2015), and for a wider study of the possibility or failure of transcultural parent–child relationship and adoptions, see John McLeod's *Life Lines: Writing Transcultural Adoption* (2015).

16 For Catherine Rovera, it is hard to say when Rhys began to write the novel; in a letter written in the 1950s, Rhys alludes to autobiographical notes she wrote in the 1930s, a manuscript entitled 'Creole' which was lost or destroyed; the only remaining fragment was written in 1938, after the trip to the West Indies (Rovera 2015: 19).

17 I am grateful to Kerry-Jane Wallart for pointing out that this echoes the fictional version of Geneva in *Wide Sargasso Sea*, Coulibri, adding layers of (un)belonging.

11

'The small things that they've not been able to talk about': An interview with Caryl Phillips about his novel *A View of the Empire at Sunset* (2018)

Kerry-Jane Wallart

At the end of the short story 'Vienne', as he is trying to escape Vienna and the debts he contracted there, Pierre sells his car and throws 'two tickets on the bed' of a hotel room in Prague. He tells the narrator, Frances/Francine, '"There you are, to Liège, to London"' (*CSS* 117). While he now resides in the United States, Caryl Phillips is often to be found in either city, among others in Europe. Not fleeing debts but roaming through a European Old World which, like Jean Rhys, he seems to feel both drawn to and estranged from.

His latest novel, *A View of the Empire at Sunset*, based on the life of Jean Rhys, was launched in Paris at the *Maison de la Poésie*, at the Shakespeare & Co. bookshop, and at the Sorbonne, in June 2018, but it is in Liège indeed that I met him and that the following interview was recorded. It was now mid-October and a thick mist had fallen on the city. Caryl Phillips was about to read a text later to be published by *Salmagundi* (issue number 199); he had been invited to the University of Liège by Bénédicte Ledent, a leading scholar on his work and a dear friend of both of us. Bénédicte had put us in touch in the first place.

The fictional essay read by Caryl Phillips that night, 'I saw Mario Balotelli in the Ghetto', addresses many of the cross-cultural circulations and aporias that the present volume, focused on Jean Rhys, tackles. While it reshuffles some distinctly Phillipsian themes (adoption and transmission, sports, journeys, solitude and odd encounters) in a quest for formal newness, it also evokes disorientation, trans-traumatic experiences and feelings of identitarian loss in ways which are somehow aligned with Phillips's rendering of 'Gwendolyn Williams' in *A View of the Empire at Sunset*, and with Jean Rhys's own favourite themes. The essayistic narrative (for lack of a better phrase) is set in Venice, a city which Jean Rhys visited and which, one assumes, she would have found familiar to some extent, because it is by the sea, because it celebrates Carnival and because it used to be the centre of a vast empire, a seat of immense colonial power and was consequently a place where foreign languages and subaltern minorities jostled at the margins.

In its own way this interview connects many more places than just London and Roseau. It constitutes a perspective on Rhys by another unplaceable writer who, a few generations later, recorded the protracted aftermath of European imperialism in all its spatial coordinates. As a female character says at the end of 'Night Out 1925', late at night on a Parisian bus, "'Same old miseries. No more splendours. Not now. […] *Et qu'est-ce que tu veux que ça leur fasse?*'" (*CSS* 327).

Kerry-Jane Wallart [KJW]: Alongside Jean Rhys, do you also read such 'colonial' modernist writers as Katherine Mansfield, or James Joyce, and would you say that their influence is woven in your novel in any significant way?

Caryl Phillips [CP]: No, I'd say neither were influences, or structural influences, when I was writing. I have read Katherine Mansfield's short stories and I have read James Joyce too. The tone of James Joyce, particularly in the conclusion of 'The Dead' in *Dubliners*, is a prose tone with an eloquence and grandeur and simplicity that, I think, any writer should try and aspire to. The idea of prose becoming poetry, and being incredibly moving not because of its content but because of the rhythm and the words, is always in my mind, in everything I write, as in that story of Joyce's. But in approaching Jean Rhys's life neither Katherine Mansfield nor James Joyce have been any particular form of influence.

KJW: Does your writing sometimes start with things rather than with characters and/or places?

CP: It often starts with things, ideas, something I've seen in a newspaper or something I've read in a history book. Or a building I've looked at and wondered about. But it rather quickly has to be filtered through characters because a novel can't be sustained with an idea, or with the content of an article in a newspaper. Novels are about people and at some point a person has to intervene to carry the idea, or carry the thought, and the full complexity of *their* life has to take over. So, it can begin with an idea, with an irritation even. But it has to soon flower into the concern of a person.

KJW: I'll pick up on that irritation and ask you about disappointment – was it, as a theme or an affect, one of your conscious starting points for the novel?

CP: Absolutely. I am a child of immigrants who came to England with a lot of hopes in the late 1950s. They believed that Europe, and Britain in particular, could offer much to them and they were disappointed by what they found and their whole lives have been clouded by that sense of 'what we hoped for did not happen'. I think that I've been aware of it in their lives, but I've also been aware of this disappointment in the lives of so many people who have migrated, particularly to Europe. The US is a country of migration and I spend most of my time there now, but my main concern relates to the migration that has come into Europe, either colonial or not colonial, in which people have expected and have been thereafter disappointed.

KJW: You visit Paris regularly. Did you specifically visit Paris before writing the Parisian scenes? And how did the snippets of French come to you – in the section entitled 'Continental Drift' for instance? Inserting bits of foreign languages is not something that you do often in your writing ....

CP: Well, I did come to Paris specifically to spend a couple of days going to all the places in Paris that I could find that I knew Jean Rhys had been to, or mentioned, such as the sometimes rather grim hotels near Gare du Nord, and the various bars in Montparnasse that she used to go and sit in, and drink in, and the hotel in Rue Vavin where she wrote most of *Quartet*. Nightclubs – there's a short story in the *Collected Short Stories* where she sees West Indians in a particular nightclub and I went to try and find that. I went to Parc Monceau, I also found the place where she used to be a nanny – but the building's no longer there. So I went to all these locations and I would stand outside and make notes, or I would go in and have a drink. In the Parc Monceau I looked around and made lots of notes about kids playing and fountains and what the grass and the gates looked like. A lot of that did not find its way into the book and I didn't expect it to. It was just a way of trying to get close to a person and seeing the world through their eyes. And so, these very specific locations were important to me. I did the same in Dominica.

In terms of the snippets of French it just seemed important to try to catch some of that dislocation that she felt. She was happy, or as happy as she could be, in Paris, and part of it is that using the French language involved hiding from English. It's about hearing other voices, hearing something that wasn't immediately judgemental of her. And the French language wasn't immediately judgemental of her – France wasn't immediately judgemental of her. England was. And so you get those little snippets of noises off-stage. You know, you get a little bit of that in her prose too. So both of those reasons, because it seemed true to how Rhys herself wrote, but it's also true to a temporary escape from the judgemental nature of English and Englishness.

KJW: I have a question that branches out from what you've just said, about the Dominican landscape – you've said that the writing of the novel was only made possible by your visit to Dominica. Did you find it to be very different from St Kitts or from other Caribbean islands that you know?

CP: I was already writing the novel when I went to Dominica, I'd already written quite a bit. The landscape of Dominica is very different from any of the Caribbean islands. It's different from St Kitts, it's different from Barbados, it has a wildness and a kind of primitive beauty about it while the other islands are a little bit manicured, and geared towards accommodating tourism, shall we say, which is a key industry in the region. Dominica just can't be bothered. It's too wild, it's too strange, it's too much its own thing geographically and that's *sort of* how I think of Rhys. She's too wild, she's too much of her own thing. So the landscape, in a strange way, to me, matched her personality. I can't imagine her coming from somewhere like Barbados or somewhere where it's a little bit more manicured. So there's something about the wildness and the unpredictability of Dominica that made me realize that so much of her sensibility is rooted not just in the Caribbean but in that particular, almost uncategorizable island. It wasn't my first trip to Dominica. I'd been there before, briefly. But it was on this particular trip that I would sit in the hotel late at night, having gone to pretty much every spot that she'd spent time in – the school, the library, the house that she grew up in. The house in the hills where she used to go with her father – having gone to all those places, I went to a place that was two hundred metres away from my hotel in Dominica: her father's grave. I knew there were sections of the book that were not written and that would have to be written. I needed something to flesh out who she was in this landscape. And those sections are the sections about the library and going to her father's grave and being in school and the headmistress talking to her. So for these sections, I would sit in the hotel at the end of the day in Dominica and make notes and I'd say, London yes, Paris yes, but these sections have to be in there, to give it a fuller picture. Even the scene towards the end of the novel where she meets the offspring of her brother's gallivanting in a hotel bar – the hotel doesn't exist anymore but the scene is there because I found out where the hotel was. I stood where the hotel used to be. I imagined what kind of a place it was. It released a lot, my being in Dominica. Not just the landscape but various specific places.

KJW: The first thing that Lenglet asks Gwendolyn when they meet in London is whether she's English – would one say that she finds an emancipation of sorts in France because at last, she's seen as English? From a French point of view?

CP: Well, I think it's really important that somebody asked her that question rather than privately keeping it to themselves. Or, exporting the answer for themselves by calling her a mongrel, or a Hottentot, or you know, some equally judgemental comment. Englishness has a way to this day of categorizing you without actually having the decency to ask you the question straight out. They'll look at you, or they'll look at your clothes, or they'll look at the way you carry yourself and they'll decide: 'you don't belong here, you're not part of this'. So the fact that somebody was prepared to ask her straight out, had seen something in her but not judged it, and was actually prepared to engage with her around difference, that I think, released something in her. Obviously Lenglet turned out to be a bit of a rogue, but his own hybrid identity and his own border crossings freed him up in terms of his sensibility so that she was faced with somebody who was probably more like her than any of the other people she was meeting.

KJW: Now, this novel, like many of your novels, is a very silent one, with few of the dialogues and noises that traverse Modernism and Rhys's texts in particular.

CP: I think the silence is really important because that's how we do our work, when we're working hard. This is what I tell my students. I always give the ones that are working with me on writing an exercise, in the second or third week. They have to think about character and I'll give them a photograph, or a poem, and I'll say,

> write me something about who that person is in the photograph, or about the person that might have written that poem. And what we're going to do now is, I'm going to give you fifteen minutes in which to sit and write it. And in that fifteen minutes we're going to be silent, because you need to understand that this is when you are working.

When there's no noise, when they are thinking – that's when they're working. They are not used to silence. Because of social media, because of TV, because of the way the noise comes from everywhere. You have to find the character through silence, there's no other way you're going to get there apart from being silent and pressing the down button on the elevator and going into that person. Now, when you feel silence, you're writing.

That's silence from the point of view of the writer. From the point of view of the lives of the characters it's interiority that I'm interested in, more than I'm interested in dialogue, or in narrative exposition. And you can get interiority in dialogue. So somebody's talking to somebody else, but I'm always interested in what they're *thinking* as that conversation is going along. So even if it is dialogue and it has to be very exterior, I'm always looking for those moments of interiority in terms of the general narrative unfolding of a piece. It is the difficult self-questioning, the moments of self-questioning, that take place in the character's life that I am interested in because that is what the character is. On a train journey, for instance, as Rhys/Gwendolyn often is in this novel: she's on a train journey and she's thinking, *and* she's looking out the window. So, I'm never interested in just looking out of the window and describing the tiny English fields and the horses, and the mist. I'm interested in what she's *also* thinking about and not just what she's seeing. And that interior landscape of a character interests me much more than, you know, 'what happens next'. And in that sense, I think, obviously, I'm much more interested in the sort of Modernism in which self-contradiction, self-examination, not exactly existentialism but that idea of being alone yet being social, is kind of the engine room of the narratives that interest me, and this is certainly the case in this novel.

KJW: About being social – what about the performance of selves, about Gwen's training as a performer? Do you see it as an emancipation or do you think that, much like what happened to Bert Williams, for example, this performance constituted a redoubled form of alienation, in gendered and social terms?

CP: It's ironic that some people are asked to perform who they are in the world and they just can't do it because who they are is subject to so much turbulence, and so much interpretation and misinterpretation around race, around gender, around class and certainly around sexuality. They're asked to perform, or expected to perform, a certain role that doesn't match who they are and it can create a kind of tragic loss, a loss of a side of who you are, a real void inside of you that you have no way of repairing because people's expectations are what they see and what they think they know of you. The longer you go on performing in that way, the more difficult it becomes to build a bridge back and make yourself singular and whole again. I think that certainly did happen in Bert Williams's life and I think that to some extent it happened in Jean Rhys's life too. You begin to perform in a certain way and obviously there's a very specific performance in Paris, as a mannequin, in London, on the stage, but there's performance beyond that, a larger kind of performance of what a female is supposed to be, in Edwardian or post-Edwardian London. Of what a white female in the Caribbean is supposed to be. You perform a certain role, her mother tells her, 'this is what is expected of you' and she's saying, 'no, I don't want to do that'. She goes to London and friends tell her, 'this is what you're supposed to do. Stop pretending you're a virgin. You've got to get to the wallet, you've got to perform in a certain way'. And then she goes to Paris and she's expected to perform again, so sometimes she agrees to the performance, and at other times she doesn't. It's a huge pressure on some people, this expectation of performance which obscures, or makes it very difficult for them to discover, who they are. Or to think of themselves as a singular, whole person. They become fractured and start to act out in all sorts of strange ways.

An Interview with Phillips About A View of the Empire at Sunset 183

KJW: Because of *Extravagant Strangers*, we know that you have been reading Jean Rhys for a long time. How long have you been thinking about writing this novel? And what led you to writing this novel now?

CP: I wasn't thinking about writing about Rhys at all – in fiction. In maybe 2010, 2011, 2012, some time around that, I had an idea of doing a story about Jean Rhys as a film. I don't know why, I just had this notion that it would make a great film. So I started looking at her life in that period from getting off the ship in 1907, until she goes to Paris after the First World War – maybe looking at the chaos of that period. It may be due to the fact that there were a lot of things in the news during that period about the lead-up to the anniversary of the First World War, it was going to be the hundredth anniversary in 2014 so there was lots of talk about what England was like during that period, and because I've always been interested in Jean Rhys maybe that's why I was beginning to think of a film. I went to see Diana Athill, who was Rhys's editor, and talked to her; I reread everything Rhys wrote, and the more I did so, the more I thought, actually, I don't want to represent this character as a performer. I want the interiority of this character, I don't want to externalize her life in dialogue and be dependent upon the actor to capture the pain and capture the interior collapse, the interior contradiction. I would write the dialogue, I would be able to write the scenes, but it would be the actor and the camera who would actually be writing the inside of her life. There's a very good French film that is very influential on me, called *The Lacemaker*.[1] And particularly towards the end of that film, the pain of that young woman's disappointment and the way she is questioning herself, and being unsure of herself, but trying to find stability is all done brilliantly by the actress and the camera. What I would like to write is what she's thinking at the end of *The Lacemaker*. I would want to write from the inside. So I thought, I want to write from the inside of Jean Rhys, I don't want to rely upon the camera and the actress.

I was writing another novel at the time, I was in the middle of writing *The Lost Child*, and I just had to put Rhys to one side and finish that novel. But I knew where I was going immediately after I finished *The Lost Child*, I was going to Rhys. But why now? Well, as I said, some temporal reasons because there was this focus on the First World War and I was thinking about it. But I was also thinking about disappointment, about so many people whose lives in Europe had been a great disappointment for them. They'd survived, they'd endured, they'd got through it, they lived perhaps a long life but they'd done so with a great deal of disappointment. Certainly my parents' generation were now beginning to die and, you know, I was looking at them, looking at older West Indians in the streets of London. And I'm wondering about that sense of what they carried with them all their lives. The small things that they've not been able to talk about. You know, just in my own family, my mother came to England via Paris and she told me she went to a hairdresser – her hair used to be to her waist. She went to a hairdresser to get her hair trimmed and, because she didn't really speak French the hairdresser cut all of her hair off and gave her money because she wanted to use the hair as a wig. So she arrived in England for the first time in her life with hair that didn't go down to her waist. But with money and disappointment, the hurt of that transaction. Again it was on my mind when I was thinking about how people coped with the journey from the Antilles to Europe and the misunderstandings and the disappointments, and the hurts that they suffered along the way. How did they manage to keep going? That's one of the things I was thinking about too.

KJW: In the novel, *A View of the Empire at Sunset*, there is a very discreet/discrete reflection on the way empires follow empires – Britain and France are on the wane, Nazi Germany is on the rise and so is the US; and yet these historical facts are also systematically sidelined. Did you feel the need to focus instead on what historians call micro-histories – on the experiences and perceptions of individuals?

CP: When I'm writing a novel I'm always aware of history, whether it's the large world events that are going on, such as the First World War, the Wall Street Crash – I'm aware of what's going on in Paris in the 1920s, of the rise of a certain political agitation in the Caribbean in the 1930s, which did contribute towards a sense of alienation that Jean Rhys had when she went back. There was a real rise among black workers throughout the Caribbean of what one might call, from her point of view, 'attitude', that wasn't there when she was a girl. So these are all historical facts and I might expand upon them. I could say a lot more about the First World War and those soldiers coming back, and her serving them soup in the canteen in Euston. I could say a lot about the effect of what Paris looked like in 1919. When you arrived there you could still see bullet holes in the buildings. But it's not about that. These are small details to give texture and period. The main thing I'm interested in is the people. And I don't want the people to be subsumed – the interior crisis of the people, what Faulkner called the human heart in conflict with itself. I don't want that to be a secondary subject behind an exploration of what England was like in 1917 with soldiers coming back or what Paris was like in 1919, in the immediate aftermath of the First World War. What was the kind of social/literary life in Paris in that period. These are all details that are there but I'm not going to focus on that. I'm just focusing on the character. If history leaks out in a mini-moment in a scene such as her looking at a soldier in a grey coat who comes in, and she's serving him and then she sees the desolation on his face, that's good enough because I think the reader can just infer the larger history from the smaller moment.

KJW: I have a last question, which must be asked a lot about that novel. Little reference is made to Gwen's writing in its relation to her life. This is not 'a portrait of the artist as a young woman'. Why such a deliberate choice? I was also struck by how much, instead of speaking, which she finds difficult for various reasons, she smiles. Might this be inspired by the title of her unfinished autobiographical text?

CP: Does she smile a lot in the novel?

KJW: She does smile, all the time.

CP: Well, I wasn't aware of that but I believe you. And I wasn't consciously thinking of it in terms of *Smile Please*. I was thinking more in the context of how smiling is a substitute for using words. Because words always get her into trouble. Beyond the accent, which introduces questions of identity she's fed up with dealing with, words tend to be misinterpreted. It's just easier to smile, it's just easier to concur. It's just easier to get through the day without saying anything if you can, without causing any discord, or creating ill will. So, perhaps that's where the smiling is coming from. I have to say, I wasn't thinking of the title of the unfinished autobiography.

As far as not dealing with her writing, you put it perfectly, it is not 'a portrait of the artist as a young woman' because I'm not really interested in tracing her development as a writer, that's more of a biographer's job, that's really not what she's about. She's like all writers: before she's a writer, she's a human being, and after she's a writer she's a human being. Writing is her way of stabilizing herself in the world. Writing is her way of quelling the storm. But I want to know what the storm is all about, I want to know where the turbulence is coming from. I'm not interested in the solution, she's giving us the solution, because we have the evidence of *her* books, *her* writing. But what we don't have in there is the evidence of the storm and the evidence of the turbulence. We can infer it from looking at *Good Morning, Midnight*, or *Quartet*, or *Voyage in the Dark*. We can guess what the fear was. The inner fear. We can guess what the demons were. That's what I wanted to explore – not how she dealt with controlling those demons, which is by writing. But before she was a writer she was a young woman who was filled with all sorts of anxieties because of her race, because of her class and her upbringing, because of her mother, because of her father. She said it perfectly: writing imposes a pattern on life. A shape. Life has no shape. But by writing you are at least able to impose some kind of a shape. But that does not mean that you've dealt with the problems. You just temporarily anchored life for a little bit. So I'm interested in the problems, not how she went about anchoring life.

Note

1 *La Dentellière* is a French film by Claude Goretta (starring Isabelle Huppert) released in 1977.

Bibliography

Alexander, Jeffrey C. (2014), *Cultural Trauma and Collective Identity*, Berkeley: University of California Press.
Allen, Grant ([1895] 1995), *The Woman Who Did*, Oxford: Oxford University Press.
Allen, Walter (1967), 'Bertha the Doomed', *New York Times*, 18 June: 5.
Als, Hilton and Caryl Phillips (2018), 'Caryl Phillips in Conversation with Hilton Als', [Podcast] The Greenlight Bookstore Podcasts 32, 8 July 2018. Available online: https://www.stitcher.com/podcast/citizenracecar/the-greenlight-bookstore-radio-hour/e/55244372 (accessed 30 July 2019).
Alvarez, Al (2005), *The Writer's Voice*, London: Bloomsbury.
Angier, Carole (1985), *Jean Rhys*, Harmondsworth: Penguin.
Angier, Carole ([1990] 1992), *Jean Rhys*, 2nd edn, Harmondsworth: Penguin.
Angier, Carole (1993), 'Weekend in Gloucestershire: Jean Rhys, Adrian Allinson and "Till September, Petronella"', *Jean Rhys Review*, 4 (1): 2–14.
Angier, Carole (2000), 'Introduction', in Jean Rhys, *Voyage in the Dark*, v–xiv, London: Penguin.
Antoni, Robert (1992), *Divina Trace*, Woodstock: Overlook Press.
Ardoin, Paul (2013), 'The Un-happy Short Story Cycle: Jean Rhys's *Sleep It Off Lady*', in Mary Wilson and Kerry Johnson (eds), *Rhys Matters: New Critical Perspectives*, 233–48, New York: Palgrave Macmillan.
Armstrong, David (2013), 'Reclaiming the Left Bank: Jean Rhys's "Topography" in *The Left Bank* and *Quartet*', in Mary Wilson and Kerry Johnson (eds), *Rhys Matters: New Critical Perspectives*, 169–85, New York: Palgrave Macmillan.
Athill, Diana (1979), 'Foreword: Jean Rhys and Her Autobiography', in Jean Rhys, *Smile Please: An Unfinished Autobiography*, 5–15, London: André Deutsch.
Athill, Diana (1985), 'Introduction', in Jean Rhys, *The Complete Novels*, vii–xiv, New York: Norton.
Athill, Diana (2012), 'Editing Jean Rhys', *Women: A Cultural Review*, 23 (4): 401–7.
Athill, Diana (2017), 'Introduction', in Jean Rhys, *The Collected Short Stories*, vii–iv, London: Penguin.
Badiou, Alain (1988), *L'Être et l'événement*, Paris: Seuil.
Bakhtin, Mikhail Mikhailovich (1981), *The Dialogic Imagination*, ed. Michael Holquist, trans. Caryl Emerson and Michael Holquist, Austin: University of Texas Press.
Baldick, Chris (1987), *In Frankenstein's Shadow: Myth, Monstrosity, and Nineteenth-Century Writing*, Oxford: Clarendon Press.

Barret-Ducrocq, Françoise (1991), *Love in the Time of Victoria: Sexuality and Desire Among Working-Class Men and Women in Nineteenth-Century London*, trans. John Howe, New York: Penguin.

Bedford, Jean (1997), 'Crown Me with Roses Pastiche', in Susan Geason (ed.), *Regarding Jane Eyre*, 335–405, Sydney: Vintage.

Benjamin, Walter ([1936] 1999), 'The Storyteller: Reflections on the Works of Nikolai Leskov', in Hannah Arendt (ed.), *Illuminations*, trans. Harry Zorn, 83–107, London: Pimlico.

Benjamin, Walter (1999a), *The Arcades Project*, trans. Howard Eiland and Kevin McLaughlin, Cambridge, MA: Belknap Press of Harvard University Press.

Benjamin, Walter (1999b), 'Franz Kafka: On the Tenth Anniversary of His Death', in *Selected Writings 1927–34*, 794–818, ed. Howard Eiland and Michael W. Jennings, trans. Rodney Livingstone, Cambridge, MA: Belknap Press of Harvard University Press.

Benjamin, Walter (2002), 'The Storyteller', in Howard Eiland, Michael W. Jennings, Gary Smith and Marcus Bullock (eds), *Walter Benjamin: Selected Writings 1935–38*, trans. Edmund Jephcott and Howard Eiland, 141–66, Cambridge, MA: Belknap Press of Harvard University Press.

Benstock, Shari ([1987] 1994), *Women of the Left Bank: Paris, 1900–1940*, 2nd edn, London: Virago.

Berg, Wolfgang and Aoileann Ní Éigeartaigh, eds (2010), *Exploring Transculturalism: A Biographical Approach*, Wiesbaden: VS Verlag für Sozial Wissenschaften.

Berman, Jessica (2001), *Cosmopolitanism and the Politics of Community*, Cambridge: Cambridge University Press.

Bernanos, Georges (1936), *Journal d'un curé de campagne*, Paris: La Palatine, à la Librairie Plon.

Berry, Betsy (1996), '*Voyage in the Dark*, Esther Walters and the Naturalistic Tradition', *Jean Rhys Review*, 7 (1): 17–25.

Beverley, John (2001), 'The Im/possibility of Politics: Subalternity, Modernity Hegemony', in Ileana Rodriguez (ed.), *The Latin America Subaltern Studies Reader*, 47–63, Durham, NC: Duke University Press.

Birat, Kathie (2016), 'Embodied Voices: Literacy and Empathy in Caryl Phillips's *Crossing the River*', in Vanessa Guignery and Christian Gutleben (eds), *Traversée d'une œuvre: Crossing the River de Caryl Phillips*, Cycnos, 32 (1): 89–105.

Bloch, Marc ([1949] 1992), *L'Étrange Défaite: témoignage écrit en 1940*, Paris: Gallimard.

Bloch, Marc ([1949] 1992), *The Strange Defeat: A Statement of Evidence*, trans. Gerard Hopkins, London: Oxford University Press.

Bloch, Marc ([1924] 2015), *The Royal Touch: Sacred Monarchy and Scrofula in England and France*, trans. J.E. Anderson, London: Routledge.

Bourdieu, Pierre (1983), *The Field of Cultural Production: Essays on Art and Literature*, Oxford: Polity.

Bourdieu, Pierre (2006), 'Cultural Reproduction and Social Reproduction', in David Grusky and Sonja Szelenyi (eds), *Inequality: Classic Readings in Race, Class, and Gender*, 257–71, Boulder, CO: Westview Press.
Bowen, Stella ([1941] 1984), *Drawn from Life*, London: Virago.
Brathwaite, Edward Kamau (1971), *The Development of Creole Society in Jamaica 1770–1820*, Oxford: Clarendon Press.
Brathwaite, Edward Kamau (1973), *The Arrivants: A New World Trilogy*, Oxford: Oxford University Press.
Brathwaite, Edward Kamau (1974), *Contradictory Omens: Cultural Diversity and Integration in the Caribbean*, Mona, Jamaica: Savacou.
Brathwaite, Edward Kamau (1975), *Other Exiles*, Oxford: Oxford University Press.
Brathwaite, Edward Kamau (1984), *History of the Voice: The Development of Nation Language in Anglophone Caribbean Poetry*, London: New Beacon Books.
Brathwaite, Edward Kamau ([1986] 1993), *Roots*, Ann Arbor: University of Michigan Press.
Brathwaite, Edward Kamau (1993), *The Zea Mexican Diary*, Madison: Wisconsin University Press.
Brathwaite, Edward Kamau (1994), *Barabajan Poems*, Mona, Jamaica: Savacou.
Brathwaite, Kamau (1995), 'A Post-Cautionary Tale of the Helen of Our Wars', *Wasafiri*, 11: 69–81.
Brockway, Lucile (1979), *Science and Colonial Expansion: The Role of the British Royal Botanic Gardens*, New York: Academic Press.
Brontë, Charlotte ([1847] 1985), *Jane Eyre*, Harmondsworth: Penguin.
Brown, J. Dillon (2010), 'Textual Entanglement: Jean Rhys's Critical Discourse', *Modern Fiction Studies*, 56 (3): 568–91.
Brown, Nancy Hemond (1986), 'Aspects of the Short Story: A Comparison of Jean Rhys's "The Sound of the River" with Ernest Hemingway's "Hills Like White Elephants"', *Jean Rhys Review*, 1 (1): 2–12.
Burnett, Paula (1986), *The Penguin Book of Caribbean Verse in English*, London: Penguin.
Butler, Judith (1993), *Bodies that Matter: on the Discursive Limits of Sex*, New York: Routledge.
Butler, Judith (2015), *Senses of the Self*, New York: Fordham University Press.
Cantwell, Mary (1990), 'A Conversation with Jean Rhys', in Pierrette M. Frickey (ed.), *Critical Perspectives on Jean Rhys*, 21–7, Washington, DC: Three Continents Press.
Carr, Helen ([1996] 2012), *Jean Rhys*, 2nd edn, London: Northcote House.
Carr, Helen (2003), 'Jean Rhys: West Indian Intellectual', in Bill Schwarz (ed.), *West Indian Intellectuals in Britain*, 93–113, Manchester: Manchester University Press.
Caruth, Cathy (1996), 'Introduction: The Wound and the Voice', in *Unclaimed Experience: Trauma, Narrative and History*, 1–9, Baltimore: Johns Hopkins University Press.
Césaire, Aimé ([1950] 1955), *Discours sur le colonialisme*, trans. Joan Pinkham, Paris: Présence Africaine.

Césaire, Aimé (2000), *Discourse on Colonialism* trans. Joan Pinkham, New York: Monthly Review Press.
Chateaubriand, François-René de ([1961] 2014), *Memoirs from Beyond the Tomb, Mémoires d'outre-tombe, 1849–50*, selected and trans. Robert Baldick, London: Penguin.
Childs, Peter (2007), *Modernism and the Postcolonial, Literature and Empire 1885–1930*, London: Bloomsbury.
Clayton, Jay and Eric Rothstein, eds (1991), *Influence and Intertextuality in Literary History*, Madison: University of Wisconsin Press.
Clifford, James (1988), *The Predicament of Culture: Twentieth-Century Ethnography, Literature, and Art*, Cambridge, MA: Harvard University Press.
Cohn, Dorrit (1978), *Transparent Minds, Narrative Modes for Presenting Consciousness*, Princeton, NJ: Princeton University Press.
Cohn, Dorrit (1989), 'Fictional Versus Historical Lives: Borderlines and Borderline Cases', *Journal of Narrative Technique*, 19 (1): 3–24.
Colette ([1910] 1990), *La Vagabonde*, Paris: Albin Michel.
Colette (1936), *Mes apprentissages*, Paris: Hachette.
Colette ([1941] 2004), *Le Pur et l'impur*, Paris: Librairie Arthème Fayard et Hachette Littératures.
Colette (1967), *My Apprenticeships; Music Hall Sidelights*, trans. Helen Beauclerk and Anne-Marie Callimachi, London: Penguin.
Colette (1968), *The Pure and the Impure*, trans. Herma Briffault London: Secker and Warburg.
Colette ([1920] 1974), *Chéri*, trans. Roger Senhouse, New York: Farrar, Straus and Giroux.
Colette (1982), *The Vagabond*, trans. Enid McLeod, New York: Farrar, Straus and Giroux.
Colette (1991a), 'A Bad Morning', in Robert Phelps (ed.), *The Collected Stories of Colette*, 111–13, trans. Matthew Ward, Antonia White and Anne-Marie Callimachi, New York: Farrar, Straus and Giroux.
Colette (1991b), 'Bastienne's Child', in Robert Phelps (ed.), *The Collected Stories of Colette*, 147–53, trans. Anne-Marie Callimachi, New York: Farrar, Straus and Giroux.
Colette (1991c), 'The Misfit', in Robert Phelps (ed.), *The Collected Stories of Colette* 170–9, trans. Anne-Marie Callimachi, New York: Farrar, Straus and Giroux.
Colette (1991d), 'The Victim', in Robert Phelps (ed.), *The Collected Stories of Colette*, 189–93, trans. Anne-Marie Callimachi, New York: Farrar, Straus and Giroux.
Coronil, Fernando (1995), 'Introduction: Transculturation and the Politics of Theory', in Fernando Ortiz, *Cuban Counterpoint: Tobacco and Sugar*, trans. H. De Onis, ix–lvi, Durham, NC: Duke University Press.
Crawl Me Blood (2018a), [Programme], Royal Botanic Gardens Victoria in association with Aphids and Melbourne Writers Festival.
Crawl Me Blood (2018b), [Site-immersive sound and video installation] dir. Willoh S. Weiland and Halcyon Macleod, Royal Botanic Gardens Victoria in association with

Aphids and Melbourne Writers Festival, 29 August 2018, Royal Botanical Gardens, Melbourne, Australia.

Damrosch, David (2003), *What Is World Literature?*, Princeton, NJ: Princeton University Press.

Dash, J. Michael (1995), *Édouard Glissant*, Cambridge: Cambridge University Press.

Dawkins, Ruth (2016), 'Close and Personal: Jennifer Livett', TasWriters, 20 October. Available online: https://www.taswriters.org/close-personal-jennifer-livett (accessed 2 March 2018).

De Caires Narain, Denise (2000), 'Caribbean Creole: The Real Thing? …', in *Essays and Studies 2000*, vol. 53, The English Association, Woodbridge: Brewer.

Deleuze, Gilles and Félix Guattari (1975), *Kafka: pour une littérature mineure*, Paris: Minuit.

Deleuze, Gilles and Félix Guattari (1987), *A Thousand Plateaus*, trans. Brian Massumi, Minneapolis: University of Minnesota Press.

Di Battista, Maria and Emily O. Wittman, eds (2014), *Modernism and Autobiography*, Cambridge: Cambridge University Press.

Dickinson, Emily (2016), *Emily Dickinson's Poems: As She Preserved Them*, ed. Cristanne Miller Cambridge, MA: Belknap Press of Harvard University Press.

Dolar, Mladen (2006), *A Voice and Nothing More*, Cambridge, MA: MIT Press.

Doubrovsky, Serge (1977), *Fils*, Paris: Galilée.

Drake, Sandra (1990), 'All that Foolishness/That All Foolishness: Race and Caribbean Culture as Thematics of Liberation in Jean Rhys's *Wide Sargasso Sea*', *Critica*, 2 (2): 97–112.

Dunning, R.C. (1924), 'Twelve Poems', *Transatlantic Review*, 2 (5): 478–90.

Ekert-Rotholz, Alice (1960), *A Net of Gold*, trans. Richard and Clara Winston, London: Jonathan Cape.

Eliot, T. S. (1964), *Knowledge and Experience in the Philosophy of F.H. Bradley*, London: Faber.

Eliot, T. S. ([1919] 1975), 'Tradition and the Individual Talent', in Frank Kermode (ed.), *Selected Prose of T.S. Eliot*, 37–44, London: Faber.

Emberley, Julia (2007), 'Material Fictions of Desire', *Fashion Theory*, 11 (4): 463–81.

Emery, Mary Lou (1990), *Jean Rhys at 'World's End': Novels of Colonial and Sexual Exile*, Austin: University of Texas Press.

Emery, Mary Lou (2003), 'Misfit: Jean Rhys and the Visual Cultures of Colonial Modernism', *Journal of Caribbean Literatures*, 3 (3): xi–xxii.

Emery, Mary Lou (2007), *Modernism, the Visual, and Caribbean Literature*, Cambridge: Cambridge University Press.

Emery, Mary Lou (2013), 'Foreword', in Mary Wilson and Kerry Johnson (eds), *Rhys Matters: New Critical Perspectives*, xi–xiii, New York: Palgrave Macmillan.

Eyerman, Ron (2001), *Cultural Trauma: Slavery and the Formation of African American Identity*, Cambridge: Cambridge University Press.

Fetterley, Judith (1978), *The Resisting Reader: A Feminist Approach to American Fiction*, Bloomington: Indiana University Press.

Fitch, Noel Riley (1983), *Sylvia Beach and the Lost Generation: A History of Literary Paris in the Twenties and Thirties*, New York: Norton.

Flanagan, Richard (2008), *Wanting*, North Sydney: Knopf.

Flaubert, Gustave (1982), *The Letters of Gustave Flaubert, 1857-1880*, ed. and trans. Francis Steegmuller, Cambridge, MA: Belknap Press of Harvard University Press.

Flynn, Nicole (2013), 'Clockwork Women: Temporality and Form in Jean Rhys's Interwar Novels', in Kerry Johnson and Mary Wilson (eds), *Rhys Matters: New Critical Perspectives*, 41-66, New York: Palgrave Macmillan.

Ford, Ford Madox (1927), 'Rive Gauche', introduction to Jean Rhys, *The Left Bank and Other Stories*, 7-27, London: Jonathan Cape.

Ford, Ford Madox ([1931] 2012), *When the Wicked Man*, Plano, TX: Read Books.

Forster, Edward Morgan ([1910] 2012), *Howards End*, ed. David Lodge, 2nd edn, Harmondsworth: Penguin.

Forster, Edward Morgan (1936), 'Notes on the English Character', in *Abinger Harvest*, 3-14, London: Edward Arnold.

Forster, Edward Morgan ([1939] 1951), 'Racial Exercise', in *Two Cheers for Democracy*, 29-32, London: Edward Arnold.

France, Anatole (1923), *On Life and Letters, La Vie littéraire: Première Série, 1919*, trans. A.W. Evans, London: John Lane and the Bodley Head.

Frickey, Pierrette M., ed. (1990), *Critical Perspectives on Jean Rhys*, Washington, DC: Three Continents Press.

Friedman, Susan Stanford (2011), 'Towards a Transnational Turn in Narrative Theory: Literary Narratives, Traveling Trope, and the Case of Virginia Woolf and the Tagores', *Narrative*, 19 (1): 1-32.

Fumagalli, Maria Cristina, Bénédicte Ledent and Roberto Del Valle Alcalá, eds (2013), *The Cross-Dressed Caribbean: Writing, Politics, Sexualities*, Charlottesville: University of Virginia Press.

Gardiner, Judith Kegan (1982-3), '*Good Morning, Midnight*; Good Night, Modernism', *boundary 2*, 11 (1/2): 233-51.

Geason, Susan, ed. (1997), *Regarding Jane Eyre*, Sydney: Vintage.

Gilbert, Sandra M. and Susan Gubar ([1979] 2000), *The Madwoman in the Attic: The Woman Writer and the Nineteenth-Century Literary Imagination*, New Haven, CT: Yale University Press.

Giles, Paul (2010), *Transnationalism in Practice: Essays on American Studies, Literature and Religion*, Edinburgh: Edinburgh University Press.

Gilroy, Paul (1993), *The Black Atlantic: Modernity and Double Consciousness*, London: Verso.

Gilson, Annette (2004), 'Internalizing Mastery: Jean Rhys, Ford Madox Ford, and the Fiction of Autobiography', *Modern Fiction Studies*, 50 (3): 632-56.

Glissant, Édouard (1981), *Le Discours antillais*, Paris: Seuil.
Glissant, Édouard (1989), *Caribbean Discourse: Selected Essays*, trans. Michael Dash, Charlottesville: University Press of Virginia.
Glissant, Édouard (1997), *Poetics of Relation*, trans. Betsy Wing, Ann Arbor: University of Michigan Press.
Gogwilt, Christopher (2011), *The Passage of Literature: Genealogies of Modernism in Conrad, Pramoedya, and Rhys*, Oxford: Oxford University Press.
Gregg, Veronica Marie (1995), *Jean Rhys's Historical Imagination. Reading and Writing the Creole*, Chapel Hill: University of North Carolina Press.
Gunning, David (2012), 'Concentric and Centripetal Narratives of Race: Caryl Phillips's *Dancing in the Dark* and Percival Everett's *Erasure*', in Bénédicte Ledent and Daria Tunca (eds), *Caryl Phillips: Writing in the Key of Life*, 359–74, Amsterdam: Rodopi.
Haliloğlu, Nagihan (2011), *Narrating from the Margins: Self-Representation of Female and Colonial Subjectivities in Jean Rhys's Novels*, Amsterdam: Rodopi.
Hanrahan, Barbara ([1977] 1986), *The Albatross Muff*, London: Chatto & Windus.
Hanrahan, Barbara (1998), *The Diaries of Barbara Hanrahan*, ed. Elaine Lindsay, St Lucia, Brisbane: University of Queensland Press.
Harris, Wilson (1983), *The Womb of Space: The Cross-Cultural Imagination*, Westport, CT: Greenwood Press.
Hearne, John (1974), 'The Wide Sargasso Sea: A West Indian Reflection', *Cornhill Magazine*, 1080: 323–33.
Heilmann, Ann and Mark Llewellyn (2010), *Neo-Victorianism: The Victorians in the Twenty-First Century*, Basingstoke: Palgrave Macmillan.
Herold, Jean Christopher (1958), *Mistress to an Age: A Life of Madame de Staël*, New York: Grove Press.
Ho, Elizabeth (2013), *Neo-Victorianism and the Memory of Empire*, London: Bloomsbury.
Hollander, Martien Kappers-den (1987), 'A Gloomy Child and its Devoted Godmother: Jean Rhys, *Barred, Sous les verrous*, and *In de Strik*, *Jean Rhys Review*, 1 (2): 20–30.
Honeychurch, Lennox ([1975] 1984), *The Dominica Story: A History of the Island*, Roseau: Dominica Institute.
Howells, Coral Ann (1990), 'Introduction: Jean Rhys', in Bonnie Kime Scott (ed.), *The Gender of Modernism: A Critical Anthology*, 372–7, Bloomington: Indiana University Press.
Hulme, Peter (1994), 'The Locked Heart: The Creole Family Romance of *Wide Sargasso Sea*', in Francis Barker et al. (eds), *Colonial Discourse, Postcolonial Theory*, 72–88, Manchester: Manchester University Press.
Hulme, Peter (2000), *Remnants of Conquest: The Island Caribs and Their Visitors, 1877–1998*, Oxford: Oxford University Press.
Issacharoff, Jess (2013), '"No Pride, No Name, No Face, No Country": Jewishness and National Identity in *Good Morning, Midnight*', in Kerry Johnson and Mary Wilson (eds), *Rhys Matters: New Critical Perspectives*, 111–29, New York: Palgrave Macmillan.

James, Louis (1978), *Jean Rhys*, London: Longman.
Jay, Paul (2013), *Global Matters: The Transnational Turn in Literary Studies*, Ithaca, NY: Cornell University Press.
Joannou, Maroula (2012), '"All right, I'll do anything for good clothes": Jean Rhys and Fashion', *Women: A Cultural Review*, 23 (4): 463–89.
Joannou, Maroula (2015), '"From Black to Red": Jean Rhys's Use of Dress in *Wide Sargasso Sea*', in Erica Johnson and Patricia Moran (eds), *Jean Rhys: Twentieth-Century Approaches*, 123–45, Edinburgh: Edinburgh University Press.
Johnson, Erica (2003), *Home, Maison, Casa: The Politics of Location in Works by Jean Rhys, Marguerite Duras, and Erminia Dell'Oro*, Madison, NJ: Farleigh Dickinson University Press.
Johnson, Erica (2006), 'Auto-Ghostwriting *Smile, Please: An Unfinished Autobiography*', *Biography*, 29 (4): 563–83.
Johnson, Erica and Patricia Moran, eds (2015), *Jean Rhys: Twenty-First Century Approaches*, Edinburgh: Edinburgh University Press.
Johnson, Erica and Elaine Savory, eds (2020), Wide Sargasso Sea *at Fifty*, New York: Palgrave Macmillan.
Johnson, Kerry and Mary Wilson (2013a), 'Introduction: Rhys Matters?', in Kerry Johnson and Mary Wilson (eds), *Rhys Matters: New Critical Perspectives*, 1–18, New York: Palgrave Macmillan.
Johnson, Kerry and Mary Wilson, eds (2013b), *Rhys Matters: New Critical Perspectives*, New York: Palgrave Macmillan.
Joyce, James ([1922] 1971), *Ulysses*, Harmondsworth: Penguin.
Judd, Alan (1991), *Ford Madox Ford*, London: Flamingo.
Kalaidjian, Andrew (2020), *Exhausted Ecologies: Modernism and Environmental Recovery*, Cambridge: Cambridge University Press.
Kaplan, Cora (2007), *Victoriana: Histories, Fictions, Criticism*, Edinburgh: Edinburgh University Press.
Kascakova Janka and Gerri Kimber, eds (2015), *Katherine Mansfield and Continental Europe, Connections and Influences*, New York: Palgrave Macmillan.
Kennedy, A.L. (2000), 'Introduction', in Jean Rhys, *Good Morning, Midnight*, v–xii, London: Penguin.
Kime Scott, Bonnie, ed. (1990), *The Gender of Modernism: A Critical Anthology*, Bloomington: Indiana University Press.
Kincaid, Jamaica (1985), *Annie John*, London: Picador.
Kincaid, Jamaica (1988), *A Small Place*, London: Virago.
Kincaid, Jamaica (1991a), *Lucy*, New York: Plume.
Kincaid, Jamaica (1991b), 'On Seeing England for the First Time', *Transition*, 51: 32–40.
Kincaid, Jamaica (1992), 'Biography of a Dress', *Grand Street*, 11 (3): 93–100.
Kincaid, Jamaica (1995), 'Putting Myself Together', *The New Yorker*, 20 February. Available online: https://www.newyorker.com/magazine/1995/02/20/putting-myself-together (accessed 13 January 2020).

Kincaid, Jamaica (1996), *The Autobiography of My Mother*, London: Vintage.
Kincaid, Jamaica (2000), *My Garden Book*, London: Vintage.
Kincaid, Jamaica (2013), *See Now Then*, New York: Farrar, Straus and Giroux.
Kloepfer, Deborah Kelly (1989), *The Unspeakable Mother: Forbidden Discourse in Jean Rhys and H.D.*, Ithaca, NY: Cornell University Press.
Kohlke, Marie-Luise (2013), 'Neo-Victorian Biofiction and the Special/Spectral Case of Barbara Chase-Riboud's *Hottentot Venus*', *Australian Journal of Victorian Fiction*, 18 (3): 4–21.
Kolodny, Annette (1986), 'A Map for Rereading: Gender and the Interpretation of Literary Texts', in Elaine Showalter (Ed.), *The New Feminist Criticism: Essays on Women, Literature, and Theory*, 46–62, London: Virago.
Konzett, Delia (2003), 'Ethnic Modernism in Jean Rhys's *Good Morning, Midnight*', *Journal of Caribbean Literatures*, 3 (3): 63–76.
Koselleck, Reinhart (2002), 'Transformations of Experience and Methodological Change: A Historical-Anthropological Essay', trans. Jobst Welge, in *The Practice of Conceptual History: Timing History, Spacing Concepts*, 45–83, Stanford, CA: Stanford University Press.
Kral, Françoise (2017), *Sounding Out History: Caryl Phillips's* Crossing the River, Nanterre: Presses Universitaires de Paris Nanterre.
Lamming, George ([1953] 1987), *In the Castle of My Skin*, London: Longman.
Lansbury, Coral (1985), *Ringarra*, New York: HarperCollins.
Ledent, Bénédicte (2012), '"Look liberty in the face": Determinism and Free Will in Caryl Phillips's *Foreigners: Three English Lives*', in Bénédicte Ledent and Daria Tunca (eds), *Caryl Phillips: Writing in the Key of Life*, 75–85, Amsterdam: Rodopi.
Ledent, Bénédicte (2019), 'There Is Always the Other Side, Always', *Wasafiri*, 34 (1): 61–6.
Ledent, Bénédicte and Evelyn O'Callaghan (2017), 'Caryl Phillips's *The Lost Child*: A Story of Loss and Connection', *Ariel: A Review of International English Literature*, 48 (3–4): 229–47.
Ledent, Bénédicte, Caryl Phillips and Daria Tunca (2019), '"A Growth to Understanding": An Interview with Caryl Phillips about Biographical Fiction', *Journal of Commonwealth Literature*: 1–13. https://doi.org/10.1177/0021989418814586.
Lehman, Robert S. (2016), *Impossible Modernism: T.S. Eliot, Walter Benjamin, and the Critique of Historical Reason*, Stanford, CA: Stanford University Press.
Lejeune, Philippe (1989), *On Autobiography*, ed. Paul John Eakin, trans. Katherine Leary, Minneapolis: University of Minnesota Press.
Levenson, Michael (1983), *A Genealogy of Modernism: A Study of English Literary Doctrine, 1908–1922*, Cambridge: Cambridge University Press.
Livett, Jennifer (2016), *Wild Island*, Sydney: Allen & Unwin.
Lohrey, Amanda (1995), 'Jane Eyre', *RePublica*, 2: 75–9.
Look Lai, Wally (1968), 'The Road to Thornfield Hall: An Analysis of *Wide Sargasso Sea*', in John La Rose (ed.), *New Beacon Reviews: Collection One*, 38–52, London: New Beacon Books.

Look Lai, Walton (1998), *The Chinese in the West Indies, 1860–1995: A Documentary History*, Mona, Jamaica: University of the West Indies Press.

Lopoukhine, Juliana, Frédéric Regard and Kerry-Jane Wallart, eds (2020), Jean Rhys: Writing Precariously, in *Women: A Cultural Review* 31 (2). Available online: https://www.tandfonline.com/toc/rwcr20/31/2 (accessed 24 August 2020).

Malouf, David (2000), *Jane Eyre: Libretto for an Opera by Michael Berkeley*, London: Vintage.

Mapping Expatriate Paris (n.d.), [digital humanities project] 'Shakespeare and Company – Project'. Available online: https://mep.princeton.edu (accessed 5 August 2019).

Marcus, Laura (1994), *Auto/biographical Discourses: Theory, Criticism, Practice*, Manchester: Manchester University Press.

Marcus, Steven (1966), *The Other Victorians: A Study of Sexuality and Pornography in Mid-Nineteenth-Century England*, New York: Basic Books.

Mardorossian, Carine (2015), 'Caribbean Formations in the Rhysian Corpus', in Erica Johnson and Patricia Moran (eds), *Jean Rhys: Twenty-First Century Approaches*, 107–22, Edinburgh: Edinburgh University Press.

Maurel, Sylvie (1998), *Jean Rhys*, London: Macmillan.

Maurois, André (1929), *Aspects of Biography*, trans. S.C. Roberts, Cambridge: Cambridge University Press.

McClintock, Anne (1995), *Imperial Leather: Race, Gender and Sexuality in the Colonial Context*, New York: Routledge.

McCracken, Donal P. (1997), *Gardens of Empire: Botanical Institutions of the Victorian British Empire*, London: Leicester University Press.

McDougall, Russell (2002), 'Australia and the Caribbean', *Australian Cultural History*, 21: 1–15.

McGarrity, Maria (2008), *Washed by the Gulf Stream: The Historic and Geographic Relation of Irish and Caribbean Literature*, Cranbury, NJ: Associated University Presses.

McKittrick, Katherine (2013), 'Plantation Futures', *Small Axe*, 42: 1–15.

McLeod, John (2011), 'Sounding Silence: Transculturation and its Thresholds', *Transnational Literature*, 4 (1): 1–13.

McLeod, John (2015), *Life Lines: Writing Transcultural Adoption*, London: Bloomsbury.

McMahon, Elizabeth (2016), *Islands, Identity and the Literary Imagination*, London: Anthem.

Metz, Jeremy (2015), 'Recrossing the Sargasso Sea: Trauma, Edward Kamau Brathwaite and His Critics', *Ariel: A Review of International English Literature*, 46 (4): 89–121.

Mignolo, Walter D. (2007), 'Delinking', *Cultural Studies*, 21 (2): 449–514.

Miller, Nancy K. (2007), 'The Entangled Self: Genre Bondage in the Age of Memoir', *PMLA*, 122 (2): 537–48.

Moon-ho, Jung (2006), *Coolies and Cane: Race, Labor, and Sugar in the Age of Emancipation*, Baltimore: Johns Hopkins University Press.

Moore, Brian L. and Michele A. Johnson (2004), *Neither Led nor Driven: Contesting British Cultural Imperialism in Jamaica, 1865–1920*, Kingston, Jamaica: University of the West Indies Press.

Moore, George (1885), *Literature at Nurse, Or, Circulating Morals*, London: Vizetelly.

Naipaul, V. S. (1972), 'Without a Dog's Chance', *New York Review of Books*, 18 May: 29–31.

Nasta, Susheila (2009), '"Beyond the Frame": Writing a Life and Jamaica Kincaid's Family Album', *Contemporary Women's Writing*, 3 (1): 64–85.

Nève, Edward de (1932), *Barred*, trans. Jean Rhys, London: Desmond Harmsworth.

Nord, Deborah Epstein (2006), *Gypsies and the British Imagination, 1807–1930*, New York: Columbia University Press.

Obeah Night (1993), [Play] dir. Paul Monaghan, La Mama, Melbourne.

Olaussen, Maria (1993), 'Jean Rhys's Construction of Blackness as Escape from White Feminism in *Wide Sargasso Sea*', *Ariel: A Review of International English Literature*, 24 (2): 65–82.

Ortiz, Fernando ([1940] 1995), *Cuban Counterpoint: Tobacco and Sugar*, trans. Harriet De Onis, Durham, NC: Duke University Press.

Oxford English Dictionary (OED) *Online* (2018), Oxford University Press. Available online: https://www.oed.com (accessed 28 May 2020).

Paravisini Gebert, Lizabeth (2007), 'Jean Rhys's "Heat" and the Tragedy of Mont Pelée', in Joyce Harte (ed.), *Come Weep with Me: Loss and Mourning in Anglophone Women's Writing*, 11–26, Newcastle-upon-Tyne: Cambridge Scholars Publications.

Parey, Armelle (2006), 'Introduction: *Jane Eyre*, Past and Present', *La Revue LISA/LISA e-journal*, 4 (4): 1–8. Available online: https://journals.openedition.org/lisa/1741 (accessed 31 December 2006).

Phillips, Caryl (1991), *Cambridge*, London: Bloomsbury.

Phillips, Caryl ([1993] 1994), *Crossing the River*, London: Picador.

Phillips, Caryl (2005), *Dancing in the Dark*, London: Secker and Warburg.

Phillips, Caryl (2015), *The Lost Child*, London: Oneworld.

Phillips, Caryl (2018a), *A View of the Empire at Sunset*, London: Vintage.

Phillips, Caryl (2018b), '*A View of the Empire at Sunset*: Coffee with Caryl Phillips', [Podcast] Interview at the Shakespeare & Company Bookshop, Paris, 22 June 2018. Available online: https://soundcloud.com/shakespeareandcompany/a-view-of-the-empire-at-sunset-coffee-with-caryl-phillips (accessed 10 September 2019).

Phillips, Caryl, ed. (1997), *Extravagant Strangers, A Literature of Belonging*, London: Faber.

Poli, Bernard J. (1967), *Ford Madox Ford and the Transatlantic Review*, Syracuse, NY: Syracuse University Press.

Powell, Joan Miller (2012), 'Hybrid Inventiveness: Caryl Phillips's Black Atlantic Subjectivity – *The European Tribe* and *The Atlantic Sound*', Bénédicte Ledent and Daria Tunca (eds), *Caryl Phillips: Writing in the Key of Life*, 87–105, Amsterdam: Rodopi.

Proust, Marcel (1984), *On Art and Literature*, trans. Sylvia Townsend Warner, New York: Carroll & Graf.

Proust, Marcel ([1913] 2002), *In Search of Lost Time Volume I: Swann's Way*, trans. C.K. Scott Moncrieff and Terence Kilmartin, revised D.J. Enright, London: Vintage.

Pulda, Molly (2011), 'A Feminist Compact: Jean Rhys's *Smile Please* and Life Writing Theory', *Contemporary Women's Writing*, 6 (2): 159–76.

Raiskin, Judith (1991), 'Jean Rhys: Creole Writing and Strategies of Resistance,' *Ariel: A Review of International English Literature*, 22 (4): 51–67.

Raiskin, Judith (1996), *Snow on the Cane Fields: Women's Writings and Creole Subjectivity*, Minneapolis: University of Minnesota Press.

Ramchand, Kenneth (1970), *The West Indian Novel and Its Background*, London: Faber.

Rancière, Jacques (2004), *The Politics of Aesthetics: The Distribution of the Sensible*, trans. Gabriel Rockhill, London: Continuum.

Ransom, W.S., ed. (1988), *Australian National Dictionary: A Dictionary of Australianisms on Historical Principles*, Melbourne: Oxford University Press.

Raymond Williams (1989), 'When was Modernism?', in Tony Pinkney (ed.), The Politics of Modernism: Against the New Conformists, 31–35, London: Verso.

Reviron-Piégay, Floriane (2018), 'Jean Rhys's *Smile Please*: Re/De Constructing Identity through Autobiography and Photography', *Ebc*, 54. Available online: https://journals.openedition.org/ebc/4364 (accessed 1 August 2019).

Rhys, Ernest (1931), *Everyman Remembers*, London: Dent.

Rhys, Jean (1924), 'Vienne', *Transatlantic Review*, 2 (6): 639–45.

Rhys, Jean (1927), *The Left Bank and Other Stories*, with a preface by Ford Madox Ford, London: Jonathan Cape.

Rhys, Jean ([1928] 2000), *Quartet*, Harmondsworth: Penguin.

Rhys, Jean ([1930] 1971), *After Leaving Mr Mackenzie*, London: Penguin.

Rhys, Jean (1931), 'The Christmas Presents of Mynheer Van Rooz', *Time and Tide*, 12 (48): 1360–2.

Rhys, Jean ([1934] 2000), *Voyage in the Dark*, London: Penguin.

Rhys, Jean ([1939] 2000), *Good Morning, Midnight*, London: Penguin.

Rhys, Jean ([1966] 1999), *Wide Sargasso Sea*, ed. Judith Raiskin, New York: Norton.

Rhys, Jean, ([1976] 1979), *Sleep it Off Lady*, Harmondsworth: Penguin.

Rhys, Jean ([1979] 1990), *Smile Please: An Unfinished Autobiography*, London: Penguin.

Rhys, Jean ([1984] 1985), *Jean Rhys: Letters 1931–66*, ed. Francis Wyndham and Diana Melly, Harmondsworth: Penguin.

Rhys, Jean (1990), '*Voyage in the Dark*: Part IV (Original Version)', in Bonnie Kime Scott (ed.), *The Gender of Modernism: A Critical Anthology*, 381–9, Bloomington: Indiana University Press.

Rhys, Jean (2017), *The Collected Short Stories*, London: Penguin.
Rhys, Jean, Black Exercise Book, Archive, Tulsa, Series 1, Box 1, folder 1, p. 11.
Rhys, Jean, 'L'Affaire Ford', Jean Rhys Archive, McFarlin Library, Tulsa University, Series 1, Box 2, folder 23.
Rich, Adrienne (1972), 'When We Dead Awaken: Writing as Re-Vision', *College English*, 34 (1): 18–30.
Richardson, Dorothy (2020), *Pilgrimage 1 & 2*, Scott McCracken (Ed.), Oxford: Oxford University Press.
Ricklefs, M.C. (1993), *A History of Modern Indonesia since c.1300*, 2nd edn, Stanford, CA: Stanford University Press.
Ricœur, Paul (1984), *The Reality of the Historical Past*, Milwaukee, WI: Marquette University Press.
Ricœur, Paul (1991), 'The Creativity of Language', in *A Ricœur Reader: Reflection and Imagination*, 463–81, ed. Mario Valdès, New York: Harvester Wheatsheaf.
Rimbaud, Arthur (1964), *Œuvres poétiques*, ed. Paterne Berrichon, Paris: Garnier-Flammarion.
Rimbaud, Arthur (2004), *Selected Poems and Letters*, trans. Jeremy Harding and John Sturrock, London: Penguin.
Robbe-Grillet, Alain (1963), 'Time and Description in Fiction Today', in *For a New Novel: Essays on Fiction*, trans. Richard Howard, 143–56, Evanston, IL: Northwestern University Press.
Roberts, J. Kimberley (1983), *Ernest Rhys*, Cardiff: University of Wales Press.
Rodney, Walter ([1972] 2018), *How Europe Underdeveloped Africa*, London: Verso.
Rodriguez, Ileana (1994), *House/Garden/Nation: Space, Gender, Ethnicity in Post-Colonial Latin American Literatures by Women*, trans. Robert Carr and Ileana Rodriguez, Durham, NC: Duke University Press.
Rønning, Anne Holden (2011), 'Literary Transculturations and Modernity: Some Reflections', *Transnational Literature*, 4 (1): 1–10.
Roosa, John (2006), *Pretext for Mass Murder: The September 30th Movement & Suharto's Coup d'État in Indonesia*, Madison: University of Wisconsin Press.
Rose, Jacqueline (1986), *Sexuality in the Field of Vision*, London: Verso.
Rosenberg, Leah (1999), '"The rope of course being covered in flowers": Metropolitan Discourses and the Construction of Creole Identity in Jean Rhys's Black Exercise Book', *Jean Rhys Review*, 11 (1): 5–33.
Ross, Kristin (1988), *The Emergence of Social Space: Rimbaud and the Paris Commune*, Basingstoke: Macmillan.
Rovera, Catherine (2015), *Genèse d'une folie créole: Jean Rhys et Jane Eyre*, Paris: Hermann.
Sade, Marquis de ([1791] 2012), *Justine*, trans. John Phillips Oxford: Oxford University Press.
Sage, Lorna (1992), *Women in the House of Fiction: Post-War Women Novelists*, New York: Routledge.

Sarraute, Nathalie ([1946] 1990), *Portrait of a Man Unknown*, trans. Maria Jolas, preface Jean-Paul Sartre, New York: George Braziller.

Saunders, Max (2013), *Self-Impression: Life-writing, Autobiografiction, and the Forms of Modern Literature*, Oxford: Oxford University Press.

Savory, Elaine (1996), 'The Word Becomes *nam*: Self and Community in the Poetry of Kamau Brathwaite and Its Relationship to Caribbean Culture and Postmodern Theory', in John C. Hawley (ed.), *Writing the Nation: Self and Country and the Post-Colonial Imagination*, 23–44, Amsterdam: Rodopi.

Savory, Elaine (1998), *Jean Rhys*, Cambridge: Cambridge University Press.

Savory, Elaine (2009), *The Cambridge Introduction to Jean Rhys*, Cambridge: Cambridge University Press.

Savory, Elaine (2015), 'Jean Rhys's Environmental Language: Oppositions, Dialogues and Silences', in Erica Johnson and Patricia Moran (eds), *Jean Rhys: Twenty-First Century Approaches*, 85–106, Edinburgh: Edinburgh University Press.

Selvon, Sam ([1956] 2006), *The Lonely Londoners*, London: Penguin.

Sharrad, Paul (2004), 'Cloth and Self-definition in Jamaica Kincaid's *The Autobiography of My Mother*', *Kunapipi*, 26 (1): 54–65.

Shklovsky, Victor ([1917] 1991), 'Art as Device', in *Theory of Prose*, trans. Benjamin Sher, 1–14, Kalkey Archive Press. Available online: https://doubleoperative.files.wordpress.com/2009/12/art-as-device.pdf (accessed 20 December 2019).

Smith, Angela (2015), '"There is always the other side, always": Katherine Mansfield's and Jean Rhys's Travellers in Europe', in Kascakova Janka and Gerri Kimber (eds), *Katherine Mansfield and Continental Europe: Connections and Influences*, 142–53, Basingstoke: Palgrave Macmillan.

Smith, Barry (1996), *Peter Warlock: The Life of Philip Heseltine*, Oxford: Oxford University Press.

Smith, Sidonie and Julia Watson (2001), *Reading Autobiography: A Guide for Interpreting Life Narratives*, Minneapolis: Minnesota University Press.

Snaith, Anna (2014), *Modernist Voyages: Colonial Women Writers in London 1890–1945*, Cambridge: Cambridge University Press.

Spivak, Gayatri Chakravorty (1985), 'Three Women's Texts and a Critique of Imperialism', *Critical Inquiry*, 12 (1): 243–61.

Spivak, Gayatri Chakravory (1988), 'Can the Subaltern Speak?', in Cary Nelson and Lawrence Grossberg (eds), *Marxism and the Interpretation of Culture*, 271–313, Urbana: University of Illinois Press.

Stanford Friedman, Susan, ed. (2018), *Turning Back to the Future in Twenty-First Century Literature and Art*, London: Bloomsbury.

Stewart, Annette (2010), *Barbara Hanrahan: A Biography*, Kent Town, Adelaide: Wakefield Press.

Stoneman, Patsy (1996), *Brontë Transformations: The Cultural Dissemination of* Jane Eyre *and* Wuthering Heights, London: Prentice Hall/Harvester Wheatsheaf.

Stuart, Andrea (2003), *The Rose of Martinique: A Life of Napoleon's Josephine*, London: Macmillan.
Stuart, Andrea (2013), *Sugar in the Blood: A Family's Story of Slavery and Empire*, New York: Knopf.
Su, John J. (2015), 'The Empire of Affect: Reading Rhys After Post-Colonial Theory', in Erica Johnson and Patricia Moran (eds), *Jean Rhys: Twenty-First Century Approaches*, 171–89, Edinburgh: Edinburgh University Press.
Sudjic, Olivia (2018), *Exposure*, London: Peninsula.
Taylor-Batty, Juliette (2013), *Multilingualism in Modernist Fiction*, London: Palgrave Macmillan.
Teresa of Avila, Saint ([1562–5] 1957), *The Life of Saint Teresa of Avila by Herself*, trans. J. M. Cohen, London: Penguin.
Thacker, Andrew (2019a), 'Of Bliss and Blushing: Cities and Affect in Katherine Mansfield and Jean Rhys', in Gerri Kimber, Isobel Maddison and Todd Martin (eds), *Katherine Mansfield and Elizabeth von Arnim: Katherine Mansfield Yearbook*, vol. 11, 163–80, Edinburgh: Edinburgh University Press.
Thacker, Andrew (2019b), *Modernism, Space and the City: Outsiders and Affect in Paris, Vienna, Berlin and London*, Edinburgh: Edinburgh University Press.
Thomas, Deborah A. (2011), *Exceptional Violence: Embodied Citizenship in Transnational Jamaica*, Durham, NC: Duke University Press.
Thomas, Sue (1994–5), 'Jean Rhys, "grilled sole," and an experience of "mental seduction"', *New Literatures Review*, 28/29: 65–84.
Thomas, Sue (1997), 'Revisionary (Post)modernist Plausibilities? Paul Monaghan's Staging of *Obeah Night* and the Film of *Wide Sargasso Sea*: A Commentary', *Jean Rhys Review*, 8 (1–2): 30–5.
Thomas, Sue (1999), *The Worlding of Jean Rhys*, Westport, CT: Greenwood Press.
Thomas, Sue (2015a), 'Jean Rhys and Katherine Mansfield Writing the "sixth act"', in Erica Johnson and Patricia Moran (eds), *Jean Rhys: Twenty-First Century Approaches*, 21–39, Edinburgh: Edinburgh University Press.
Thomas, Sue (2015b), 'Transforming *Jane Eyre*: Its Australian Stage Adaptations', *Australian Literary Studies*, 30 (3): 134–48.
Thurman, Judith (1999), *A Life of Colette: Secrets of the Flesh*, New York: Ballantine Books.
Tiedemann, Rolf (1999), 'Dialectics at a Standstill', in Walter Benjamin, *The Arcades Project*, trans. Gary Smith and Andre Lefevere, 929–45, Cambridge, MA: Belknap Press of Harvard University Press.
Tolstoy, Leo ([1885] 2005), 'Strider: The Story of a Horse', in *Master and Man and Other Stories*, trans. Ronald Wilks and Paul Foote, 67–107, London: Penguin.
Tunca, Daria (2017), 'The Poetics of Invisibility: A Stylistic Analysis of Caryl Phillips' *Foreigners: Three English Lives*', *Ariel: A Review of International English Literature*, 48 (3–4): 159–86.

Walcott, Derek (1986), *Collected Poems 1948-1984*, New York: Farrar, Straus, & Giroux.
Wallart, Kerry-Jane (2016), '"Saving Bodies"—Performance in *Crossing the River*', in Vanessa Guignery and Christian Gutleben (eds), *Traversée d'une œuvre: Crossing the River de Caryl Phillips, Cycnos*, 32 (1): 173-88.
Weiland, Willoh S. and Halcyon Macleod (n.d.), [residency diary] *Fresh Milk Barbados*, St. George, Barbados.
Wide Sargasso Sea (1993), [Film] dir. John Duigan, Laughing Kookaburra Productions, Australia.
Wide Sargasso Sea (1997), [Chamber opera] by Brian Howard, performed by Chamber Made Opera, Melbourne.
Wittman, Emily O. (2014), '"Death before the Fact": Posthumous Autobiography in Jean Rhys's *Good Morning, Midnight* and *Smile Please*', in Maria Di Battista and Emily Wittman (eds), *Modernism and Autobiography*, 185-96, Cambridge: Cambridge University Press.
Woman in the Attic (1987), [Play] dir. Peter Freund, by Gabby Brennan and Polly Croke, performed by Whistling in the Theatre, Anthill Theatre, Melbourne.
Wyndham, Francis (1966), 'Introduction', in Jean Rhys, *Wide Sargasso Sea*, 5-13, London: André Deutsch.
Wyndham, Francis (1984), 'Introduction', in Francis Wyndham and Diana Melly (eds), *Jean Rhys: Letters, 1931-1966*, 9-12, London: André Deutsch.
Yelin, Louise (2017), 'Migrant Subjects, Invisible Presences: Biography in the Writings of Caryl Phillips', *Ariel: A Review of International English Literature*, 48 (3-4): 103-28.
Young, Iris Marion (2005), *On Female Body Experience*, Oxford: Oxford University Press.
Zimmerman, Emma (2019), 'Uncanny Cities: Urban Geographies and Metropolitan Life', in Benjamin Kohlmann and Matthew Taunton (eds), *A History of 1930s British Literature*, 31-43, Cambridge: Cambridge University Press.

Index

After Leaving Mr Mackenzie 2, 74
   Indonesian reference 81–2, 84, 86
   modernist novel 5, 84, 160
   Quai des Grands Augustins 54
   slave figure 86, 90–1
Allen, Grant 23
Allen, Walter 36
Allinson, Adrian 54
Als, Hilton 160–2, 165, 173
Althusser, Louis 163
Anderson, Sherwood 52
Angier, Carole
   biography based on fiction 31, 65
   flawed biography 173
   Rhys's biographer 15–16, 31–2, 87
   Rhys's modernist novels 57–8
   Rhys's poetic language 152
   Rhys's prison sentence 137
   Rhys's relationship with Ford 62
   Rhys's stay in Paris 52, 54
Arthur, Sir George 102
Athill, Diana 87
   Rhys as translator 17
   Rhys meeting Joyce 58
   Rhys's autobiographical work 65–6, 130, 144
   Rhys's editor 183
A View of the Empire at Sunset 9–11, 83, 143–55, 159–74, 177–86

Baker, Josephine 25
Baldick, Chris 99
Barnes, Djuna 52
Barret-Ducroq, Françoise 24
Baudelaire, Charles 83, 107
Bauman, Zygmunt 8
Beach, Sylvia 8, 51–3, 55, 58–9
Benjamin, Walter 44, 75, 89
   dialectical images 35, 83–4, 91
   importance of anecdote 46–8
Benstock, Shari 30, 52

Bernanos, George 65, 66
Bishop, Morchard 65
Bliss, Eliot 57
Bloch, Marc 8, 35–8, 40–3, 46–7
Bloom, Harold 55
Blue Marble photograph xi
Bonaparte, Napoleon 17–18, 77–8
Booth, Charles O'Hara 102
Bourdieu, Pierre 55, 161
Bowen, Stella 18
Brathwaite, Edward Kamau 10, 109–25
Briffaut, Herma 20
Broch, Hermann 151
Brontë, Charlotte 9, 95, 99–100, 130–1
Butler, Judith 130, 163

Camus, Albert 35
Cantwell, Mary 66, 130
Carco, Francis 2, 3, 62
Caribbean Great Houses 104–8
Carr, Helen 7–8, 35, 36, 57, 66, 72, 137
Caruth, Cathy 110, 113
Césaire, Aimé 2, 52, 125
Chaplin, Charlie 45
Childs, Peter 6
Clifford, James 122
Cohn, Dorrit 145–7, 151, 155
Colette, Sidonie-Gabrielle 8, 17–24
Conrad, Joseph 52, 81, 84–5, 107
Covici, Pascal 62
Crawl Me Blood 96, 104–8
Creole
   Modernism 83, 84
   Rhys's background 6, 10, 15–16, 83, 110–19, 131–3
   white 16, 18–20, 109–10
Cross, Felix 105, 107

Damrosch, David 95
de Beauharnais, Joséphine 8, 17–18
de Beauvoir, Simone 8, 52

Index

de Jouvenel, Bertrand 19
de Sade, Marquis 28–9
de Staël, Madame 77
Dell'Oro, Erminia 8
Dickinson, Emily 1, 2, 35, 49, 57
Dillon Brown, J. 6
Drake, Sandra 113
Du Maurier, Daphne 62
Duigan, John 100
Dumas, Alexandre 41
Dunning, R.C. 53
Duras, Marguerite 8

Ekert-Rotholz, Alice 89
Eliot, George 100
Eliot, T. S. 55, 67, 112, 115, 123–4
Emberley, Julia 128
Emery, Mary Lou 2, 35
Eyerman, Ron 15

Flanagan, Richard 103
Ford, Ford Madox 54, 66, 67, 71, 84
    affair with Rhys 62, 160–1
    connection with Rhys in Paris 52–3
    portrayal in *Quartet* 18, 62, 65
    Rhys's language skills 17, 62
    Rhys's notebooks 7
    Transatlantic Review 53
Forster, E. M. 4, 166
Fowles, John 95
Franklin, Lady Jane 101–2
Franklin, Sir John 101
Friedman, Susan Stanford 96–7

Gardiner, Judith 57, 58
Gilbert, Sandra 115–16, 160
Gillard, Julia 103
Gilson, Annette 70
Glissant, Édouard 109–10, 119–21, 124
    poetics of relation 112–13, 125
'Goodbye Marcus, Goodbye Rose' 53
Good Morning, Midnight 53, 128–9, 131, 149
    alcoholism 44
    BBC version 87
    colonial oppression 4
    compared to *L'Étrange défaite* 35–40, 46

    ending of 58, 74
    experiences of defeat 8
    Indonesian references 82, 85–6
    letter writing 76
    life writing 77–8
    modernist novel 5
    narrative structure 44
    nationality issues 69–72
    Parisian setting 16, 24, 60–1, 72
    power structures 46
    restaurant scene 85–6, 90–1
    sexual behaviour 27–31
    time issues 72–5
    title of 35, 57
    use of anecdote 47–9
Gregg, Veronica 27, 113, 173
Grigson, Geoffrey 56
Gubar, Susan 115–16, 160

Haliloğlu, Nagihan 73
Hanrahan, Barbara 9, 96–9
Harris, Wilson 120
Hearne, John 4
Hemingway, Ernest 51, 58
Heseltine, Philip 54
Ho, Elizabeth 98
Howard, Brian 100
Howells, Coral Ann 57
Hugo, Victor 17, 41
Hulme, Peter 81, 87, 91, 110
'Hunger' 39
Huxley, Aldous 54

'Illusion' 39
Indonesia 81–92

James, Henry 52
James, Louis 30
Jane Eyre 57, 95, 99, 130–1
    revisioned by modern authors 100–2
Jenkins, Elizabeth 57
Johnson, Erica 1
Johnson, Michele A. 105
Joyce, James 2, 3, 30, 51–2, 58, 178
Jung Moon-ho 90
Jynel, Natasha 107

Kafka, Franz 44–6
Kaplan, Cora 95
Kappers-den Hollander, Martien 62
Kennedy, A. L. 35
Kincaid, Jamaica 10, 127–36, 139–41
Kipling, Rudyard 2
Kirkaldy, Peggy 56, 87
Kohlke, Marie-Louise 160
Konzett, Delia 73
Koselleck, Reinhart 36

L'Étrange défaite 35–8, 40–3, 46–7
Lacan, Jacques 52
Lai, Wally Look 4
Landoy, Henry 18
Ledent, Bénédicte 159, 177
Lehman, Robert S. 48
Lehmann, John 56–7
Lehmann, Rosamond 57
Lejeune, Philippe 69
Lenglet, Ella Williams *see* Rhys, Jean
Lenglet, Jean 16, 54, 62, 170, 180–1
Lessing, Doris 8
'Let Them Call it Jazz' 39, 136–8
Livett, Jennifer 10, 96, 101–4, 107–8
Lohrey, Amanda 9, 96, 100–2, 107–8
Lopoukhine, Juliana xi

Macleod, Halcyon 10, 96, 107
Malouf, David 103
Mansfield, Katherine 2, 3, 51–2, 57, 178
Marcus, Steven 98
Maupassant, Guy de 7–8
Maurel, Sylvie 149, 160
McClintock, Anne 165
Melly, Diana 95
Modernism
    Anglophone 52
    Creole 83, 84
    English 84
    French 8, 61
    Indonesian lineage 82, 84
    literary 9
    male 58
    postcolonial 10, 109–25
    reaction against biography 68
    status of Rhys 55
Moerman, Ellen Ruth 81, 86–8

Moerman, Job 86–7, 89
Moerman, Maryvonne 9, 81, 86–9
Monaghan, Paul 100
Moore, Brian L. 105
Moore, George 54
Moran, Patricia 1
Morrison, Toni 8
Mouttet, Louis 168

Naipaul, V. S. 4, 71
Nasution, Abdul 86, 89
Nazi occupation of France 41–2
Newman, Zahra 107

'Obeah Night' 122

Paravisini-Gebert, Lizabeth 168
Parey, Armelle 107
Paris
    Jean Rhys conference xi–xii, 11
    Rhys's life in 179, 182
Phillips, Caryl 9–11, 83, 143–55, 159–74, 177–86
'Pioneers, Oh Pioneers' 3
Poe, Edgar Allan 52
Proust, Marcel 7, 67–8

Quartet 53
    ending of 74
    Ford's reaction to 65
    letter writing 76
    modernist novel 5
    Parisian setting 16, 24–7
    portrayal of Ford 18, 62
    Rhys meeting Joyce 58
    Rhys's relationship with Ford 62, 160

Raiskin, Judith 90
Ramchand, Kenneth 4
Rees, Gwendolyn 7
Regard, Frédéric xi
Reviron-Piégay, Floriane 172–3
Rhys, Ernest 54
Rhys, Jean
    affair with Ford 62, 160–1
    autobiographical material 66–7, 69–75, 79
    Caribbean author 4, 6

chorus girl 21, 24
colonial oppression 4
concept of strangeness 38–9
cosmopolitanism 5
Creole background 6, 10, 15–16, 83, 110–19, 131–3
diasporic writing 2
Dominican oigins 3–4, 15–16, 37
excluded from Caribbean canon 110–11
fictionalized in *A View of the Empire at Sunset* 143–55, 159–74, 177–86
French connections xii, 5, 7–8, 59–61
French language skills 3
French translations 61–3
Indonesian links 81–92
influence on Australian writers 96–108
letters of 95
life in Paris 179, 182
links with Mansfield 3
literary networks 56–7
marriage to Lenglet 16, 17
marriage to Smith 57
meeting Joyce 58
modernist writer 2–4, 6, 84, 160
neo-Victorian fiction 95–108
poetic language 152
prison sentence 137
schooling 16
significance of clothing 128–30, 132–3, 137–9
similarities with Colette 20–4
subjugation of women 129
translating Carco 3
travels 3
use of anecdote 46–9
views on writing 75–6
Rhys, Owen 15–16
Richardson, Dorothy 38, 52
Richepin, Jean 59
Ricoeur, Paul 122
Ridge, Lola 56
Rimbaud, Arthur 9, 56, 59–61, 72, 77
Rodney, Walter 42
Ross, Kristin 60

Sarraute, Nathalie 52
Sartre, Jean-Paul 56

Sayers, Dorothy L. 52
Scott, Bonnie Kime 57
Scott, Dennis 120
Senior, Olive 173
Sewell, Anna 77
Shakespeare and Company bookshop 8, 51–5, 57–9, 63, 177
Shakespeare, William 107
Sheridan, Brinsley 56
Shklovsky, Viktor 6
Sleep it Off Lady 53
Smile Please 10, 78, 163–4, 166–9
  act of writing 21, 161
  autobiographical nature of Rhys's novels 130, 144, 160
  Caribbean background 4, 11, 171–2
  dress 131–6
  publication of 144
  Rhys's language skills 16–17
  Rhys's views on biography 67
Smith, Lancelot Grey Hugh 16
Smith, Leslie Tilden 57
Smith, Stevie 56, 57
Snaith, Anna 2
Spivak, Gayatri Chakravorty 98, 100, 114, 160, 173
Stanford Friedman, Susan 160
Stein, Gertrude 52
Stuart, Andrea 17–18, 21
Su, John 163
Sudjic, Olivia 79
Swinnerton, Frank 56

Taylor-Batty, Juliette 62
'Tea with an Artist' 39
'Temps Perdi' 5, 6
The Albatross Muff 96–9
'The Christmas Presents of Mynheer Van Rooz' 56
'The Day they Burned the Books' 2
The Left Bank and Other Stories xii, 52
'The Sidi' 4
The Zea Mexican Diary 10, 117, 123
Thomas, Deborah A. 105
Thomas, Sue 27, 145, 149, 173–4
Thurman, Judith 19, 22
Tiedemann, Rolf 35
'Till September, Petronella' 54

'Tout Montparnasse and a Lady' 39, 62
Transatlantic Review 53, 58
'Trio' 39
Tunca, Daria 144

Vaz Dias, Selma 55, 87
Verlaine, Paul 9, 56, 57, 59–61, 77
'Vienne' 4, 53, 58, 177
Voyage in the Dark 2, 11
   autobiographical basis 66, 68, 160
   Caribbean background 4, 5
   cosmopolitanism 5
   ending of 54, 74, 98s
   French authors 59
   importance of clothing 127–8
   letter writing 76
   poetic language 152

Walcott, Derek 107, 118, 120–2, 173
Wallart, Kerry-Jane xi, 162, 178–86
Weiland, Willoh S. 10, 96, 107
West, Rebecca 56
Whitman, Walt 3
'Who Knows What's Up in the Attic?' 81, 82, 91
Wide Sargasso Sea xi, 7, 9–10, 166–7, 170, 174
   Australian affiliations 99–100
   Caribbean background 4, 5, 104–8, 121–4
   coolies 90–1
   cosmopolitanism 5

Creole background 81, 87–8, 97, 103–4, 110–12, 115–16, 121
   cultural identity 114–15, 117–21
   decolonization 89
   ending of 58, 60, 74
   Indonesian references 81, 86, 90
   influencing adaptations of *Jane Eyre* 9, 95
   Introduction 66
   late modernist novel 95, 113–14
   literary influences 5, 57
   'other woman' angle 124, 143
   postmodern novel 130
   reviews of 36
   Rhys's motives for writing 55
   world literature 96, 160
   writing of 58, 83, 86–7, 161, 173
Williams, Bert 144, 182
Williams, Gwendolyen Rees 11
Williams, Raymond 38
Wittman, Emily 78
Woolf, Virginia 71, 161
Wyndham, Francis 7, 63, 67, 137
   Introduction to *Wide Sargasso Sea* 66
   Rhys writing *Wide Sargasso Sea* 58
   Rhys's letters 95

Yelin, Louise 144
Young, Iris 127–8

Zola, Émile 59

www.ingramcontent.com/pod-product-compliance
Lightning Source LLC
Chambersburg PA
CBHW072234290426
44111CB00012B/2091